日本語ナビで読む洋書

What is Global Leadership?

疾風怒濤の現代、リーダーに求められるスキルとマインドセットとは何か？

Ernest Gundling,
Terry Hogan and Karen Cvitkovich
英文編集：Kay Jones　ナビゲーター：山久瀬洋二

IBC PUBLISHING

装　幀 = 斉藤　啓（ブッダプロダクションズ）
英文編集 = Kay Jones
編集協力 = iTEP Japan

日本の読者のために

本書は、一見ビジネススクールで提供される専門書のような印象を与える。その印象からくる分かりにくさを乗り越えるには、現在世界の主流となっている企業での国境を超えた組織開発への知識を学習する必要がある。

一般的に、日本の組織は社員がいて、管理職があり、その上に経営陣が指揮をとるというピラミッド型が主流である。国の内外を問わず、支社と本社との関係も同様だ。しかし、企業が世界に進出するにあたって、現地での多様な文化や常識を理解しながら、現地でのモチベーションを上げてゆくには、ただ駐在員がピラミッドの「部品」として派遣され、年月を経て帰任するだけの組織では機能しにくい。さらに、現地での優秀な人材をピラミッド型企業では抜擢しにくく、そのことが日本企業の国際化を遅らせている。

また、企業は常に自らのリソースを効率的に成長させるために、M&Aも繰り返す。M&Aされた企業をどのように組織に組み込むかを考えたとき、無理やりピラミッドの中に押し込んでは人材を有効に活用することはできない。かといって、放置放任のまま、支社や買収先を本社の戦略に統合できずにいれば、それはそれで効率も削がれ、企業としてまとまった戦略を遂行できない。

従って、多くの国際企業では、「ピラミッド型」の組織から「マトリックス型」の組織へと組織構造を変革してきた。

もっといえば、世界をカバーする大きな傘があり、プロジェクトや職制ごとに、その傘の中で世界に点在する「統括機能」がある。そして世界中の社員はその統括機能のレポートラインに従って業務を行うのである。それは海外の支社でも同様だ。海外の支社の社員は、それぞれ世界各地にレポートラインをもちながら、その国の中では支社としての組織をもつ。この交錯した組織構造がマトリックス型の組織の特徴である。

本書を読み進めるためには、この「マトリックス型」組織という考え方を理解する必要があるのである。

ここでいうグローバルリーダーとは、例えば支社に派遣された現地のトップである。しかし、彼ら、彼女らの部下はそうしたトップではなく、海外の統括機能に従って仕事を行い、レポートをする。その組織全体をリーダーがまとめなければならないのである。だからこそ、現地の社員には様々なステークホルダーとの関係があり、同時に国内の顧客などといった地元との関係も共存する。

このように一見中核の存在しない複雑な組織をどのように運営し、成長させるか。さらに、現地で将来のリーダーをいかに育成するかが、本書が分析し、提言する課題なのである。

文化の違いを理解し、さらに会社としてのビジョンやモラルを現地に導入し、かつ現地が独立し、現地にも新たなリーダーを育て、自立して活動しながら世界レベルの作業に貢献できるリーダーシップを育てるにはどうしたらよいかというのが本書のテーマである。

グローバルリーダーシップという概念は日本には馴染みの薄いテーマのようでいて、世界と仕事をし、海外に進出する企業にとっては、避けては通れない学習事項なのである。

こうした前提を理解すれば、本書がMBAの学習書ではなく、我々企業人にとって必須の課題を提示した極めて斬新なビジネス書であることが理解できるのではないだろうか。

本書は、原文を日本人向けにリライトし、さらに日本語訳をつけた。日本語訳といっても逐語訳ではなく、より原文の意図を日本人が理解しやすいよう、超訳という形式をとった。つまり、著者の意図を理解した上で、その内容を文章の進行に沿ってまとめていったのである。英文にひっかかったときは、この超訳にて著者の意図を理解すればよい。また、超訳からリライトされた英文に戻り、超訳と比較しながら目を通してゆくと、仮に英文を完読しなくても、グローバル企業の人事、マネージメント、人材開発に関する英語やその表現に直に触れることができるはずだ。その経験こそが、海外との業務や交流のノウハウを育成することに大いに役立つのではと期待している。

山久瀬洋二

Contents

はじめに

急激な環境の変化にさらされる国際企業は、今までになく迅速にそうした状況に対応しなければならなくなっている。

企業に働く人々に、時代遅れのリーダーシップの概念を変革し、そうした世界の実情に合わせてゆくことは喫緊の課題である。

今まで自国だけで完結してきた価値観とは異なる、あらゆる状況に対応し、複雑で様々な機能をもった「十全な対応力」の養成が必要だ。その新しい能力が、リーダーシップの未来へのレパートリーとして、自国で開発された様々なスキルに付加されなければならない。

国際社会でこうした能力を備え、成功したリーダー達は、次の10の要件を共有し、それを行動に移している。

1）　自己文化への認識力
2）　予期せぬ事態への受容性
3）　人間関係を通した目標達成力
4）　フレームシフト力
5）　オーナーシップの拡大
6）　将来のリーダーの育成
7）　適応と価値を付加する能力
8）　コアバリューと柔軟性
9）　境界を越えた影響力の発揮
10）　第三のソリューションの提供

顧客のニーズ、サプライチェーンの課題、社員のモチベーション、競合関係、道徳律の標準化、法的枠組みなど、様々なテーマが世界各地の異文化環境で、さらには国境を越えてリーダー達に対応を迫ってくる。そしてこれらの課題にいかに対応し、解決してゆくかがグローバルリーダーの能力として問われているのだ。

新たな時代が求めるグローバルリーダーシップとは何か。これからその詳細を語ってゆきたい。

CHAPTER ONE

Why Global Leadership?

An interesting set of trends drives the current focus on **global leadership**. Many companies have gone through enormous changes in response to dynamic economic events. They have shaken up their operations and increased, reallocated, or limited investments to cope with market changes. These **megatrends** have created a new landscape for the world and have made an impact on the ways companies conduct their business.

As plans are shaped, the task of determining priorities and deploying limited resources has never been more crucial. The challenge for most companies, which tend to react quickly to the changing global landscape, is getting their employees to change as rapidly. The ability to deal with complexity in many forms requires frequent rebuilding of **previous skill sets** and a new or expanded range of leadership behaviors. There is a need for **leaders with the vision and skills** to function in a world with many boundaries marking differences across a spectrum of business and culture: customer needs, supply chain issues, competition, legal frameworks, educational systems, and so on.

Three Megatrends

In the dynamic global landscape, full of **uncertainty as well as clearer** trend lines, what are the key currents that we need to track, and what are their implications for global leadership strategy? Futurists have their leanings and temperaments, and they paint different scenarios as well as more general pictures of where we are headed. Some focus on technological developments and their implications, others look at social trends or analyze geopolitical forces. Futurism provides a unique license to speculate without feedback on predictions, which can only be assessed years later.

第１章

なぜグローバルリーダーシップが必要なのか？

ダイナミックな経済情勢の中、今**グローバルリーダーシップ**が注目されている。市場の変化に応じ、企業は様々な戦略を練ってゆかなければならない。**メガトレンド**は、世界に新たな風景を生み出し、企業のビジネスの進め方に影響を与えてきた。

従業員の取り組み方を迅速に変えることが、国際情勢の変動に即座に対応するために必要だ。**既存の業務スキル**の向上を常に図りながら、同時に新しい、そして幅広い役割を担うリーダーシップ・スタイルを開発しなければならない。顧客ニーズ、サプライチェーンの課題、競合、法的枠組み、教育制度など、ビジネスや文化の領域に、様々な境界線が存在する世界で役割を果たせる**ビジョンとスキルを持ったリーダー**の育成が不可欠なのである。

３つのメガトレンド

ここで、今世界で顕著になっている３つのメガトレンドについて考えたい。

不確実性と明確、そしてダイナミックに変化する世界情勢の中で、追いかけるべき重要なトレンドは何か、それがグローバルリーダーシップ戦略に与える影響は何か、様々な予測が検討される。しかしその予測が評価されるのは数年先である。現在予測不能な事態が今後も発生する可能性が高く、不測の事態とは別に、ビジネスのトレンド自体の予測不能な変化も継続するはずだ。

The future will probably bring events that cannot be predicted based upon present estimates, as with recent unanticipated events such as armed conflicts, terrorism, financial crises, and environmental disasters due to either natural or human causes. Along with these events, there are also more predictable trends that are likely to continue. And the future is already present in certain locations if we have the eyes to understand it and the imagination to anticipate where it could take us.

Three predictable megatrends have been impacting the global business environment for decades. These trends are **population growth in the developing world, changes in the balance of the gross domestic product** (GDP) between developed and emerging markets, and **rapid urbanization** in Asia and Africa. Each trend holds implications with which few, if any, corporations have fully come to terms.

MEGATREND #1: POPULATION GROWTH IN THE DEVELOPING WORLD

Our planet is in the middle of the **greatest boom in human population** in all of human history. Demographers project that from 1950 to 2050 the world's population will have more than tripled from 2.5 billion to over 9 billion. Such trend lines are slow to change, and even though the rate of population growth has decreased in some locations over the last decades, it is still probable that we will hit or exceed 9 billion within our lifetimes or those of our children.

What is less recognized is that virtually one hundred percent of this population growth is occurring in the **developing world**. The number of people in the developed world was under a billion in 1950, and the population of those countries in 2050 will probably be little more than a billion. So almost the entire increase of six and a half billion people over this hundred-year span will be in countries that represented one and a half billion people in 1950. This trend has implications for future markets, consumer demand, workforce demographics, and much more. Consider the implications of the fact that that nine out of ten of the world's children under fifteen currently live in developing countries.

As their markets and the people they lead continue to reflect this demographic transformation, **present and future leaders** will be increasingly unable to cope unless they change their approach to leadership.

ここで、何十年にもわたってグローバルなビジネス環境に影響を与えてきた、**3つの予測可能なメガトレンド**を紹介する。第1は、**新興国の人口増加**、第2は、先進国と新興国の**国内総生産（GDP）のバランスの変化**、最後にアジアとアフリカの**急速な都市化**である。ほとんどの企業でこれらのトレンドに完全には対応しきれていない。

メガトレンド1：発展途上国の人口増加

世界は**人類史上最大の人口増加現象**の中にいる。1950年に25億人だった世界の人口が、2050年には90億人を超えるかもしれない。

しかも人口増加は、ほぼ100%**発展途上国**で起きている。15歳未満の子どもの9割が発展途上国に住んでいるという事実だ。これが将来の市場、需要、労働人口などにどのような影響を与えるだろうか。

現在と将来のリーダーは、こうした状況を加味しながらリーダーシップの手法を変えてゆく必要があるだろう。

MEGATREND #2: CHANGES IN THE BALANCE OF GDP

Companies accustomed to earning the bulk of their **revenues** in North America and Europe might argue their biggest customers and business opportunities are still where they have always been, and downplay the significance of developing countries' population growth. However, along with the shift of the world's population has come a change in the **global GDP balance**. Estimates suggest the combined GDP of the emerging economies already exceeds that of the developed world, and this trend will accelerate.

These emerging economies are still adding fresh legions of **middle-class consumers**, estimated at more than half a billion people, and their numbers will soon exceed the population of Europe. What makes this trend dangerous to ignore is that production and consumption patterns in the emerging markets are no longer focused on **commodities**,[*1] but now include products and services regarded as "high tech." For example:

- Developing countries dominate both mobile phone and PC sales.
- China has by far the world's largest number of internet users, with India in second place.
- The largest automotive market in the world is China.

MEGATREND #3: RAPID URBANIZATION IN ASIA AND AFRICA

For the global economy, it makes a big difference where people live and what their occupations are. Rural populations engaged in subsistence agriculture are less likely to purchase or provide goods and services delivered across geographic boundaries. When people move to an urban center, however, their lifestyles become more caught up in the **global network of commerce**. For instance, they may work in factories that produce goods for customers on the other side of the world, and they gain the purchasing power to buy clothes, foods, and consumer items produced elsewhere, while the **natural resources** of a local farming community are no longer available.

North America and Europe had a majority of their populations living in cities in 1950, and they have since become more urban, with over seventy percent of their inhabitants now living in urban centers. In contrast, Asia and Africa were predominantly rural throughout the twentieth century, and are now transforming into urban societies. We are presently witnessing the growth of cities in the world's **emerging markets**[*2] of a size and scale never

メガトレンド2：GDPのバランスの変化

収益を北米やヨーロッパなどの先進国に頼る企業が顧客やビジネスチャンスは従来通りの場所にあると主張しても、**世界のGDPバランス**の変化に直面することは避けられない。人口の増加に伴い、新興国のGDPはすでに先進国のGDPの合計を上回り、その傾向は加速する。

新興国では、5億人を超える**中産階級の消費者**が増え、その数はまもなく欧州を凌駕する。このトレンドを無視できないのは、新興国市場の生産や消費のパターンが変わっていることだ。もはや**コモディティ**に焦点を当てるのではなく、ハイテク商品を含むようになっているのだ。下記の事例に注目したい。

- 携帯電話やコンピューターの主な販売先は発展途上国である。
- 国別で最もインターネットユーザー数が多いのは中国で、それに続くのはインドである。
- 世界最大の自動車市場は中国である。

メガトレンド3：アジアとアフリカの急速な都市化

今後ますます都市部は**グローバルな商取引網**に巻き込まれていく。

例えば、都市部の人々は、世界の反対側に住む消費者向けの商品を生産する工場で働き、他地域で生産された消費財を購入するが、地元の農村の**天然資源**の多くはもはや入手できない。

北米や欧州では、都市部に住む人口比率がこの70年で70%を超えている。一方、アジアやアフリカでもその傾向がさらに加速する。世界の**新興市場**はかつてない都市化を経験し、消費者は、自分たちのニーズや用途に合った製品やサービスを、過去には不可能と考える価格帯で購入しようとしている。

＊1 原材料、農作物、鉱業品など、商品価値が普遍化されたもの。

＊2 エマージング市場とは経済が発展途上にある国や地域の金融市場のこと。

before seen. Consumers in these markets are demanding different products and services, developed for their needs and applications, and at prices regarded as impossible by most multinational corporations.

Implications for Strategy: The Need for a Global Mindset

Population growth, GDP shifts, and urbanization are driving a transformation in the **risks and opportunities** faced by **commercial enterprises** worldwide. Global leadership is becoming an essential capability because such changes can only be understood and met with a **global mindset**. Companies will become obsolete if their responses are ineffective.

The three megatrends outlined here have a combined impact that is affecting almost every aspect of life. **Climate change**, **energy supply issues**, **deforestation**, **water shortages**, **fisheries depletion**, and **migration pressures** can all be linked to changes in population, GDP, and urbanization. We are witnessing an increase of so-called "tragedies of the commons" in which a person or even a country may derive short-term benefits from an activity that degrades our natural heritage. While all people have a responsibility to address these issues, commercial enterprises must learn how to manage their businesses through the changes that have occurred and those yet to come.

For business leaders with an outlook shaped by the last century's events, it is essential to adapt to such trends. Many executives still rely on an out-of-date mental map. Executives and their organizations must learn to re-evaluate and reshape their responses to the following kinds of questions:

- Where are our key markets?
- What are the companies that matter to us?
- What are the major sources of innovation?
- Who are the model global leaders?

MINDSET CHANGE: WHERE ARE OUR KEY MARKETS?

A list of the largest cities in the world in 1900 would include London, New York, Paris, Berlin, and Chicago, with the only non-Western city being Tokyo. On the list projected for the next decade, there are no U.S. or European cities among the top ten.* The largest urban areas are now or soon will be places such as Mumbai and Kolkata, India; São Paulo, Brazil;

グローバルなマインドセットへの問いかけ

3つのメガトレンドは、世界の**企業**が直面する**リスクであり**チャンスでもある。この状況を理解し企業活動を発展させるためには**グローバルなマインドセット**が必要であり、グローバルリーダーシップのスキルを持つことが不可欠だ。

しかも3つのメガトレンドは、**気候変動**、**エネルギー供給不足**、**森林破壊**、**水不足**、**漁場減少**、**移民の流入**に結びついている。

前世紀の発想のままでいるビジネスリーダーは、新たな適応が必要だ。経営幹部と組織は、以下のマインドセットを意識しているか、再検討されたい。

- 鍵となる市場はどこにあるのか？
- 自分たちにとって重要な企業とは何か？
- イノベーションの源泉は？
- 模範となるグローバルリーダーは誰か？

マインドセットの転換：鍵となる市場はどこか？

1900年当時の大都市は、ロンドン、ニューヨーク、パリ、ベルリン、シカ

＊2021年の統計（マクロ・トレンド）では、東京、デリ（インド）、上海（中国）、サンパウロ（ブラジル）、メキシコシティ（メキシコ）、ダッカ（バングラデシュ）、カイロ（エジプト）、北京（中国）、ムンバイ（インド）、大阪がトップ10となっている。

Chongqing and Shanghai, China; and Jakarta, Indonesia. Each of these will have a population exceeding 15 million. Corporate managers raised in a world where the 1900 list was still dominant may have trouble finding major developing world cities on a map, let alone traveling or living in them and having a sense of their marketplace dynamics. And yet these are the markets of the future. Any **effective global strategy** will need to take them into account, considering which locations to target and how to achieve success in a place that may have different consumer tastes, supply chain resources, or pricing standards.

MINDSET CHANGE: WHAT ARE THE COMPANIES THAT MATTER TO US?

Knowing the **competitive landscape**[*1] is an important part of any strategy and a necessary part of leadership skills. We tend to focus on "the usual suspects"—companies that have been rivals for many years and are based in our home market or another developed economy location. Yet strategy experts warn that the most dangerous competition can enter a market from **another industry** or as a **start-up.**[*2] There is a global version of this phenomenon, which is the **emerging market** company that was not on anyone's radar screen, but is growing and could soon become a force around the world. Such companies are **potential competitors**, but also **possible customers**, suppliers, or partners.

A veteran of the electronics industry once described how his Western firm had been satisfied with its high rate of business growth in Japan, a promising market for the company at that time. Simultaneously, a small local competitor was growing at almost double that rate, although it was still too minor to be regarded as a threat. That "small local competitor" continued to prosper and became the global giant Sony; meanwhile, the rival from its own country that the Western firm had been focused on has faded into obscurity, in part due to its lack of success in foreign markets. In the Chinese automotive market today, for instance, there are growing manufacturers and parts suppliers that could become future giants.

To what extent are the people who shape strategy in your organization aware of the threats as well as the opportunities presented by firms that are growing but are still relatively unknown outside their home countries? Global team members from emerging market countries will demonstrate their value when viewing such a list, as they will probably have a good

ゴなどで、非西洋都市は東京のみだった。しかし、今後10年間で、アジアや南米などの大都市の規模が拡大し、トップ10の座を奪うだろう。

これこそが未来の市場だ。従って**グローバル戦略の策定**には、改めてターゲットとする場所を特定し、消費者の好みやサプライチェーンのリソース、価格基準が異なる可能性のある地域で成功を収める方法の検討が必要だ。

マインドセットの転換（1）：自分たちにとって重要な企業はどこか？

競合環境を知ることはリーダーシップ・スキルにも不可欠である。

我々は、長年の競合他社をライバルとみなし注目しがちだ。しかし、**異業種**、あるいは**スタートアップ企業**が最も強敵となる可能性がある。誰もマークしていなかった**新興市場**の企業が世界を席巻する可能性もある。これらの企業は**潜在的競合**であるとともに、**潜在的な顧客**、サプライヤー、パートナーにもなり得る。

自国以外では無名の成長企業がもたらす脅威とビジネスチャンスをどの程度認識しているかを問いかける必要がある。

＊1 市場（の）勢力図。market landscapeで「市況」となる。

＊2 ベンチャー企業とは違い、イノベーションを起こして、短期間で成長する企業。

understanding of the competitive landscape.

MINDSET CHANGE: WHAT ARE THE MAJOR SOURCES OF INNOVATION?

There is a myth in the **developed world** that **emerging market firms** are **imitators** rather than innovators, and that their products and services are nearly always copies of those invented elsewhere. There is some truth to this claim, but it is increasingly the case that **significant innovations** come from developing rather than developed countries. A disruptive innovation is a product that is introduced at a low price and includes adequate functions, and which through continuous improvement threatens and possibly replaces products regarded as high quality.

The term "**trickle up**"[*1]—the opposite of the idea of technology that "**trickles down**"[*2] from advanced economies to the rest of the world—is used to describe the effects of these products. For example, General Electric's Healthcare India operation designed a portable electrocardiogram device for the local market to be sold at one-tenth the price of larger, more sophisticated products used in North America and Europe. That same product has been introduced into Germany, reversing the trickle-down pattern. Similarly, the Chinese company BYD has introduced a battery-powered car into the Chinese automotive market at a lower price than those advertised for competing Japanese and U.S. products—and BYD made its product available to consumers sooner.

The value of **continuous improvement** should also not be underestimated. A series of innovations introduced by **small players** can have a **disruptive effect** over time, particularly in markets where large numbers of components are assembled to create the final product. Over the years, markets for major industries such as automobiles, shipbuilding, home appliances, and telecommunications have been turned upside down by "imitators" that gradually became skillful at continuous improvement. Companies such as Toyota, Hyundai Heavy Industries (shipbuilding), Haier (home appliances), and Huawei (telecommunications) are now powerful global competitors. Firms seeking to do business in emerging markets, and even in developed economies, must create combinations of breakthrough pricing, adequate technology, and continuous improvement over long periods in order to **remain competitive**.

マインドセットの転換（2）：イノベーションの主な源は何か？

先進国では、**新興国企業**はイノベーター（改革者）ではなくイミテーター（**模倣者**）であるという通説がある。しかし、途上国から**大きな破壊的イノベーション**が起きるケースが増えている。低価格で十分な機能を備え、継続的な改善によって、従来の市場に取って代わるプロセスを指す。

「**トリクルアップ**」とは、先進国から世界に「**トリクルダウン**」するという考え方とは逆の、破壊的イノベーションを起こすことを示す言葉である。

例えば、GEヘルスケア・インドは、現地向け携帯型心電計を設計し、北米や欧州の大型で高性能な機器の10分の1の価格で販売し、やがてドイツでも販売されるようになった。

また、中国のBYDは、日米の競合製品よりも低価格のバッテリー駆動自動車を自国の自動車市場に投入し、自社製品をより早く消費者に提供した。

継続的改善も大切だ。**小企業**の一連のイノベーションは、特に多数の部品を組み合わせて最終製品を生産する市場で、**破壊的影響**を及ぼす可能性がある。自動車、造船、家電、通信といった主要産業の市場は長年、継続的改善に長けた「模倣者」に逆転されてきた。トヨタ自動車、現代重工業（造船）、ハイアール（家電）、ファーウェイ（通信機器）などが、強力なグローバル企業に成長した。企業は、画期的な価格設定、十分な技術開発、長期的な改善を組み合わせ、**競争力を維持**することが求められる。

＊1 社会の経済的中・下層に富を与えれば、上層まで利益がいきわたる。

＊2 上層（大企業や金持ち）が潤えば、下層（庶民）も潤う。

MINDSET CHANGE: WHO ARE THE MODEL GLOBAL LEADERS?

The Western business press has celebrated a few current or former top executives in its "hall of fame" for model global leaders over the past couple of decades. But without **continual revitalization**, the companies linked with their names may one day look like the list of the world's largest cities in 1900. In fact, most of the largest corporations from the first half of the twentieth century have faded into obscurity. Other executives and firms merit increasing recognition.

It is worth looking to **developing markets** to expand our view of model executives, because there are individuals who deserve inclusion and because employees in other parts of the world may find such people and their careers easier to identify with and to emulate. In India, Narayana Murthy of Infosys and Azim Premji of Wipro started corporations and achieved considerable success. Each helped to build two of Asia's most respected companies from humble beginnings, and they are admired not only for their business acumen but for their ethics and contributions to social causes.

In China, Zhang Ruimin, the CEO of Haier, turned a broken state-owned enterprise into one of the world's most formidable home appliance companies. Liu Chuanzhi, chairman of Lenovo, built up a domestic Chinese computer-maker to the point where it accomplished the purchase of IBM's personal computer division and is now among the world's top five industry players. Such names represent the variety of careers and characters that can be seen with an expanded perspective.

Conclusion

Leadership was formerly a topic reserved for the **corporate and political elite**, and leading in a global context was not a reality even for many people in top-ranking jobs. Now, global leadership has become the target of much wider attention. Not only executives in line to step into top leadership roles, but also **mid-level "high-potential" employees**, **MBA candidates**, and even **university undergraduates** receive training in this area. There are various factors related to this transformation.

マインドセットの転換（3）：グローバルリーダーは誰か？

継続的な活性化がなければ、偉大な経営者が育てた企業でも、いつか凋落するかもしれない。実際、20世紀前半の大企業のほとんどは今では忘れさられている。

途上国市場には模範となるべき人材が存在し、そうした人材とその経歴を、世界の他地域の社員は自身と結びつけて模範とするだろう。インドでは、インフォシスのナラヤナ・ムルティとウィプロのアジム・プレムジが会社を立ち上げ、大成功を収めた。小さな企業をアジア有数の企業に育てた両氏は、ビジネスへの鋭い洞察力はもちろん、倫理的、社会的貢献に対しても称賛を集めている。

一方、中国では、ハイアールのCEO張瑞敏（チャン・ルエミン）が倒産寸前の国有企業を世界最強の家電企業に生まれ変わらせた。また、レノボ会長の柳伝志（リウ・チュアンジー）は、中国国内のコンピューターメーカーを成長させ、IBMのパーソナルコンピューター部門を買収し、同業界の世界トップ5に躍り出た。彼らは、新たなグローバルリーダーの代表例である。

結論

かつては、リーダーシップは**政財界やエリート**向けのテーマだった。ましてやグローバルリーダーシップはさほど注目されなかった。しかし、現在ではグローバルリーダーシップは、経営幹部、**将来性の高い中堅社員**、**MBA候補者**、さらには**大学の学部生**までが、以下の理由でその育成のノウハウを学んでいる。

- Organizations seeking to leverage trends and to grow their business in key global markets have prioritized the need to build their **global leadership pipeline*** and will make significant investments for this purpose.
- The idea of "**leadership at all levels**" suggests that there are many roles in which leadership capabilities can be used.
- Global leadership and its secrets are appealing to those who seek to move up the career ladder.
- Large-scale corporate and educational budgeting practices sometimes make it easier to receive funding for an important topic such as global leadership than for more mundane skills like project or performance management.

Whatever their organizational roles, only leaders with **global vision and skills** will be able to position their enterprises to cope with the three megatrends outlined here and their implications for global commerce and leadership. A sense of the **strategic implications** of population growth, GDP shifts, and urbanization will provide an important compass to steer through stormy economic times. In addition to knowing the most crucial markets, companies, sources of innovation, and examples of leadership, leaders will need to tap sources of talent and find ways to develop the skills of people on the other side of their world.

- グローバルに事業を拡大しようとする組織は、**グローバルリーダーシップのパイプライン**を築く必要性に着目し、多額の投資を行うはずである。

- **「あらゆるレベルでのリーダーシップ」**という考え方は、リーダーシップ能力を活用できる役割があちこちに存在していることを示唆している。

- グローバルリーダーシップの概念はキャリアアップ志向の人を引きつける。

- 大企業や教育機関の予算編成においては、プロジェクト管理やパフォーマンス管理などの一般的スキルよりも、グローバルリーダーシップのような重要なテーマに対する取り組みのための予算を確保するほうが容易な場合がある。

グローバルな洞察力とスキルを持つリーダーだけが、ここで概説した3つのメガトレンドに着目し、グローバルな企業活動に対応できるようなる。

人口増加、GDPシフト、都市化のメガトレンドの**戦略的意味**を理解することは、経済の激変期を乗り切る羅針盤を持つことになるからだ。同時に、我々は才能ある人材を発掘し、世界の反対側にいる人々のスキルを伸ばす方法を見つけなければならない。

＊安定的にかつ効率よく次のリーダーを生み出し続ける仕組みのこと。

CHAPTER TWO

What's Different About Global Leadership?

Most leaders have received formal or informal leadership training. As their roles expand to include global responsibilities, the question arises, "What's different about global leadership?" Supporters of various leadership development approaches are not necessarily aware of or in discussion with one another, and there is confusion about the distinction between **leadership in general** and **global leadership** in particular.

Leadership: Common Approaches

Political rulers and military strategists of earlier eras drew upon numerous sources of advice, some of which still exert influence today. The topic of leadership is fascinating in part because there are many approaches and examples that have been held up as models. Leaders engaged in commerce have received guidance in various forms, including instruction through the religious traditions of Judaism, Christianity, and Islam.

The focus in this section will be on leadership approaches in the post-World War II West that have gained **common currency**[*1] in the business arena and have been applied, with mixed results, in many countries around the world. There has been a special fascination with these models, even in places such as Japan, the Middle East, and Northern Europe, due to the size and success of the U.S. economy, the reach of its business schools, and the spread of its brand names. As the global balance of economic power shifts, people who once looked to the U.S. for reference points have begun to explore other leadership perspectives as well.

LEADERSHIP AND MANAGEMENT

John Kotter[*2] of the Harvard Business School outlined an approach that

第2章

グローバルリーダーシップの特徴は？

そもそも、グローバルリーダーシップと一般的なリーダーシップとはどこが違うのだろうか。

リーダーシップとは：共通のアプローチ

本章では、第二次世界大戦後の西欧諸国において、ビジネスの場に**共通の思想**をもたらし、適用され、世界各国で様々な成果を収めてきたリーダーシップのスタイルに焦点を当てる。アメリカ経済の規模と成功、ビジネススクールでの研究、ブランド名の普及などから、あるいは世界の経済力のバランスが変化するにつれて、アメリカを基準にしていた人々も、日本、中東、北欧など他国のリーダーシップについて学ぶようになってきているからだ。

リーダーシップとマネジメント

ハーバード・ビジネス・スクールのジョン・コッターは、著名な学者とし

＊1 一般化された共通の考え方、信念。

＊2 企業におけるリーダーシップ論の権威として有名。

has gained the most widespread recognition over the past twenty years. According to Kotter, leadership involves coping with change by **setting a direction, aligning people**, and **motivating and inspiring**. Management, on the other hand, focuses on coping with difficulties through **planning and budgeting, organizing and staffing**, and **coordinating and problem solving**.

From a global leadership perspective, Kotter's description of leadership is helpful, but it is incomplete. It does not address issues such as how to read futures for divergent markets, communicate with people used to a different communication style, or identify future leaders who live far away from headquarters.

LEADERSHIP AT ALL LEVELS

Beyond the general definition of leadership as setting and explaining a vision, aligning the organization, and motivating employees, there is also the question of to whom these activities apply. Leadership is sometimes seen as applying only to top executives. Noel Tichy's* idea of "leadership at all levels" represents a different stance: he claims that the most effective companies are the ones that work to cultivate leadership capabilities at each level of the organization.

Tichy's emphasis on this open, **multilevel approach to leadership** development has been adopted by many corporations. They have invested time and resources to improve the capabilities of **"high-potential" individuals**, which has created an industry of leadership development professionals and approaches. At the same time, the fashionable focus on leadership at all levels has led to confusion about the nature of leadership and has caused some people to underestimate the value of the vital workhorse skills of good management. Given the choice between attending a leadership development program or a standard management course, ambitious young employees are attracted to leadership, even though they lack management experience. And those who have risen to high levels in an organization may feel that they no longer need to manage, as ordinary management skills are beneath them.

A useful way to sort out the confusion and to continue to recognize the value of management skills is to distinguish between "leaders" and "leadership," and between "managers" and "management." Regardless of whether one's position in the organization is that of leader or manager, both leadership and management skills are necessary. Even top executives are involved

てリーダーシップによって、**方向性を定め、人々をまとめ、モチベーションを高め、刺激を与え**変化に対応する一方、マネジメントは、**計画と予算編成、組織化と人員配置、調整と問題解決**を通じて難しい課題に取り組むことであると集約している。しかし、コッターのリーダーシップの説明は、異なる市場の将来をどう読むか、異なるコミュニケーションスタイルに慣れている人々とどうやってコミュニケーションを図るか、本社から遠く離れた地域の未来のリーダーたちをどう特定するかといった問題に対応していない点に課題が残る。

あらゆるレベルのリーダーシップ

リーダーシップには、ビジョンを設定し、それを明確化し組織をまとめ、社員のモチベーションを高めるという一般的定義がある。ここで、リーダーシップが、経営陣だけに適応されるのではなく、「あらゆるレベルのリーダーシップ」をという、ノール・ティシーの理念を考えよう。彼によると、極めて優れた企業は組織の各レベルでリーダーシップ能力を育成する取り組みを行っているという。

ティシーが重視するオープンで**多層的なリーダーシップ**の開発を模範とした多くの企業は、**有望な人材**の能力開発に時間と資源を投じてきた。だが一方で、例えば、若く意欲的な社員は、マネジメント経験がなくてもリーダーシップを取ろうと思うかもしれず、逆に上のレベルにいる社員は、通常のマネジメントスキルは自分のレベルでは必要ないと感じるかもしれないといった課題が残る。

これを整理し、マネジメントスキルの価値を明確にするには、「リーダー」と「リーダーシップ」、「マネージャー」と「マネジメント」を区別しなければならない。実は、地位にかかわらず、リーダーシップもマネジメントスキルも共に必要だ。

＊ミシガン大学教授、リーダーシップ論が専門で、GE、シェル、コカ・コーラなどでコンサルタントとして活躍。

in budgeting, assigning tasks, and tracking and evaluating performance; meanwhile, a junior-level manager may take charge of a project or team for which it is necessary to establish a vision or direction, communicate that to others, and motivate team members. The balance of leadership and management skills may shift as one's roles change, and some people are better at one set of skills than the other; but most jobs at any level continue to call for both.

Although Tichy's "leadership at all levels" has been popular and influential, it has also created difficult moments for global customers and counterparts in more **hierarchical countries** when they meet a young "leader" who appears to be in his or her first management role. At its best, Tichy's idea fosters the rapid empowerment and development of young leaders with great promise. Defects arising from its misapplication include a muddling of leadership and management as well as **culture clashes** between those who consider themselves leaders and others who regard them as just another junior employee.

Ram Charan* and his coauthors have helped to explain the changing requirements of positions at various levels in large organizations. Their model highlights what a leader needs to value and be spending time on at a particular stage (e.g., helping others get work done versus doing it themselves). The authors describe leadership stages through which a person moves from being an **individual contributor** to a **front-line management** role, takes on the responsibility of guiding other managers, and learns how to head a **function, business, group**, or an **enterprise**. For example, a person previously in charge of a function who must now lead a business will have to deal with new problems, set strategies for growth and profitability, value other functions equally, and deal with visibility as well as scrutiny from above and below.

Intercultural Views on Leadership

Intercultural training and theory have approached leadership from another direction; they help to link common approaches to leadership with the challenges of leading in a **global context**. The basics of the intercultural approach include understanding **one's culturally based values**, beliefs, and assumptions, and perceiving how others behave according to their **cultural lens**.

ティシーの「あらゆるレベルのリーダーシップ」は有名で影響力もあるが、管理職になったばかりの若い「リーダー」が、**階層意識の強い国**の顧客やカウンターパートに対応する際には課題が残る。彼の理念は、うまく機能すれば将来性のある若いリーダーに早い段階で権限を付与し、成長を導ける。しかし、それを誤用すれば、リーダーシップとマネジメントの混同を招き、自分自身をリーダーと考える人と、彼らを下位社員と見なす人との間の**文化的衝突**が起きかねない。

ラム・チャランとその共著者を見ると、リーダーが何を重視し、特定の段階、たとえば、仕事を自分でやるのではなく、他の人が仕事を成し遂げるのを助けるなどでどう時間を費やすべきかがわかってくる。著書では、**一般社員**から**第一線に立つ管理職**に昇格し、他のマネージャーを指導する役割を引き受け、**機能**、**事業**、**グループ**、あるいは**企業**を率いる方法を学ぶリーダーシップの段階について紹介している。例えば、事業を指導する役割を持つ者は、新たな課題に取り組み、成長と収益を向上させるための戦略を策定し、他の部門のことを考え、上下からの監視と精査にも対応しなければならない。

リーダーシップにおける異文化間の見解

異文化トレーニングと理論は、リーダーシップに異なる方向からアプローチする。それは、**グローバルな背景**に直面したときに、どういうリーダーシップをもって組織をリードするかという課題に光を当てる。異文化のアプローチの基本は、まず**自分の文化に基づいた価値観**、信念、前提条件を認識し、他の人がその**文化的視点**に従ってどのように行動するかを考えなければならない。

＊ハーバード・ビジネススクールとノースウェスタン大で教鞭をとった世界的に著名なビジネス・アドバイザー。

DIMENSIONS OF CULTURE

Some people focus on cultural contrasts, comparing countries and individuals using various dimensions of culture. While such cultural contrasts are useful to anyone working across borders, they can also be applied to the concerns of people in leadership roles. For example, a team leader who seeks to implement a change process in a **multicultural organization** would be advised to consider attitudes toward risk-taking that are shaped by different cultures and to plan culturally appropriate strategies for handling them. **Cultural knowledge** can be used to shape leadership tasks such as communicating a vision, motivating employees, and evaluating potential future leaders. Leaders working in diverse environments ignore such cultural points at their peril.

CULTURES WITHIN CULTURES

Any national culture is full of **complexity** and **contradictions**. Beyond differences among cultures, leaders need to be able to see **cultures within cultures**—for example, the practices of different ethnic groups—as well as variations among individuals. These factors can affect **consumer tastes**, brand appeal, and so on.

This **diversity** calls for flexible leadership that takes into account the behavior of employees from the same country who represent different points on a cultural spectrum. China's historical cultural patterns could be called **interdependent**, for example; until a few decades ago most Chinese lived within a communal structure that encompassed jobs, housing, health care, and community. However, a side effect of the country's **one-child policy**, along with economic reforms, has been the creation of the "Little Emperor" generation of only children. Members of this generation behave more independently in comparison with their elders, although perhaps not in comparison with people from cultures that have prized independence for generations. Such generational differences within China create challenges even for Chinese people who are in leadership roles, let alone foreigners trying to work with Chinese colleagues.

Global Leadership

Prior approaches to leadership do not provide **adequate answers** for leaders facing the full force of globalization in which any or all of the following may occur.

文化の様々な側面

まず、文化的側面を理解することは、国境を越えて業務に携わるには有用であり、リーダーシップの役割を担う人の不安解消にも役立つだろう。例えば、**多文化組織**で変革プロセスを実施するリーダーは、異文化によるリスクを取る心構えを検討し、これに取り組むために文化的に適切な戦略を策定するとよいだろう。それは、**文化的知識**は、ビジョンを共有し、モチベーションを向上し、将来のリーダーが誰かを評価するといったリーダーシップの課題に取り組む上で役に立つ。しかし、中には、危険を覚悟でこうした文化的要素を無視する者もいる。

文化の中の文化

あらゆる国の文化は**複雑**で**矛盾**に満ちている。リーダーは、文化の違いだけでなく、**文化内の文化**（民族ごとの慣習の違いなど）や個人間での文化の違いを見極めなければならない。文化の中の文化は、**消費者の好み**や、ブランドアピールなどに影響を与えるはずだ。

このような**多様性**に対応するには、同じ国の中でも異なる文化圏の従業員の行動様式を考慮した柔軟なリーダーシップが必要である。例えば、中国の歴史的な文化パターンは**相互依存的**である。数十年前まで、ほとんどの中国人は、職場、住居、医療、地域社会を含む共同体内で生活していたが、経済改革とともに**一人っ子政策**の副作用が発生した。この世代の人の価値観は、何世代にもわたって受け継がれてきた文化を持つ人とは異なっている。このような中国内の世代間による違いは、中国人と仕事をする中国人以外の人はもちろん、リーダーシップの役割を担う中国人にとっても難しい課題となっている。

グローバルリーダーシップとは

以下の少なくとも１つに該当する環境にいるリーダーは、従来のアプローチでは、**適切な答え**を得ることができない。

- **Disruptive technologies** come from different countries, including ones not previously a source of competitive threat.
- Robust and assertive global stakeholders all seem to have **vested interests** in the direction of the business.
- An effective vision must identify and capitalize on **similarities and differences** between customer and employee needs in developed and emerging countries.
- Authority based on **organizational structure** is supplanted by the need to work horizontally and exert authority through a global network of relationships.
- **Dispersed development projects** may involve a dozen multicultural teams in various continents and time zones.
- Historical **silos*** housing technical expertise must be linked to generate distinctive products and services through cross-border systems thinking.
- **Contradiction and ambiguity** have become the norm, and besides making decisions with a finite set of "unknowns," leaders need to try to prepare for "unknown unknowns."

As the necessities of leading in a global context have become more obvious and more urgent, scholars and consultants have carried out studies to delineate the characteristics of effective global leaders.

Research has done much to deepen our understanding of global leadership. Nonetheless, these frameworks still have several key limitations:

- Global leadership competencies are often not distinguished from more general competencies that leaders need in any role.
- Leadership characteristics are often described in broad or abstract ways, making it difficult to cultivate and utilize them in a practical way.
- The requirements for leadership roles are often mixed with more general management or intercultural skills that are needed by anyone working in a diverse environment.

Given the rising priority of global business opportunities in many

■**破壊的技術**が、以前は脅威でなかった国など様々な国からもたらされている。

■強固で自己主張の強いグローバルなステークホルダーが、すべての事業の方向性において**既得権益**を持っているようである。

■先進国と新興国における顧客と従業員のニーズの**類似点と相違点**を特定し、それを生かした優れたビジョンを必要としている。

■**組織構造**に基づく権限は、水平方向に機能しグローバルな関係のネットワークを通じて権限を行使する必要性へと変化しようとしている。

■**分散型の開発プロジェクト**に異なる大陸と時間帯の複数の多文化チームが関わりそうだ。

■技術的な専門知識を蓄積した**サイロ**を、国境を越えたシステムと思考を通じて特徴のある製品やサービスを生み出していくことが求められる。

■**矛盾と曖昧さ**は日常となっており、リーダーは限定された「未知のこと」によって意思決定をするだけでなく、「未知であることが認識されていないこと」に備える必要がある。

このようにグローバルな視点でリーダーシップを発揮するノウハウの育成が緊急の課題となっているものの、今なおいくつかの基本的制限も残っている。

■グローバルリーダーシップを発揮する能力と、一般的なリーダーシップでの能力とが区別されないことが多い。

■リーダーシップの特性は、広く抽象的に表現されることが多く、実践的な方法で育成、活用することが難しい。

■リーダーシップの役割に対する要件は、多様な環境で働くすべての人に必要とされる一般的なマネジメントスキルや異文化スキルと混同されがちである。

人々はグローバルなビジネスチャンスの優先度が高くなるにつれ、これま

＊飼料の貯蔵庫の意味から転じて、組織のことを考えず自分の部門のことだけ考えること。

industries, there is temptation to take whatever has been successful to date and give it a "global" label. Executives sometimes assume that their leadership styles can be exported.

Flaws have been listed in studies focused on global leadership, and suggest that future research examine "whether and how global leaders differ from domestic leaders," and "what effective global leaders do." People working in global leadership roles may become impatient with competencies, survey tools, or forms of advice that are similar to what they have learned in previous jobs as domestic leaders, and it is equally if not more essential to respond to their practical priorities and concerns.

Research Background: What Is Distinctive About Global Leadership?

Based on the contributions and limitations of previous studies, we have been focused on two questions:

- What is global leadership, and how is it different from leadership in general?
- How can effective global leadership behavior be disseminated throughout an organization?

PARTICIPANT DEMOGRAPHICS

To address these questions, we approached fourteen major global organizations. We asked company representatives to select interviewees with the following characteristics:

- Service in a key leadership role as a current or former international assignee
- At least eighteen months of experience on assignment
- Evaluated by the organization as highly successful in their roles

We interviewed approximately seventy international assignees selected by their companies according to these criteria. Eighty percent of interviewees had been on more than one international assignment. Most were in positions as a country or regional director, or head of a major business or functional group.

で成功してきたあらゆるものに「グローバル」というレッテルを貼りたくなる誘惑にかられる。経営幹部は、自分たちのリーダーシップ・スタイルを広めることができると考えがちだ。

しかし、グローバルリーダーシップに焦点を当てた調査では、そこに複数の欠陥が確認されており、今後の研究で、「グローバルリーダーとドメスティックリーダーの違い」や「優れたグローバルリーダーが実践していること」を検証することが示唆されている。

そもそもグローバルリーダーシップの特徴は何だろう。はじめに２つの課題に焦点を当てた。

研究の背景：グローバルリーダーシップとは何か？

研究では、以下２点に焦点を当てた。

- グローバルリーダーシップとは何か。それは通常のリーダーシップとどう異なるのか。
- 効果的なグローバルリーダーシップを組織全体に広めるにはどうすればよいか。

参加者の特徴

この課題に答えるために、14の大手グローバル組織にアプローチし、以下のような特徴を持った人を選んでもらった。

- 現職または元海外赴任者として重要な役割を担っている人
- 赴任経験が18カ月以上の人
- その役割において組織内で高く評価された人

The interviewees came from twenty-six countries and were on international assignments to thirty-two different country destinations. This mixture enabled us to identify themes that emerged across the board rather than characteristics of a particular nationality or destination.

RESEARCH FINDINGS: A BRIEF OVERVIEW

The consensus among our interviewees was that global leaders must perform tasks similar to those of leaders in any location, yet they must be able to shift strategies, business processes, and personal styles to fit different cultural environments along with a broad range of employee backgrounds and motivations.

Many also noted that a different level of effort was required to perform in their global leadership capacity compared with a domestic leadership role.

Global leadership behaviors are vital and yet easy to **underestimate.** The people who most need to acquire them may downplay their significance by emphasizing similarities to general leadership. While there is overlap between global leadership behaviors and more generic leadership and intercultural skills, it is also possible to describe a combination of behaviors that are characteristic of effective global leadership.

Analysis of the interview data revealed that certain behaviors were mentioned repeatedly when leaders described what they had learned while working in a global context.

One initial observation about these **global leadership behaviors*** is that they begin with "**seeing differences.**" Those who acquire the capabilities associated with beginning stages are more likely to be successful at subsequent stages.

POTENTIAL APPLICATIONS

A common message we heard from interviewees is that the insights and experience they gained while serving in global leadership roles have been **insufficiently leveraged** by their employers. However, these individuals were eager to share their insights.

Dissemination of global leadership skills throughout an organization requires a **shift in mindset.** Companies needing to expand their presence in global markets must learn to start every major effort with its global

インタビューを受ける人の出身国は計26カ国、業務の対象となった国は計32カ国であった。この組み合わせによって、特定の国籍や地域の特性ではなく、全体的に浮かび上がったテーマを明らかにすることができた。

調査結果の概要

インタビューに応じた人の意見で一致していたのは、グローバルリーダーはそれぞれの地域のリーダーと同様の業務を遂行しつつ、異なる文化的環境、スタッフの背景やモチベーションに合わせて戦略や業務プロセス、自らのスタイルを変換させなければならないということである。

また、多くの人は、グローバルリーダーシップ能力を発揮するためには、国内のリーダーシップとは異なるレベルの取り組みが必要だと指摘した。

グローバルリーダーシップの行動様式は極めて重要であるが**過小評価**されやすく、中には、一般的なリーダーシップとの類似性を強調して、その重要性を軽視する人もいるかもしれない。グローバルリーダーシップと、一般的なリーダーシップや異文化スキルとの間には共通のものもあるが、優れたグローバルリーダーシップの特徴である行動との組み合わせについても考察しなければならない。

まずは、**グローバルリーダーシップ行動**における最初の考察を「**違いを見る**」ことから始めたい。早い段階で「違いを見る」能力を身につけた人は、その後の段階で成功する可能性が高い。

潜在的な用途

インタビューで異口同音に指摘されたのは、グローバルリーダーシップの役割を果たしながら得た見識や経験を、雇用主が**十分に活用**していないという点だった。

組織全体にグローバルリーダーシップ・スキルを浸透させるには、**マインドセットの転換**が必要である。グローバル市場で存在感を拡大する必要がある企業は、グローバルな課題を既存の課題の「**付け足し**」と見なすのではなく、

＊役職や肩書きに関わらず、若手社員であってもとれる行動。自ら動くことで他に影響を与える行動。

implications in mind instead of seeing global issues as an "**add-on**" to what exists. Possible areas for integrating global leadership behaviors into key organizational systems and processes include:

- Executive meetings
- Orientations for leaders of global teams and global projects
- Coaching/**mentoring*** for global leaders and international assignees
- Employee recruitment and retention policies

Having a shared understanding of and commitment to a consistent set of global leadership behaviors could also serve to better align these efforts across different functions.

GLOBAL LEADERSHIP: BENEFITS

Weaving a global viewpoint throughout an organization is increasingly a necessity. Our interviewees spoke about the benefits of the global leadership behaviors they learned as well as the value they offer for companies competing in the world's fastest-growing markets.

Sample Benefits of Global Leadership

- Global market awareness; better sensors
- Perspective on the organization
- Knowledge of global business drivers
- Effectiveness in a diverse environment
- Innovation

これを念頭に置いて以下のあらゆる方法や場所で重要な取り組みを始めなければならない。

- ■経営会議
- ■グローバルチームやグローバル・プロジェクトのリーダー向けオリエンテーション
- ■グローバルリーダーや国際業務担当者向けのコーチングとメンタリング
- ■従業員の採用と維持の方針

一貫したグローバルリーダーシップ行動について共通の理解とコミットメントを持つことで、異なる機能間での取り組みの整合性を高めることができる。

グローバルリーダーシップ：有用性

実際、インタビューに応じた人々は、自分たちが学んだグローバルリーダーシップに従った行動が、グローバル市場への意識と優れたセンサーをもち、組織を改革し、事業自体の原動力を育成し、さらに多様な環境に適応しながら、イノベーションを達成するために有用であると語っている。

＊ 職場における人材育成の方法。指導者（熟練者）が、新人（未熟者）に助言し、自発的な発達を促す。

グローバルリーダーシップのメリット

- ■グローバル市場の意識の改善
- ■組織への視点を持つ
- ■グローバルな視点からビジネスの優先事項を知る
- ■多様な環境での効果
- ■イノベーション

CHAPTER THREE

Seeing Differences

Effective global leadership begins with the ability to see the differences that are most likely to make a difference. When companies do not notice or address differences in global markets, inappropriate solutions from headquarters tend to fill the knowledge gap. Leaders in a global environment must cultivate vision that places their previous leadership experience in context and enables them to sort through factors to identify and deal with the issues most crucial to success.

Global Leader: Fernando Lopez-Bris, John Deere

Fernando Lopez-Bris is the manager of Product Engineering for John Deere in its Coffeyville, Kansas, plant, which makes power transmission equipment.

Fernando's role involves design control in his division. His unit does the engineering for the product lines, and works with a sister factory in Mexico. His job is to oversee multiple projects and to provide support for all engineering teams, while handling budgeting, personnel, and other tasks. Before coming to the United States, Fernando performed a similar job in Spain, but with a different product range in Deere's agricultural division.

Fernando describes his previous leadership style as "pulling" rather than "pushing." He feels that by setting an example of hard work along with basic principles, you can expect people to follow this example rather than needing to "**crack the whip**."

Although Fernando had considerable leadership experience before

第3章

違いを知る

まずは、「違い」を見極める能力について考える。企業が文化の異なる市場に気づかず、対応できないとき、本社が独断でそのギャップを埋めかねない。グローバル環境では、従来の経験に照らし合わせ、成功するために最も重要な問題点を特定し、これに対応するための要因を見つける洞察力を培うべきだ。

フェルナンド・ロペス-ブリスの事例

フェルナンド・ロペス-ブリスは、ディア・アンド・カンパニーのトランスミッションを製造するカンザス州コフィービルの工場のマネージャーだ。

フェルナンドは設計管理の担当で、その部署ではメキシコにある関連工場と協働している。中でもフェルナンドの仕事は、複数のプロジェクトを監督し、すべての技術チームをサポートしながら、予算や人事などのタスクを処理することだ。アメリカに来る前、スペインでもフェルナンドは同じような仕事を経験している。

フェルナンドは、以前のリーダーシップのスタイルを「プッシュ」ではなく「プル」と表現する。ハードワークの手本を示すことで、「**鞭を打つ**」のではなく、周りが従ってくれると思っていた。

彼は、アメリカに赴任するまでは、スペインで同様の業務に携わり、

coming to the United States, his current role has exposed him to a broader range of circumstances and stresses.

"All situations, if you are directly exposed to them, reveal your abilities. The more situations you are exposed to, the better skills you gain. As a leader, you learn how you work under stress. In the U.S., the expectation is that you will stand up and work even harder in a crisis situation."

This exposure to a range of experiences has also provided Fernando with a broader perspective on global markets. "In Europe, all of our operations are smaller than in the U.S., so you don't expect to sell a U.S. eight thousand to nine thousand model tractor frame there. But the six thousand model will sell in Europe. It was developed for Europe, based on knowledge of the European market. You need to understand that small farms don't have the money for the big tractors. A global company understands markets and acts accordingly. You can't drive the business the same in the U.S., Russia, China, or Africa."

Along the way, Fernando has encountered numerous other challenges stemming from cultural contrasts in communication and leadership styles. He has found that Spanish culture is more indirect. But the U.S. expectation is for clear and precise information, so long as it's not perceived as rude. He misses business relationships that are developed around food. "In Spain, a meal is two to three hours at minimum. You talk and have food; sometimes you need to be less formal in order to capture the whole picture."

Fernando observes that his work experience in Japan made it easier for him to adjust to the United States. "In the U.S., I started by interacting with colleagues and neighbors to appreciate and understand the culture. This helps you to understand your own culture, and you realize the differences. We take everything for granted when working domestically. But abroad, everything gets put into perspective."

Cultural Self-Awareness

The first step toward seeing differences is to **develop cultural awareness.** It includes the realization that our leadership practices are shaped by our environment, and that there are different ways of getting things done in

渡米前にすでに十分なリーダーシップ経験を持っていたが、現在の役割はより幅広い環境の中で多くのストレスを伴うものだったという。フェルナンドは、多様な経験によって、グローバル市場に対する幅広い視野を持つことができた。

「企業は市場を理解し、それに従って事業を展開する。世界の異なる地域で同じように事業を行うことはできない」

彼は、スペインの文化はアメリカの文化より間接的だという「違い」に気がついた。アメリカではそれが無礼だと見なされない限りは明確で正確な情報が期待される。彼は食事をしながら間接的に情報を得ていたスペインの風習を懐かしむ。

「スペインでは食事に少なくとも2時間から3時間かける。食事をしながら話し合う。全体像を把握するためには堅苦しくない雰囲気が必要なこともある」

フェルナンドは日本での仕事の経験が、アメリカでの適応を容易にしたとも考える。「アメリカでは、同僚や隣人と交流して、文化を理解することから始めた。これは、自分の文化を理解し、他の文化との違いを理解するのに役立つ。国内で働いている時は、何でも当たり前だと思っていても、他国へ行ったらあらゆることに対して釣り合いの取れた見方が必要だ」

第一の条件 自文化への認識力

「違い」は他の**文化への洞察を深める**ことで見出せる。インタビューでは、多くの人がグローバルな役割を担ったとき、初めて自らが良しとするリーダーシップ・スタイルが特定の文化背景の産物に過ぎなかったことに気づいた

other locations. Many of our interviewees remarked that their global roles enabled them to see themselves and their leadership styles for the first time as the product of a particular cultural context. As Fernando Lopez-Bris indicates, being exposed to a wider set of circumstances requires leaders to check for similarities and differences with what they know, or think they know, and to change their expectations.

Cultural self-awareness may be stimulated through the questions that others ask. As another leader from a firm based in Asia said:

> "You learn to see your country and yourself from an outsider's point of view. When I talk to other Asians or Europeans, people ask me about my country with questions like 'Why do you do things this way?' When you are asked, it is difficult to answer."

Other leaders, perhaps because of their executive status or reputation, don't get such questions and must reach out. The recipe for failure is to be "**stuck inside yourself.**" There is often a "**new normal**" to which one needs to become accustomed concerning the values of a different country, organization, or individual. As one interviewee said, "You need to go back to zero and consider how to apply your expertise and values—you can't command or criticize others based on your fixed ideas or assumptions."

Insights from Global Followers

I saw people who were prominent leaders at home who crumbled in global roles, while others who started at more mid-level positions rose to the top. Those who failed were **inflexible**, and did what they were told to drive an existing process. They couldn't get the job done and couldn't understand why. This pattern of behavior turned into a downward spiral. The people who failed tended to have little or no previous global experience, and had never spoken a second language. They had not been exposed to different cultures; our executives thought we could plop them out in the world and they would be surrounded by the company bubble.

と述べている。フェルナンドが指摘するように、異なる状況に直面したとき、自分が知っていることや知っていると思っていることの共通点と相違点を確認し、自らの期待自体も変えることが必要になる。

自らの文化についての認識は、他人からの質問によって深められる。アジアに拠点を置く企業の別のリーダーは、「他の文化の人と話していて、自分の国について『どうしてこのようなやり方をするのか？』と質問されても、答えに詰まることがよくあった」と語ってくれる。

自分の殻に閉じこもらず、異なる国、組織、人の価値観に慣れる必要のある「**ニューノーマル（新常態）**」が存在することを知っておこう。インタビューでは「ゼロに戻って、自分の専門知識と価値観をどう適用するか検討する必要がある。固定観念や仮定で他人に指示したり批評するべきではない」という意見もあった。

グローバルフォロワーからの洞察

ある現地スタッフは、自国で著名なリーダーだった人たちがグローバル環境では成果を上げられず、逆に中間的な役割でスタートした人たちがトップに上がっていくのを見てきたと語る。

「失敗した人は、**柔軟性がなく**、既存のプロセスを進めるために言われたとおりのことをやっている」

「彼らは任務をやりとげられず、その原因もわからないので、悪循環に陥った。失敗した人は、過去にグローバルな経験がほとんどないか全くなく、外国語を話したことや異なる文化にさらされたことがなかった。幹部らは、彼らを世界に送り出せば会社というあぶくのなかでうまくやってゆくだろうと考えていた」

What Are the Differences?

Academics who try to describe the different circumstances that global leaders face tend to use the term "**complexity**." While having to deal with complexity is not necessarily unique to a global role, the nature of the challenges faced by people in global leadership roles is different, and includes factors such as the following:

- Physical distance
- Language
- Institutions: educational, legal, political, and religious
- Cultural values

People working across boundaries in leadership roles are likely to encounter difficulties sooner in their careers and with greater intensity than those working domestically. If they are not able to place their leadership experience in perspective and adapt to these new environments, their chances for success are slim. Each leader who takes on more complex responsibilities must reassess assumptions and patterns of behavior that are influenced by his or her upbringing, work experience, and past successes.

For example, when managers are attached to product requirements from their home markets, there is a good chance that their teams will underperform or sink under the weight of conflicts. This is true of leadership styles, too, as it is necessary to modify one's approach to working with team members in different locations. Similarly, if managers remain focused on the major competitors they are accustomed to seeing in established markets without taking into account the threat posed by fast-growing new emerging market competitors, their business could be blindsided by innovations that arise from unanticipated directions. Only by **distancing themselves from their experiences** and assuming a **broader perspective** can people serve as effective global leaders.

Tips from Global Leaders

The global leaders we interviewed offered additional advice related to **cultural self-awareness** and why and how it should be cultivated. The following are the themes we heard most frequently:

何が違うのか？

グローバルリーダーシップが直面する様々な状況を説明しようとする学者たちは「**複雑性**」という言葉を使用する傾向がある。複雑性に取り組まなければならないのは、グローバルな役割を担う人だけではないが、グローバルリーダーシップの役割を担う人々は、以下のような少々異なる課題に直面する。

- 物理的距離
- 言語
- 制度：教育、法律、政治、宗教
- 文化的価値

海外勤務のリーダーは、国内勤務のリーダーよりもキャリアの早い段階でより厳しい課題に直面しがちだ。新しい環境に適応できなければ、成功はできない。まずは、自分の過去の成功体験に影響される思い込みや行動のパターンを見直してみよう。

例えば、マネージャーが自国市場の製品スペックに固執していると、チームの業績が低下しかねない。アプローチを変える必要があるのだ。同様に、マネージャーが、急成長する新興市場の新たな競合相手の脅威を考慮せずに、既存市場で見慣れた大手の競合相手だけを意識していると、突如予期せぬ脅威にさらされる。**自分の経験から距離を置き、広い視野**を持たなければ、優れたグローバルリーダーとしての役割を果たせない。

グローバルリーダーからのアドバイス

グローバルリーダーたちは、**文化的自己認識**と、それがなぜ、どのように育成されるべきなのかをアドバイスしてくれた。

- **You can't change a country, and your country is not the center of the universe.**

  "Culture never adapts to you; you have to adapt to country and organizational culture."

  "I was seeing so many different cultures, that the world is so different, while still trying to achieve results locally. I learned that I cannot change people."

- **Previous patterns of success may not work in a new environment, and rigid adherence to these is likely to be fatal.**

  "You need to have self-awareness of your style, humility, and confidence to recognize that style can change and adapt if necessary."

- **There are different ways of looking at the same thing, and various ways to accomplish the same goal.**

  "I learned that the perception of reality is dependent on the cultural lens you are using. Other cultures are not programmed in the same way—you need to learn that."

  "I came to the realization that different people will look at the same thing and understand it differently."

- **It is good to experience differences early and often.**

  "It's important to accept that other cultures are different but have good reasons to be different. The earlier you have this experience, the deeper it gets into your mindset."

- **Question your approach without giving it up; what matters the most is to get the job done.**

  "You may be trained to think you know the right way to do something. But that may not work because you are in a different culture. You need to be able to question yourself without losing yourself."

  "You need to be watchful, aware, proactive, always questioning your approach. 'Is it working?' You need to be focused on getting the job done; not getting it done your way."

■ **国を変えることはできない。自分の国が世界の基準ではない。**

「文化は決してあなたに合わせることはない。あなたが国や組織の文化に適応しなければならない」

「多くの異なる文化を見てきた。地域によって様々な違いがあるが、それでもその場所で結果を出さなければならない。人を変えることはできないので」

■ **過去の成功パターンが新しい環境で有効だとは限らないし、それに固執することが致命的になる可能性は高い。**

「自分のスタイルを自覚し、必要となれば自分のスタイルを変えて適応することを認める謙虚さと自信を持たなければならない」

■ **同じものに対し様々な見方があり、同じ目標を達成する方法も様々である。**

「自らの文化背景というレンズを通して物事を見ていたことに気がついた。他の文化が同じようにプログラムされているわけではないことを学ぶべきだ」

「同じものを見ても、人によって理解が異なることに気づいた」

■ **早い段階から頻繁に自分とは違うものを経験するのはいいことだ。**

「様々な文化があるが、それにはそうした文化を生み出す十分な理由があるということを受け入れることが重要だ。その経験が早ければ早いほど、自分のマインドセットに深く取り入れることができる」

■ **自分のアプローチを疑問視する。一番大切なのは任務を成し遂げることだ。**

「正しい方法が何かという訓練を受けていても、文化が異なればその方法は有効でないかもしれない。自分を見失わず自問できるようになる必要がある」

「注意深く、意識的に、積極的に、常に自分のアプローチに疑問を持つ必要がある。『これでいいのか？』と。任務を成し遂げることに集中するべきで、自分のやり方にこだわってはいけない」

Invite the Unexpected

Seeing differences also requires leaders to invite the unexpected. One of the benefits of cultural self-awareness is that it contributes to a learning posture that is open to new information and experiences. When one's way of doing things is seen as the product of a particular context, then it is natural to be curious about other styles of leadership and business practices relevant to leading elsewhere.

READINESS TO LEARN

If the standard recipe for global leadership failure is taking what worked in one environment and applying it elsewhere, then the answer is found through proactive inquiry about relevant aspects of another country's history and institutions.

A **passion for learning** is infectious, and leaders who demonstrate they care about their global colleagues and the places they live find that their **counterparts** respond with openness. Many of the "getting to know you" questions that local colleagues or clients ask during informal conversations are intended to gauge the level of commitment that a global leader is signaling toward a given market. Lack of interest in historical or cultural sites or an unwillingness to witness lifestyles or to try local delicacies is often interpreted as a sign that the visitor does not take the country's market seriously. Business counterparts may interpret such limited interest as an indicator of the level of effort and follow-through that the leader will apply to the business.

To some extent, curiosity is innate and can be traced to character traits that started early in life. However, those who have had little exposure to working across borders can also learn how to learn, beginning with simple choices related to travel schedules, lodging, meals, and transportation while in another country. It is one thing to arrive the day before a meeting, stay in a first-class hotel, and travel in a chauffeured limousine; it is another to arrive a day or two early or stay late in order to visit key cultural sites, select a place to stay that local businesspeople might use, and discover how to navigate the subway system.

Knowledge regarding history, politics, and social networks contributes to informed business decisions while making local counterparts forgiving of errors. More importantly, identifying existing strengths of the local

第二の条件 予期せぬ事態への受容性

違いを認識するために、リーダーが予想外の事態に身を投じることも必要だ。新しい情報や経験を受け入れようと常に従順に学ぶ姿勢をもてば、異文化へのアンテナをしっかり働かせることができるはずだ。一つの方法にこだわらず、そこでの他のスタイルのリーダーシップやビジネス手法に関心を持つことが必要だ。

学ぶ姿勢

ある環境で成功した方法を別の環境で適用しようとすることが、グローバルリーダーシップのよくある失敗の原因だとすれば、その解決策は他国の歴史や制度やその背景を調べることによって見出すことができる。

学習への情熱は他の人にも伝わる。現地の同僚を理解しようと努めるリーダーには、**相手**（カウンターパート）は寛容になるはずだ。歴史的、文化的遺産への興味がなかったり、現地の生活様式を学習し、地元の料理を食べてみたいと思わないことは、その国の市場への参入を真剣に考えていないことの表れと解釈されることが多い。

たとえ、国境を越えて仕事をすることに不慣れな人でも、1、2日早めに到着するか長めに滞在して、重要な文化遺産を見学したり、地元のビジネスパーソンが利用する宿泊場所を選んだり、地下鉄を経験してみてはどうだろう。

歴史、政治、社会的ネットワークに関する知識は、ビジネス上の決定に寄与するのと同時に、現地のカウンターパートから自らのミスを許してもらえることにも繋がる。さらに重要なのは、現地の組織やそのメンバーの既存の

organization and its members, as well as points of local pride, can tap into sources of energy and enthusiasm that are not available when trying to standardize "global" practices. Instead of learning about each other, global counterparts **learn from each other**.

Ultimately, such learning influences a leader's personal values, business practices, and lifestyle.

Insights from Global Followers

It is easy to distinguish between the leaders who are going to do well and those who aren't. The ones most likely to succeed have a thirst for knowledge and ask good questions. They are prepared for the informal questions that customers might ask early in the conversation: "What's your favorite city here? Have you tried the food and what do you like best?" Such questions can be anticipated and should be considered before people look stupid with answers like, "I don't know; I have jet lag." No one is interested in your jet lag. The leaders who do well want to get out and talk to customers and see the business environment. Instead of saying, "That's not how we do it at headquarters," which people don't want to hear, they say instead, "Here's what seems to be going well based on what I've learned, and here's a small thing that maybe we could change."

SEEING WHAT WE DON'T EXPECT TO SEE

Beyond proactive inquiry, global leaders must also learn that human beings see what we expect to see, and that discipline and training are required to notice the unexpected. There is a psychological reason for this. People leading busy lives process so much information and so many stimuli on a daily basis that they would overload without mental shortcuts. Our minds incorporate mental models[*] that help us to filter out unnecessary information, focus on the most important facts, and concentrate on responding to those matters. But what about vital messages from an **unknown domain**? Leaders risk missing critical data and framing problems in a way that leads to

強み、地域に対して誇れるものを特定することで、「グローバル」な慣習を標準化することでは得られないエネルギーと熱意の源を引き出すことができる。お互いについて学ぶのではなく、**お互いから学ぶ**のである。

グローバルフォロワーからの洞察

ある現地スタッフは、成功するリーダーとそうでないリーダーを見分けるのは簡単だと指摘する。成功するリーダーは、知識に貪欲で良質な質問をする。顧客が会話の早い段階で尋ねてくる可能性のあるくだけた質問に備えている。

「ここで一番好きな所はどこですか？　地元の料理はどうですか？　何が一番好きですか？」このような質問には事前に答えを考えておくべきだ。優れたリーダーであれば外に出て顧客と話し、ビジネス環境を知りたいと思うものだ。「これは本社のやり方ではない」というのは誰も聞きたくないので、その代わりに「私の経験に基づいてうまくいくと思うやり方や、私たちが変えられるかもしれないちょっとしたコツを紹介したい」と言えばいいのだ。

予想外のことに気づく

そもそも人は自分が見たいと思っているものだけを見がちなので、予期せぬものに気づくには真摯な訓練が必要だ。多くの情報やストレスに見舞われ忙しい生活を送っている人は、不要な情報を排除し、最重要な事実に焦点を当てて問題の対処に集中するためのメンタルモデルが備わっている。しかし、**未知の領域**から重要な情報を入手した場合はどうか？　グローバル環境でフィルタリングのメカニズムを中断し、変更する準備ができていないと、重要

＊物事や人に対して持つ何らかのイメージ。人はこれに照らして意思決定をする。

incomplete solutions if they are not prepared to suspend or modify filtering mechanisms in a global context.

To discover unfamiliar aspects of local cultural and market environments that will be crucial for solving business problems, it is essential to anticipate them and to **position oneself** by casting a wide net for contacts and other sources of information. Common examples of the unexpected in a global business context include:

- New competitors in expanding markets
- Potential new customers that are unknown or underestimated at headquarters
- Consumer tastes that require substantial product modification
- Supply chain issues with product quality or labor practices

The Chinese market is rich with examples of the unexpected that Western firms have encountered. Amazon.com found that the Chinese online merchant Dangdang became an effective competitor due in part to its use of bicycle couriers. Dangdang's fleet of couriers responds to consumer tastes by delivering merchandise in person and handling cash-on-delivery payments from consumers who like to see the physical product before they pay and prefer not to use credit cards. Haier, now one of the world's top five appliance makers, has surprised its multinational competitors with innovations such as a washing machine that can be used to clean vegetables—perfect for rural Chinese consumers. Tencent QQ, the most popular instant messaging (IM) service in China (where IM is often preferred over email), has led the way in monetizing its social network of several hundred million users by selling memberships that allow users to create avatars, play online games, raise virtual pets, and listen to music.

The difficulty of perceiving the unexpected is increased in many countries by the tendency to place people in global leadership roles on a pedestal and to follow their directions regardless of whether their decisions are seen as the best course of action. This happens in part based upon respect for hierarchy, and also because this can relieve those in subordinate roles from being accountable.

な情報を見落とし、不完全な解決策につながるような問題を生み出すことになりかねない。

ビジネス上の問題を解決するために重要な現地への文化的な理解や、市場環境の未知な点に気づくためには、それを予測し、情報提供者や他の情報源に対してネットワークを広げ、自分自身の**立ち位置を確立**する必要がある。以下がグローバルなビジネス環境における予期せぬ事象の例だ。

- 拡大する市場における新たな競合相手
- 本社で知られていない、あるいは過小評価されている潜在顧客
- 大幅な製品改良を必要とする消費者の嗜好
- 製品の品質や労働慣行に関するサプライチェーンの問題

中国には欧米企業にとって予想外の事例が豊富にある。アマゾン・ドットコムにとってのダンダンがよい例だ。中国のオンラインショップ、ダンダンは、宅配に自転車を使うことで顧客をつかんだ。野菜を洗浄できる洗濯機など革新的な製品で競合の多国籍企業を驚嘆させ、現在では世界トップ５に入る家電メーカーのハイアール、中国で最も人気のあるインスタント・メッセンジャー（同国では電子メールよりもインスタント・メッセンジャーが好まれる）であるテンセントQQなどはそうした事例の代表だ。

多くの国では、グローバルリーダーを偶像化し、彼らの決定が最善かどうかにかかわらず指示に従い、予期せぬ事態を招くことがある。これは、階層制度を尊重する文化のせいでもあるが、職位が下の人が責任を転嫁する方便でもある。

"We've tried to implement programs that worked at home, but they failed here. We face challenges in a tough economy. I don't know all the answers and we need to work things out together. But people look to you for answers. You have to get to the point where people will tell you you're wrong and explain why. That only happened to me after the first year on the job."

The bottom line for global leaders is that they need to be able to step aside from their status and expertise to experience what one leader called **"the opening of your head"** that makes you able to understand different perspectives and not work in such a linear way. "If you can sum up different perspectives, you end up with a better product."

LANGUAGE AND CULTURAL INSIGHT

Our interviewees emphasized language skills as a crucial vehicle for leaders to understand other cultures and to develop effective business relationships. Although they acknowledged the effort required, they pointed out that **culture is often embedded in language**, and one cannot be understood without the other.

"It is a mistake to think you don't need to learn the language or the culture. Thinking is reflected in language, and you can't understand things without that."

The value of language may come as unwelcome news to those who do not have the time, ability, or desire to study another one, or who may deal with so many countries that it is impossible to learn enough to achieve fluency. However, even **modest attempts** at language learning are appreciated by **global colleagues**. "Learn a hundred words and use them; people will love you." More in-depth language study is not only a road to deeper insight, but a demonstration of commitment to doing business in a country while building lasting ties with local colleagues.

"If you immerse yourself in the culture and language, you will get into **flexibility, adaptability**. If someone seeks to learn the language, it is humbling; difficult. But those who do are able to cross through barriers and gain humility and the open mindset that is a natural by-product of the process."

「厳しい経済状況の中で困難に直面している。私はスタッフたちと一緒に解決しなければならない。しかし人は私に回答を求める。自分が間違っていて、それがなぜなのかを教えてもらえるようになるのに、私の場合1年かかった」

グローバルリーダーにとって重要なのは、自分自身の地位や専門性から離れて、あるリーダーが「**意識を開く**」体験をし、直線的な考え方ではなく、様々な考え方を理解することである。異なる考え方を取りまとめることができれば、より優れた製品を生み出すことができるのだ。

言語と文化の重要性

語学力を重要視する声も無視できない。外国語の習得には努力が必要であるが、**文化と言語は切り離せず**、一方が欠けるともう一方も成立しないという。

「言語や文化など学ぶ必要がないと考えるのは間違いだ。思考は言語に反映される。物事を理解する上で不可欠だ」

言語の重要性は、多忙なビジネスの現実に直面している人にとってはありがたくないことかもしれない。しかし、言語学習への**ささやかな挑戦**でさえも、**世界中の同僚**からは高く評価される。「単語を100個覚えて使うことによって、現地の人たちとの関係を向上できる」。言語学習は、地域への知識を深めるだけではなく、現地のスタッフと永続的な関係を構築しながらその国でビジネスを行うことへのコミットメントを示すことになる。

「文化と言語の習得を通して、**柔軟性**や**順応性**が身に付く。外国語を学ぶことは容易ではないが、障壁を乗り越えられれば、そのプロセスの自然の副産物としてオープンなマインドセットと謙虚さを身に付けることもできる」

TIPS FROM GLOBAL LEADERS

Here are some further comments and points of advice regarding the theme "invite the unexpected":

- **Ask lots of questions and listen while holding your experience in check so that you can hear new messages.**

  "I ask questions, listen more than I speak, and start with the assumption that I am probably not right."

  "It is challenging to hear different messages—to hear new messages that others are sending and cultural differences you need to be aware of; you need a more open filter."

- **Try to read nonverbal reactions, and don't fill the silence.**

  "The key is the ability to listen to other people in the broadest sense: perspective, arguments, even in hidden speech, culture. Don't jump to conclusions before getting the rationale behind their behavior—investigate."

  "Listen to subtleties and watch for cues. That skill translates to every culture."

- **Look for hidden issues and power dynamics.**

  "I had to take it deeper in terms of observations. There were a lot of **power dynamics** that were not obvious, so it took longer to figure things out."

- **It is sometimes best to acknowledge what you don't know.**

  "You have to be able to recognize that you don't know everything. Consumer shopping habits are different. To come in and start giving directions is foolish."

  "What was helpful—I would call people and tell them that I did not know, but that I am open to learning. In this way I was trying to get people to raise issues and explain the culture, get them to tell me how they would deal with a situation."

- **Listening is more likely to motivate than other methods.**

  "If they don't believe you are listening, they won't work for you. You can threaten them only so much."

グローバルリーダーからのアドバイス

「想定外のことを招き入れる」というテーマについてさらに以下のようなコメントとアドバイスがあった。

■ **自分の経験を語るのではなく、相手に質問をして相手の話に耳を傾けてコミュニケーションを図ることが大切だ。**

「自分が話すよりも、質問して相手の話に耳を傾ける。自分はたぶん正しくないという仮定から始めることだ」

「いろいろな話を聞くのは難しいことだ。他人から発信される新しいメッセージや異文化を理解しなければならない。心を開いて受け入れる必要がある」

■ **言葉にならない反応を読み取る必要がある。沈黙を破ってはならない。**

「大切なのは、広い意味で他人の意見に耳を傾ける能力だ。これには考え方、主張、言葉の向こうにある意味、文化も含まれる。言動の背後にある論理的根拠を確認せずに結果に飛びついてはいけない」

「注意深く耳を傾け手掛かりを探る。このスキルはあらゆる文化に通じる」

■ **表面に現れない課題やダイナミクスを見つける。**

「もっと深く観察すべきだった。はっきりしない**力関係**が多く潜んでいるから」

■ **知らないことを認めたほうがよい場合も多々ある。**

「消費者の購買習慣は多様。来たばかりでいきなり指示を出すのは愚かだ」

「人々に声をかけて『私は知らなかったけれど、学びたいと思っている』と伝えたことが役に立った。問題を提起してもらい、文化について説明してもらい、状況に対応する方法を教えてもらおうとした」

■ **耳を傾けることは最もやる気を起こさせる方法だと思う。**

「自分の話を聞いてくれていると信じられなければ、あなたのために働きたいとは思わないでしょう。脅して何かをさせることには限度がある」

CHAPTER FOUR

Closing the Gap

Once leaders have identified the differences as well as the similarities between their global context and what they may have been accustomed to in their home countries, they must learn how to address the differences in order to achieve their organizational objectives. The first step is to find ways to close the gap between themselves and their counterparts from other cultures, both through building strong personal relationships and through finding ways to shift their communication styles, leadership styles, and strategies.

Results Through Relationships

Although personal relationships are important in any leadership role, our interviewees noted that global leaders must rely on others to a greater extent because, in a foreign environment, they lack the local knowledge or skills that they would have in more familiar territory. Leaders who regard relationship-building as a **no-brainer** to be checked off the list would do well to consider the nuances and the multiple aspects of this behavior in other cultural environments: putting relationships before tasks, more interdependence or relying upon relationships to get the work done, leveraging relationship networks, and seeking out cultural guides who can help to trace a path through new territory by providing trustworthy advice. In certain cultures relationship-building is seen and cultivated in ways similar to a skilled art form or craft. Building relationships across organizational silos, stakeholder groups, and markets requires a similar focus and skill set.

第4章

ギャップを埋める

リーダーは、グローバルな環境と母国での相違点と類似点を特定したら、組織の目標を達成するために、そのギャップへの対処法を学ぶ必要がある。まずは、強固な人間関係を築き、コミュニケーション・スタイル、リーダーシップ・スタイル、戦略を適切に転換する方法を見つけ出すことだ。

人間関係を通じた成果

母国以外の職場環境では、慣れ親しんだ場所であっても知識やスキルが不足しているため、グローバルリーダーは現地の人々により頼らなければならない。人間関係の構築にそう**頭を悩ます**必要はないと考えているリーダーは、異文化環境におけるこの行動のニュアンスや多面性を考慮しなければならない。例えば、業務に取り組む前に、人間関係を築き、相互依存関係を深め、そのネットワークを活用し、信頼できるアドバイスを提供して新しい領域への道筋を示す手助けをしてくれる文化的ガイドを追求するなどだ。

Global Leader: Hannah de Zwaan, Northern European Manufacturer

Hannah de Zwaan works for a Northern European manufacturer in the corporate headquarters. She is a project manager responsible for new products from the design phase through their introduction to market. In addition to her native language, she speaks English, German, and French.

Previous roles for Hannah included working in the logistics area as a manager of managers, controlling order flow, and taking responsibility for the warehouse. Hannah was asked to join the leadership team that was moving an arm of its operations from headquarters to the Czech Republic. As the project manager for this transfer, she had a huge change-management role that included both ramping up production in the Czech Republic and closing the facility at headquarters. She moved on to logistics management of the supply chain for a factory with over a thousand employees. Although she had been slated to return to headquarters, Hannah was asked to stay to supervise the opening of a European regional center for the company in the Czech Republic, and built this center with an outsourcing partner and a large stakeholder group.

Hannah describes her original leadership style as that of a typical Nordic egalitarian leader: "very much engaging in open discussion and involving staff in decisions." She allowed the people who worked for her a great deal of freedom, but she also asked them to take on a lot of responsibility.

After moving to the Czech Republic, Hannah felt alone in the beginning. "You are leaving your personal network and you are leaving your boss and your job networks." She also notes she was not prepared for how her new Czech colleagues would react to her. "My husband and I skipped the cultural training because we were in a hurry. We said, 'Let's get there and see what things are like.' I would not recommend this, although it was helpful to me to have lived abroad before." At first Hannah kept a low profile, telling employees what the task was and taking time to observe how they performed. "Once you have been there for one or two months, you see who the driver is, what games are played. Taking this time in the beginning to observe gives you good knowledge. You need to be able to step outside yourself and get into the other person's head. Your way of

ハナ・デ・ズワンの事例

ハナは北欧のメーカーの本社で、新製品のデザインから市場導入までを担当するプロジェクト・マネージャーだ。母国語に加え、英語、ドイツ語、フランス語を話す。

ハナは、本社からチェコへの運営の移管を担うリーダーシップ・チームとして、同社の欧州地域センターを開設する監督者としてチェコへの赴任を要請された。

彼女自身のリーダーシップ・スタイルは、典型的な北欧の平等主義的なスタイルであり、開かれた議論に積極的に参加し、スタッフにも決定に関わってもらうというものだった。部下に多くの自由と責任を与えていた。

しかし、チェコに移った当初、ハナは以前の人間関係から離れ、チェコの同僚たちの反応も見えず孤独だった。

ハナは、最初は目立たないように彼らの取り組みを見守る。

「1、2カ月経つと、現地の人間関係が見えてくる。最初に時間をかけて観察すると多くの知識を得られる。自分の殻の外に出て、相手の立場で考えた」

doing things is one of many."

Although initially it was useful to observe, Hannah found she had to **alter her leadership style** in order to be effective. She discovered that her Czech employees were reluctant to take initiative. The **quantity and quality of information** expected from a leader was also different from her headquarters experience. "Where I come from, people want to be informed about everything, but when I was in the Czech Republic, at first I over-informed employees. I was used to **democratic management**, but this did not work at all in the Czech Republic. The most difficult task was being responsible for eighty blue-collar workers who spoke no English. At first I had a warehouse manager, but he left, so I needed to deal with employees myself. I had to go out on the warehouse floor, take a box, show how to pack it. They respected me and did what they were told to do. Because of the cultural differences I had to change my leadership style and become stricter, more directive, and provide clearer deadlines." Hannah discovered that she also had to differentiate between working with her production manager and with blue-collar workers. "You have to be able to switch as needed to get results."

Hannah found herself sharing her hard-won understanding of both sides of the cross-cultural interaction. "I had colleagues from headquarters come to deliver training in the Czech Republic. They kept saying that Czech people are so different, but I would respond, '**From their standpoint**, you are different.'" She also worked hard to manage others' expectations. "A lot of my time was used in setting the right expectations of people in other parts of the company, including headquarters. It is difficult for them to imagine what it is like, what is possible, what the price levels are, how the culture works. Being a bridge-builder and aligning expectations took time."

Many aspects of Hannah's leadership role were not easy, including her dealings with vendors outside the company. "You have to be tough. I was the first woman general manager. I had to deal with the manager of a local company who was not cooperating. He saw me as a stupid female, and tried to slow things down and give me a lower budget." She also struggled with the Czech language. "I ended up speaking a mixture of Czech and English to communicate. I tried to learn Czech, but it is a difficult language. So I learned what I could and used it, and they respected me for this."

第一段階の観察の結果、ハナは、成果を上げるためには自分の**リーダーシップ・スタイル**を変える必要があることに気づいた。チェコのスタッフは自立して判断したがらず、彼らが期待する**情報の量と質**も、本社での経験と違っていた。

「北欧の人はあらゆる情報を欲しがるが、チェコは違った。私の**民主的な運営方法**ではうまくいかなかった。難しかったのは、英語が通じない80人の現場の人たちをまとめることだった。当初はマネージャーがいたが、彼が去った後、私がスタッフと対応した。倉庫へ出向いて箱の梱包方法を教えることもあった」

「彼らは私に敬意を払い従った。文化の違いに対応するには、リーダーシップ・スタイルを変え、より厳しく期限を設定した多くの指示を出す必要があった」

ハナは、マネージャーと一般の職員とで接し方を区別する必要性も悟った。

「チェコでの研修のために本社から来た同僚は、『チェコの人たちは変わっている』としょっちゅう言っていたが、私は『**彼らから見れば**、変わっているのは私たちのほうだ』と答えた。また、本社を含め、他部署の人々に、現場がどんなものか、何が可能か、どんな価格帯が適切で、文化がどのように機能するかを想像させるのは難しい。両者の期待値を一致させるのには時間がかかった」

社外ベンダーへの対応も容易ではなかった。

「タフでなければならない。私は初の女性のジェネラル・マネージャーだった。協力的でない地元企業のマネージャーは、彼は私のことを無能な女性だと見なして、物事を遅らせて低予算を掲示しようとした」

ハナはチェコ語にも苦労した。

「結局はチェコ語と英語を混ぜて話した。チェコ語は難しく、できる範囲で学び使ったが、そんな私に彼らは敬意を払ってくれた」

On balance, however, Hannah says she came to have great affection and respect for the culture and the qualities of the people. "My best experience was in the last nine months when I recruited a lot of people—they are now a high-performing team. The key to success was that by then I had learned a few lessons about Czech culture and history. The lack of initiative, for example, is linked to the communist period in their history." She also learned the importance of personal relationships for many aspects of leadership, including how to give effective feedback. "You need to be able to give positive but corrective feedback. This is difficult when you are with a Czech employee whom you don't know. I took time to get to know employees before giving feedback. I could be honest and direct because I knew the employees."

Hannah observes that her experience in the Czech Republic has caused her to take a more **holistic approach** to leadership, and to enjoy having a job where she can see a task through from beginning to end and be responsible all the way. "The job involved a large role expansion with open borders, many stakeholders, and work with different departments and competing interests. I had good training in being alone and making tough decisions, which gave me more confidence. Now I also have a much better business understanding because I saw things from more than one side."

Among Hannah's current direct reports back at headquarters, there are six managers with six different nationalities. She says, "I felt it was so easy to get to know them, to start a dialogue and engage in small talk because I can imagine how they feel being here, what kind of problems they have being new to this country and not knowing the language." Her frame of reference as a leader has broadened. "Sometimes I look at issues from the Czech point of view now and think that in my home country we discuss things too long!"

RELATIONSHIPS FIRST

A number of interviewees commented that they made the mistake of focusing on the **task at hand** rather than starting with a foundation of strong personal relationships—a practice that is considered to be common sense for doing business in many parts of the world. An interviewee said, "Working

やがて、ハナはチェコの文化と人々に親愛と尊敬の情を抱き始める。

「例えば、指導力の欠如の背景には共産主義時代の影響があることなど、チェコの文化や歴史について学んだこともとても役に立った」

また、効果的にフィードバックする方法などにも文化的配慮が必要だった。

「問題を改善するためにはフィードバックを与える必要がある。これを未知のチェコのスタッフに対して行うことは難しい。フィードバックする前にスタッフと知り合うよう時間をかけた。スタッフを理解し、人間関係を構築していれば正直に率直にフィードバックができる」

ハナは、チェコでの経験からリーダーシップに対してより**包括的なアプローチ**を取れるようになったと述べている。

「複数の側面から物事を見ることで、ビジネスへの理解も深まった」

現在本社に勤務するハナのもとには、6つの国籍の6人のマネージャーがいる。

「彼らと対話し世間話をするのは容易なこと。この国にいることをどう感じているか、新しい国で言葉が通じないことの困難さなど、私には想像できるから」

リーダーとしてのハナの視野は広がった。

第三の条件 人間関係を通した目標達成力

多くの人が、強固な人間関係を築く前に、**目の前の仕事**に集中しがちだ。これは、バーチャルチームでも対面でもどちらにも当てはまる。

in Europe with the French, I was task focused and people didn't respond. I needed to invest in the relationship before they would move." This appears to be true whether contacts are virtual or take place in person; relationship and task are linked.

While it is easy to accept the notion that relationships are important, for global leaders the timing and the manner in which they are created are often different from their previous experiences. **Task-oriented leaders** begin to feel trust toward others who complete tasks as promised within deadlines and who do each task well. **Relationship-oriented leaders** build trust by learning about their counterparts: their values, the way they think, their families, organizations, and extended networks. Relationship-oriented people also, of course, like to see work finished successfully and on time. Ultimately, it is difficult to say which method is more efficient. Relationship-building takes more time in the initial stages, but tends to save time later through close collaboration and avoidance of rework that may be needed when business partners do not fully understand one another.

Following local relationship-building practices is crucial not just for getting to know people, but for setting a tone that the leader is willing to join in and become a part of the group. Acceptance of others through sincere cultivation of personal relationships tends to be reciprocated in acceptance of a new leader.

> "You are always being tested abroad, not intentionally, but it is part of trust building. If you go in with the perception they are beneath you, you will have a huge problem."

As relationships are built across linguistic and cultural barriers, vital tasks soon become more feasible. Hannah de Zwaan noted that it became easier to provide direct critical feedback to her Czech colleagues—in spite of their more indirect communication style—as she got to know them better and learned the local practices for what could be said when.

> "Be more open to people, not only at work. My colleagues need to talk to me, and not just on the job; it took me a long time to learn this. People want to learn from you or give advice—you need to be open to this."

人間関係が重要であることは容易に受け入れられても、グローバルリーダーにとって、人間関係を構築するタイミングや方法は、それまでの経験とは異なる。**職務重視のリーダー**は期限重視で、きちんと取り組んでいる人を信頼する。**人間関係重視のリーダー**は、相手の価値観、家族、組織、ネットワークなどを知ることで信頼を築く。関係構築は、初期段階では時間がかかる。しかし、構築後は緊密な協力体制によって時間を節約し、他文化への無知からくるやり直しや修正を回避できる。人間関係を真摯に構築して他の人を受け入れることは、新しいリーダーとして自分を受け入れてもらえることにつながる。

現地の人間関係構築の慣行に従うことは、人と知り合うためだけでなく、リーダーが仲間に入り、その一員になることを望んでいるという雰囲気を感じてもらうためにも重要だ。

「意図的ではないにしろ、他国ではグローバルリーダーは常に試されている」

言語や文化の壁を越えた関係が合築されると、仕事がスムーズに進むようになる。ハナはチェコの人が間接的なコミュニケーション・スタイルであるにも関わらず、直接批判的なフィードバックもできるようになった。

Insights from Global Followers

When new leaders are appointed to global roles, we watch to see what is most important to them. Are they in a hurry to build their resume with a "success story" and move to a higher position? Sometimes we have to clean up afterward because the effects of their actions only appear later. Or are they interested in us, in our market, and in our customers? We don't want to take people to see our most important clients who are going to push too hard and not show personal interest. If they are willing to get to know the employees and customers here and to work with us, then we can help them with many contacts that they don't know about. On the other hand, if they are in a hurry and not interested in us, we can help them feel comfortable and respected while they are living on an island, with the main business happening elsewhere. We know what we are doing in this market, and don't want them to be involved too closely if they are going to get in the way. Leaders come and go, and we have to live with the results of their actions for a long time.

INTERDEPENDENCE

Beyond the value of relationships for a global leader in establishing his or her credibility, they take on greater significance because of the leader's **increased reliance on others** in unfamiliar organizational and market settings for information, guidance, leverage, and implementation.

A sign of a failed global leader is the person who works long hours to compensate for the perceived shortcomings of colleagues from other countries because "they don't get it." A paradox which emerged from many of our conversations with **effective leaders** was that they were less sure than in previous roles that they could get things done themselves, but more confident they could accomplish their objectives through working with others. Thus, global leadership is a profoundly interdependent job. To recognize and cultivate this interdependence is the groundwork for progress.

LEVERAGING RELATIONSHIP NETWORKS

Good relationships accelerate the forging of new connections across

グローバルフォロワーからの洞察

新しいリーダーがグローバルな役割に任命されたとき、私たちは、彼らが何を重要視しているかを見る。自分たちの市場や顧客に興味を示さず、本国での昇進のために、ただ強引にビジネスをこなそうとするリーダーを、私たちは大切な顧客に会わせたくない。また、もし彼らが急いでいて、私たちに興味がないのであれば、リーダーを孤立したままでも心地よく尊敬されているお客様とみなし、主要なビジネスは別の場所で行っても構わないと私たちは思う。リーダーたちは来ては去るが、彼らはリーダーの帰国後もその人が残した結果に対応していかなければならないのだ。

相互依存

未知の組織や市場で業務を進めるとき、グローバルリーダーは**他者に多くを依存**しながら、信頼を勝ち得てゆかざるを得ない。相互依存関係が大切だ。

失敗するグローバルリーダーの兆候は、自らのニーズを理解してもらえないと思うあまり、自分だけが長時間働く。**優れたリーダー**は、現地で他の人とうまく協働し、目的を達成している。このように、グローバルリーダーシップは相互依存を強く求めるものだ。相互依存関係の認識と育成は、前進するための基礎となる。

ネットワークの活用

良好な人間関係は、**地域や職能ライン**を越えた新たなネットワークの構築

regional and functional lines. Accessing strong local networks through relationships can have an effect on business results. Many enterprises have been built up over generations through relationships based upon family connections, places of origin, educational backgrounds, and long-term friendships. It makes a difference whether you are seen as **an insider or as an outsider** from the perspective of people linked within these networks. If your relationships with counterparts are such that they feel comfortable sharing key contacts from within their networks, this can become an invaluable **personal and professional asset.**

FINDING A CULTURAL GUIDE

A number of interviewees also mentioned the value of establishing a relationship with another person who can serve as a **sounding board** and answer questions about standard practices in an unfamiliar environment. This person might be a well-connected local counterpart who is a business veteran, or a fellow executive from one's country who is sufficiently open and experienced in working globally to have a balanced view.

> "It's good to have someone with whom you can speak regularly and get reactions and a second opinion from, or someone who can tell you that you are wrong. Otherwise, the pressure of general business can affect your **judgment and decision making**. There are things that may feel right at the time, but which then take a lot of undoing to fix. It is better to talk to a third party and get a neutral, objective point of view."

The best **cultural guides** can balance outsider and insider perspectives: they know the **local culture**, yet can also see it from a **visitor's viewpoint** and understand what others might find difficult. If you are comfortable with your guide, yet he or she seems unclear about local practices, it could be that this guide is better at relating to you than to the local culture. On the other hand, some would-be guides, however **well informed and well intentioned,** are so caught up in their own world view that they are not able to describe how things work to outsiders, and may find the explanation process exasperating. Depending on the **dominant communication style** in a particular culture, leaders who seek advice from qualified individuals may not get it without adjusting their own styles. When the cultural guide is trying to deliver a message, you still need to be able to "hear" it.

を促進する。現地の多くの企業は、家族、出身地、学歴、長期的な友好関係に基づいて何世代にもわたって事業を展開してきた。これらのネットワーク内で結びついている人々の視点によって、自分が**部内者か部外者か**が変わってくる。相手との関係構築によって、ネットワーク内から重要な取引先を共有できるのであれば、これは非常に貴重な**個人的、ビジネス的資産**となる。

カルチャーガイド（相談相手）を探す

インタビューに応じた多くの人が、未知の環境での一般的な習慣についての質問に答えてくれ、**相談相手**になってくれる人との関係確立の重要性を強調する。このような人は、現地で広い人脈を持つカウンターパートである場合もあれば、偏見がなく、グローバルな職務経験とのバランスを心得た自国の同僚である場合もある。

> 「定期的に話をして、感想や意見を共有してくれ、間違っている時は指摘してくれる人がいるのはありがたい。相談する人がいないと、ビジネスのプレッシャーによって、自分の**判断や意思決定**がぶれてくる。その時には正しいと感じるかもしれないが、それが適切でなかった場合、修正するために多くの労力を費やしかねない」

優れた**カルチャーガイド**（相談相手）は、**現地の文化**に精通しているが、**部外者の視点**から見て何が難しいかを理解している。グローバルリーダーが満足していても、地元の文化よりもリーダーとの関わり方が上手なだけの人は相談相手としては適さない。また、ガイド志望者には、**情報が豊富で好意的**でも、自分の世界観にとらわれすぎ、部外者にどう作用するのかを表現できず、効率的に説明できない人もいる。**強いコミュニケーションスタイル**を持つ文化では、リーダーは、自分のスタイルを変えなければ、有能な人からアドバイスや情報を得られないこともある。相手のスタイルを理解して「聞きだす」ことができなければ意味がない。

Frame-Shifting

Another way to close the gaps across national and cultural borders when major differences are identified is to start **frame-shifting**. Once leaders have come to view themselves as the product of a particular cultural context, are positioned to listen for the unexpected, and have built strong relationships with their global counterparts, they must learn to shift their perspectives and leadership methods to better fit different circumstances. Successful global leaders are nimble enough to take on new frames of reference and to modify their approach to various environments without losing sight of their **business objectives**.

COMMUNICATION STYLE

The first stylistic challenge that emerges for many global leaders is how they communicate. This area overlaps with general intercultural communication issues that affect anyone working across borders. However, leaders have an urgent need to get certain kinds of communication right, including asking others to take on tasks, and **giving and receiving critical feedback**.

Direct versus Indirect Communication

Fernando Lopez-Bris described how he learned to ask U.S. employees more directly to take on overtime tasks, whereas in Spain he was accustomed to taking a more **roundabout approach**. Other leaders face the opposite challenge: if they are used to a direct approach, they need to learn how to understand and work with employees who are indirect. **Subtle communication style** differences have greater consequences than is often recognized. Some interviewees commented that leaders in Northern Europe tend to be more direct than those in the United States, but that leadership styles in the United Kingdom are indirect and reserved in comparison with Northern Europe and the U.S. They also pointed to distinctions within South and Central America.

> "Argentina and Brazil are more confrontational. In Central America, there is a more **passive-aggressive stance**. In my experience, the partners I worked with there would sometimes say yes, but just not do it."

第四の条件 フレームシフト力

国や文化の壁を越えて相違点を特定し、ギャップを埋めるもう1つの方法は、**フレームシフト**を実施することだ。リーダーが、自身を特定の文化的背景の産物だと認め、想定外のことに耳を傾け、他のグローバルリーダーたちと強力な関係を築いたら、異なる状況に合わせて視点を変え、リーダーシップを発揮する方法を学ばなければならない。成功しているグローバルリーダーは、**事業目標**を見失うことなく、迅速に新しい視点や基準を受け入れ、多様な環境に合わせてアプローチを修正する、つまりフレームシフトをすることができる。

コミュニケーション・スタイル

特に、コミュニケーション・スタイルの違いは、多くのグローバルリーダーが直面する最初の課題のひとつである。これは、異文化間のコミュニケーションの問題と部分的に重なっている。特にリーダーは、他の人に仕事を依頼したり、**重要なフィードバックを与えたり受けたり**といったコミュニケーションを適切に行う必要性に迫られている。

直接的vs間接的コミュニケーション

従業員に残業を依頼する場合、スペインでの**遠回しな表現**に慣れていたフェルナンド・ロペス-ブリス（p.41参照）は、アメリカではより直裁なコミュニケーションの方法をいかに学んだかを語ってくれた。

逆も真なりだ。直接的アプローチに慣れているリーダーは、間接的アプローチが必要なスタッフを理解し、協働する方法を学ぶべきだ。**微妙なコミュニケーションスタイル**の違いが、重大な結果をもたらすことが多い。インタビューでは北欧のリーダーはアメリカのリーダーよりも直裁にコミュニケーションをする傾向が強いが、イギリスのリーダーは北欧やアメリカと比較して間接的で控えめだという意見があった。また、中南米の中での違いを指摘する声もある。

> 「アルゼンチンとブラジルと比較して、中米は、より**間接的に相手に挑んでくる**傾向が強い。私の経験では、現地の同僚がYesと言っても、実際はそうでなかったことが何度もあった」

Even within the same country there are different **levels of directness** depending upon the situation, and each country has its version of common-sense communication standards taken for granted by insiders but not easily discernable to others. Situational factors may include whether you are in the **workplace** or in a **social setting** and the closeness of a relationship. In some countries it is customary for a leader to be critical of a subordinate but it is unacceptable for a subordinate to be critical of a leader except in certain social settings. Other ways to handle critical messages may be to convey them through third parties or in private. And causing embarrassment or loss of face, even when unintended, can lead a team or organization to turn on its leader.

Use of Questions

Leaders with global experience frequently describe how they have learned to use questions differently. They may ask more questions, pose questions in more than one form, or employ questions to challenge or to provide feedback.

What is the best course of action in countries where it is considered proper to agree with your boss **regardless of your true feelings**, and where subordinates are reluctant to bring bad news of any kind? Here a refined questioning approach that probes without interrogating can make the difference for a leader between knowing what is going on and having no idea.

Gaining Commitment

Most global businesspeople have heard about the "yes" that means "no," and the "maybe" that means "forget about it." Less known is the display of passion or emotion that means little. Leaders seeking commitments from customers or employees are likely to hear these messages and must alter their interpretations and responses based upon an understanding of the local communication style.

> "I thought that I had a dispute, but then a colleague explained to me that the guy was agreeing with me in a Greek way. He said, 'I disagree with you!' but then said exactly what I had said."

Leaders struggling to work across **diverse communication styles** are often up against more than just direct or indirect manners of speaking. A subordinate providing what seems like vague answers or information may be

同じ国の中でも状況によって**率直さのレベル**が異なることがある。これを部外者が理解することは困難だ。それには、そこが**職場**か**社交的な場所**か、関係が緊密かどうかといったことなどが関係する。一部の国では、リーダーが部下に対して批判的な指摘はできるが、特別な社会的環境を除き、部下がリーダーに対して批判的であることは困難だ。第三者を通したり、当事者だけで重要なコミュニケーションを取ったりすることもある。意図せずとも、気まずい雰囲気になったり恥をかかせたりすれば、リーダーはチームや組織から非難されるかもしれない。

質問する

グローバルな経験を持つリーダーは、地域によって質問の仕方をどのように変えたかという話をよくする。より多くの質問をし、様々な形式で問いかけ、異議を唱えたりフィードバックを与えたりするために質問をする。

部下が**本心に関わらず**上司に同意することが当然だと考えている国や、上司に悪い知らせを伝えたがらない国において、最良の方法は何か。問い詰めることなく情報を入手するための洗練された質問の仕方は、何が起こっているかを知っている場合と何も知らない場合で異なってくる。

合意（コミットメント）を得る

グローバルな環境で働く人の多くは、「No」を意味する「Yes」や、「忘れてください」を意味する「たぶん」を聞いたことがあるだろう。

コミットメントを顧客や従業員に求めるリーダーは、このような言葉を聞く可能性が高く、地域のコミュニケーションスタイルを理解した上で、対応する必要がある。

多様なコミュニケーションスタイルが存在する中で業務に取り組むリーダーは、直接的あるいは間接的な話し方の問題以上のことに直面することも多い。それは態度など**非言語に秘められた**メッセージだ。部下は、リーダーが

relying on other, **nonverbal cues** to convey his or her meaning while assuming that the leader has a shared understanding of the unspoken context. If the leader comes from a more **low-context and verbal culture**, he or she may not have the mental tools to look for the unspoken sources of meaning, so misunderstandings can, and often do, occur. Global leaders must develop new ways to search out and hear messages coming to them in unfamiliar ways.

LEADERSHIP STYLE

The need to "frame-shift" in terms of communication practices is linked with more **comprehensive shifts** in leadership style. Leaders who are trained in a **consultative approach** that informs and draws upon the expertise of other team members might find that colleagues in another country expect them to take a more **directive stance**; failing to do so may be seen as a sign of weakness or lack of capability. Similarly, a person used to being positioned as an expert technical resource may need to shift to a broader team leadership perspective or vice versa, and the expressive style that worked in one country must be toned down in another.

- **Consultative/directive:** "I learned to modify my leadership style in order to be effective in other cultures. In Mexico, they expected a more **authoritarian style** of leadership. This is the opposite of my U.S. MBA training. My style did not work in Mexico—the U.S. **participatory style** was viewed as ineffective."
- **Specialist knowledge/general team leadership:** "In Mali, leadership was based on technical skills and **leading by example**; in Benin, it required more of a **team approach**, so I learned more about team leadership."
- **Emotional expression:** "In Mexico it is about emotion; I could use an emotional **devil's advocate** approach to challenge people. This style flopped in Indonesia. They use small teams, give homework, and are non-confrontational."

Frame-Shifting and Generic Leadership

Frame-shifting for global leaders at times seems to contradict standard practices associated with generic leadership. For example, a key element of a leader's role in the generic sense is that he or she should provide a vision that gives the organization a clear sense of direction. Yet some of the leaders

暗黙のメッセージを共有していると思い込んで、漠然とした答えや情報を非言語的な方法に頼って伝えてくる可能性もある。リーダーが、**文脈が低く**、より言語に依存してコミュニケーションをとる地域の出身である場合、非言語が語る本当の意味を探しにくく、誤解が生じる可能性がある。グローバルリーダーは、未知の方法で語りかけるメッセージを見つけだし、それを読み取る訓練が必要だ。

リーダーシップ・スタイル

コミュニケーションにおける「フレームシフト」の必要性は、リーダーシップ・スタイルのより**包括的な変化**に関連している。部下や同僚の知識を参考にし、それを活用する**相談型のアプローチ**に慣れたリーダーは、他国の同僚からより**指示的なスタンス**を期待されていることに気付かないこともある。相談型アプローチは、軟弱で能力不足の兆候と見なされるかもしれないのだ。

- **相談型/指示型**　メキシコでは、より**権威主義的な**リーダーシップが期待されているが、アメリカでのMBA研修では正反対のことを学ぶ。アメリカ式の**参加型スタイル**は効果的でなく、私のやり方は通用しなかったという指摘があった。

- **専門知識/一般的なリーダーシップ**　マリでは、リーダーシップは技術的なスキルと**模範的なリーダーシップ**が求められたが、ベニンではより**チームでのアプローチ**が必要だったので、チームリーダーシップについて学んだ。

- **感情表現**　メキシコでは感情的に**あえて反対する**というアプローチで人と議論したが、これはインドネシアでは通用しない。インドネシアでは議論は好まれず、小人数のチームを使い、課題を与えながら進めた。

フレームシフトと一般的なリーダーシップ

グローバルリーダーのフレームシフトは、一般的なリーダーシップによる標準的な慣行と矛盾することもある。例えば、一般的な意味でのリーダーの重要な役割のひとつは、組織に明確な方向性を示すビジョンを提供すること

we interviewed, especially those with experience in **communist or formerly communist countries**, commented that the notion of "vision" reminded employees of propaganda. Vision also seemed to matter less in places where strong personal relationships and the mutual obligations that come with them are the first priority. Leaders had to start instead by focusing on other factors such as building personal loyalty, and explain their vision at a later date or not at all.

- Vision/personal loyalty:

  "Once you build up a loyal group of people, you set the expectation and it gets done, with no questioning. At home I spent time building consensus. In Russia, they line up if they trust you."

  "In most of Latin America, our U.S.-centric model didn't work. There, it was more the patrón relationship of employer to employee, the loyalty factor. The leader is there to take care of them, and they take care of you. Other leaders didn't adapt and failed. Once you develop the patrón relationship, loyalty kicks in and you get results."

Leadership in the generic sense means driving change, and this includes changing organizational systems to create better alignment. However, in a global context, leaders who set out to drive organizational transformation may find that they have to cope with larger **bureaucratic** and **political systems** that are not going to change, and which dictate many of the processes that their organizations must follow.

- Changing the system / beating the system:

  "You have to understand the culture you are working with and adapt your style. Russians have always lived in a situation where the system of life is rigid, so they had to get their needs met while the system stayed the same. In my country we change the system because we have that option… Russians are more clever about getting through an awful system, figuring out circuitous ways to get from point A to point B."

Pace and Timing

Another frame-shifting topic often raised by global leaders pertained to pace and timing. Their pace of work did not match that of their colleagues

である。しかし、インタビューでは、特に**共産主義国や旧共産主義国**での経験があるリーダーから、「ビジョン」の概念は従業員にプロパガンダを思い起こさせるものだとの指摘があった。ビジョンは、強固な人間関係とそれに伴う相互の義務が最優先される地域では、それほど重要ではない。リーダーは、個人的な忠誠心の構築といった他の要素に注力することから始めなければならず、ビジョンについては後回しにするか、全く触れないかのどちらかでなければならないという。

■ビジョン／個人的な忠誠心

「自国では、コンセンサスを作り上げることに時間をかけたが、ロシアでは、信頼している人には従ってくれる」

「ラテンアメリカのほとんどの地域では、アメリカ中心のモデルは機能しなかった。そこでは、雇用者と被雇用者とのパトロン的関係、つまり忠誠心が大切だった。リーダーはスタッフを保護し、スタッフはリーダーを大切にする。これに順応できないリーダーは役割を果たせなかった」

さらに、国によっては大きな**官僚制度**や**政治制度**に対応しなければならないことに気づくかもしれない。

■ 制度の改革

「職場の文化を理解し、自分のスタイルを適応させなければならない。ロシア人は、常に厳格な制度の中で生活してきた。体制が変わるまでの間は、その制度の中でニーズを満たさなければならなかった。私の国では、制度を変革するということは別に困難なオプションではない。しかし、ロシア人は、A地点からB地点まで回り道をしながら、ひどい制度を乗り切ることに長けている」

ペースとタイミング

フレームシフトに関してグローバルリーダーたちが取り上げたもうひとつのテーマはペースとタイミングについてだった。

in another country, and their sense of timing was off. Work habits vary, and there are locations around the world where the norm is to start work at mid-morning, catch up socially, do some light work, and break for lunch—but then the employees will work until late in the evening. So global leaders must learn to accelerate or decelerate their daily schedules, and to make decisions sooner or later than was their habit. The penalties for getting the timing wrong are serious; a number of people mentioned that this could become a costly error.

> "I have received feedback about my fast pace. The feedback is that I need to slow down and work at other people's pace."

> "Issues related to style and culture matter. If you are too execution focused, and want everything done in your own time, you will get stonewalled, nothing will happen. I have seen accomplished people come and offend everyone and nothing gets done."

Such shifts in leadership style may be required permanently in order to work smoothly with colleagues in other parts of the world. On the other hand, in cases where leaders had been working with the same group of people over many months or years, some reported that as relationships deepened they were able to revert to a more natural style.

Insights from Global Followers

It was a relief to meet a leader who was willing to shift her approach to doing business in this market. So many people who come here seem to be proud to say, "This is the way I am, and I'm sure you'll get used to it. This is our corporate culture. This is the way we do business." They are so tied to the approach that has made them successful in other places that they are unable to see what is in front of them, and end up lowering the motivation of their employees because they have no idea what is going on. But our new leader was well informed about the market, had learned a bit of the language, and spoke English in a way that was easy for us to understand. She was also willing to take her time to learn more and make the right decisions. I

グローバルリーダーの仕事のペースが、他国の同僚のペースと合わず、タイミングがずれていたというのだ。仕事の習慣は様々で、午前の遅い時間帯に仕事を始めて、雑談をし、軽い仕事をこなし、昼休みを取るが、その分夜遅くまで働く地域もある。こうしたタイミングを間違えた場合の代償は深刻だ。

「ペースが早すぎるというフィードバックをもらった。ペースを落として、他の人と同じペースで仕事をすべきだということだった」

「スタイルと文化の問題だ。業務の遂行を重視しすぎ、すべてを自分の都合のよい時間に終わらせようとすれば、協力してもらえず、何も変わらない」

このようなリーダーシップ・スタイルの転換は、世界の他の地域のメンバーと円滑に仕事を進めるために常に考慮する必要がある。一方で、リーダーが同じグループの人たちと長期にわたり協働し、人間関係が深まるにつれて、より自然なスタイルに戻れたという例もある。

グローバルフォロワーからの洞察

自分をシフトさせてくれるリーダーに出会えて安心できた。多くの人がここに来る人たちは「私はこうだ、きっと慣れるだろう」と誇らしげに言う。「これが当社の社風で、これが私たちのビジネスのやり方だ」

これでは、他の場所で成功してきたやり方に縛られすぎて、目の前のことが見えなくなってしまい、結果的に社員のモチベーションを下げてしまう。しかし、私たちの新しいリーダーは、市場のことをよく知っていて、現地の言葉も少しは覚えていて、私たちにも理解しやすい英語を

could see that she was asking good questions and listening, not just about the business but about people's personal lives. She asked to see an average home, so I invited her to my house to meet my wife and family. We traveled on a crowded train, and she said that this trip and being in our home helped her to better understand some of the consumer preference data that we have been providing. Our managers in this country are young and inexperienced, and they need more guidance than managers in other places; we talked about how to ensure that on future visits and through virtual communication she could arrange more formal and informal training opportunities. We also began to discuss strategies for shrinking our product footprint and setting prices differently in order to respond to customer requests.

LEADERSHIP STRATEGY

In addition to communication and leadership styles, frame-shifting extends to the strategic approach that a leader takes to working in different markets. If a **sign of intelligence** is being able to hold two contradictory ideas in the mind at the same time, global leaders who recognize major differences between country and regional markets must be able to shape strategies for other markets that sometimes run contrary to the strategies born at home. There are many possible reasons that strategic shifts could be required:

- **Distinctive products** or services have various levels of appeal in global markets.
- New environments present different customer requirements for product features, quality, cost, and delivery.
- Local innovations offer fresh opportunities.
- The local organizational support system or supply chain may be inadequate to implement strategies conceived in other locations.
- **High economic growth** in one region in contrast to a stagnant or slowing domestic market can create the need for different strategies for employee recruitment, retention, and development.

話してくれた。ビジネスのことだけでなく、個人的な生活のことも含めて知ろうとしてくれていたことがわかった。彼女は平均的な家を見たいと言ったので、彼女を私の家に招待した。満員電車で移動し、我が家にきたことで、私たちが提供しているコンスーマーの嗜好データがよく理解できたと言っていた。この国のマネージャーは若くて経験が浅く、他の国のマネージャーよりも多くの指導を必要としているのだ。

リーダーシップ戦略

ふたつの矛盾したアイデアを同時に頭の中に持てることが**知性の証し**であるならば、国と地域の市場の大きな違いを認識しているグローバルリーダーは、他市場のために自国で生まれた戦略と正反対の戦略を策定できるはずだ。戦略のシフトが必要となる理由を以下に示す。

- **差別化した製品**やサービスはグローバル市場の様々な場所で訴求力を持つ。
- 新しい環境では、製品の機能、品質、コスト、配送など異なる需要がある。
- 地域のイノベーションが新たな機会を提供する。
- 地域の組織的支援システムやサプライチェーンは、他の地域で立案された戦略を実施するには不十分な可能性がある。
- 国内市場の停滞や減速とは対照的に、特定の地域における**高い経済成長**は、従業員の雇用、維持、育成のための異なる戦略の必要性を生み出す可能性がある。

Given this kind of **volatility**, leaders must constantly weigh the potential costs of adaptation against the size and potential of each market, and strategic flexibility is essential. This happens not only with individual leaders but with teams assigned to new markets, especially when they feel pressure to get things done quickly. Their style of action and sense of timing can undermine their ability to conceive of a viable strategy.

> "The initial team fails in most countries where we are trying to start up operations. The expectations are so high for immediate action that they fall over themselves trying to do things and fail because they are not accustomed to doing nonstandard things."

Frame-shifting on the strategic level is easy to grasp by considering some examples.

EXAMPLE 1: **SOFTWARE ROLLOUT IN JAPAN**

A major software firm found that its Japanese customers had expectations for high-quality initial product releases and would not tolerate software bugs that were perceived less critically by customers in other regions, including the company's home market. There were several painful and expensive experiences in which customers found bugs that they demanded be rectified, and the company had to fly software engineers to Tokyo to work with its local engineers to fix the bugs. The software company later modified its strategy for approaching the Japanese market. Among other things, they paced product release schedules differently in Japan to ensure that any problems that emerged could be addressed; they also arranged for their Tokyo-based software engineers to participate at an earlier stage in product development in order for them to increase their knowledge and contribute to the development team's awareness of Japanese customer needs.

このような**不安定性**を考慮すると、リーダーは市場に適応するための戦略的な柔軟性が不可欠となる。これは、個々のリーダーだけではなく、新しい市場を担当するチームにも当てはまる。行動スタイルとタイミングを誤れば、実行可能な戦略を立案する能力を低下させる可能性がある。以下の指摘に注目したい。

> 「私たちが事業を立ち上げようとしているほとんどの国で、最初のチームは失敗している。迅速な行動への期待が非常に高いがゆえにつまずいて失敗する」

ここで、戦略レベルにおけるフレームシフトについてわかりやすい例をいくつか示す。

事例1：**日本でのソフトウェア販売**

ある大手ソフトウェア企業は、日本の顧客が製品の初期段階から品質の高さを求めており、同社の国内市場や他地域の顧客にとってそれほど重大ではないソフトウェアのバグを許容しない。そのため労力と経費のかかる対応を何度も強いられた。同社は、その後日本市場に対するアプローチ戦略を修正し、日本での製品リリーススケジュールを他地域と違うものにした。また、東京を拠点とするソフトウェアエンジニアを開発の早い段階から参加させ、製品知識を高めてもらい、日本の顧客のニーズに対する開発チームの認識向上に寄与させた。

EXAMPLE 2: **SELLING IN CHINA**

A Western consumer products company in China that distributed its products door-to-door found that its business model was adopted by Chinese associates and consumers. The networking skills of its Chinese salespeople made it natural for them to sell products through their personal ties, and to recruit others to sell in a similar fashion. For several years the company expanded in the Chinese market. The model was so successful that many local imitators sprung up selling all kinds of products door-to-door, often escalating the business model to create multi-layered Ponzi schemes. The Chinese government then banned door-to-door sales, permitting only brick-and-mortar retail operations. So in order to stay in China, the Western company that had helped to create the market was forced to abandon the approach that had made it famous worldwide and sell through more traditional and less lucrative retail outlets. After years of lobbying and working to reassure ministry officials that the industry could conduct itself responsibly, the government allowed door-to-door operations to resume on a limited basis by licensed entities only.

In both of these cases, the leaders in charge of these businesses had to make fundamental shifts in their operating strategies to accommodate different and even changing market circumstances. In the absence of such strategic frame-shifting, they would have lost market share or have been unable to do business altogether.

Working with a new country or market environment requires a new frame of reference and action. In a different setting, leaders may have to distance themselves from deep-rooted patterns of action on multiple levels: communication style, leadership style, and strategy. And this is not a one-time shift but something that needs to become a regular pattern in order for a person to alternate between established markets and emerging markets.

事例2：**中国での販売**

欧米の消費財メーカーの中国支社が、製品を訪問販売したところ、そのビジネスモデルが中国の取引先や顧客に採用されていることがわかった。このビジネスモデルは大きな成功を収めたため、現地で多くの企業があらゆる種類の商品を訪問販売しはじめ、このモデルをエスカレートさせて多層的なポンジ・スキームと呼ばれる投資詐欺を作り出した。その後、中国政府は訪問販売を禁止し、実店舗での小売事業のみを認めた。そのため、その欧米企業は、市場を有名にした手法を捨て、従来通りの収益の低い小売店を通じて販売することを強いられた。業界が責任をもって事業展開できることを省庁に納得させるために何年もかかり、政府は認可を受けた組織だけが限定的に訪問販売を再開することを認めた。

いずれの事例でも、これらのビジネスを担当するリーダーは、市場の特性や市場環境の変化に合わせて、事業戦略を根本的に変えたのだ。このような戦略的フレームシフトは、シェアを維持し、事業を継続する上で必要だった。

このように、新しい国や市場環境で事業に取り組むためには、新しい基準や行動の枠組みが必要である。これは1回限りのシフトではない。既存市場と新興市場を行き来するリーダーにとって必須の定例シフトパターンとなるだろう。

CHAPTER FIVE

Opening the System

Once significant differences between markets and business practices have been identified, it is often necessary to address **systemic issues** in order for a global business to expand. Leaders can close the gap between themselves and their global counterparts through more personal steps such as cultivating strong relationships and frame-shifting. However, they must also look to expand the circles of ownership and accountability for solutions across boundaries, and in so doing support the development of future leaders who may have different backgrounds and styles. Employees who are potential sources of new leadership talent in locations far from headquarters can be sensitive to the suggestion they are carrying out a strategy that has been decided elsewhere, or that they are lacking vital information that is considered too sensitive for them to know.

Global Leader: Diawary Bouare, CARE

Diawary Bouare is a veteran of a number of global assignments within CARE.* He is now the country director in Sierra Leone for an operation involving 200 employees. In 2000, Diawary was the first national staff member from CARE Mali to be assigned to another country as a Global staff member. He was also one of the first CARE employees from Africa to hold a senior leadership position in a country operation in Asia. Diawary has come a long way from his underprivileged upbringing, which included a sixteen-kilometer round-trip walk to school and back.

While working for CARE in Mali, one of Diawary's jobs was to lead partnership and institutional capacity building. This was a challenging task, as he had to manage changes inside CARE and create a viable process

第5章

体制をオープンにする

市場や商習慣の違いの特定のあとは、グローバルビジネスを展開するには**組織的課題**に対処しなければならない。リーダーは、関係構築やフレームシフトなどの個人的対応によって自身と海外の相手とのギャップを埋める。しかし、リーダーは現地の人材のオーナーシップ（当事者意識）と責任の拡大を目指すために、様々な異文化背景を持つ将来のリーダーの育成を支援しなければならない。リーダーシップの才能を発揮する可能性を持ちながら本社から離れた地域で働くスタッフは、本社からの決定が一方的に押し付けられたり、情報が共有されたりしないことに敏感になりがちだ。

デアワリー・ボアレの事例

デアワリーは、長年CAREでグローバル業務に取り組んできた。2000年、彼はマリから初のグローバルスタッフメンバーに任命され、他国に配属された。マリでの勤務は、CARE内部の変更を管理し、潜在的パートナーを評価するプロセスを作成するという困難なタスクだった。

「CAREでは変化をもたらすことのできる新しい視野を持つ人々を雇用した。当時、私は数少ない同国の国籍を持つ一人として、私との人的

＊国際ケア機構。国際的な人道援助を行なっているNGO。

for assessing potential partners. "We were introducing a new working approach at CARE, and this was a threat to CARE job security because we were now working with NGO partners. Change cannot always happen with the same staff, so we brought in people with new perspectives to help bring change. And as one of the few local nationals on the leadership team at that time, I was also facing pressure to subcontract, recruit friends, and so on. Friends came to me to get a position, but I told them to go through the process based on their accomplishments. Local NGOs were using personal contacts to try to convince me to have them partner with CARE. But I had to refuse and say that our decisions are based on process, not on preference. When I was reviewing a partner's progress, there was always political pressure to give good reviews. It is routine for me now to do the right thing, and to demonstrate the rationale behind this. I can develop social relationships but don't compromise principles. This has been successful—people respect you in every difficult situation."

Based upon his performance in Mali, Diawary moved to a project manager position in nearby Benin, working with local NGOs on good **internal governance**, **transparency**, and quality of service delivery. He became country coordinator for CARE operations in Benin, channeling CARE funds through a meticulous process to ensure that they were properly used. He changed his approach to fit this new environment and role. "In Mali my leadership style was based on technical skills, leading by example. In Benin, I had to take more of a team approach and so learned about leading a team and how to adjust myself to be a team player." Again his efforts met with success, and he began to take on wider responsibilities as civil society sector coordinator for CARE Gulf of Guinea, covering Ghana, Togo, and Benin.

Diawary's next career role was to become assistant country director in Burundi, in a post-conflict context in Central Africa that is still rife with ethnic tensions (Burundi shares a border with Rwanda). In this new leadership role, he says, "I had to change again. I had a direct approach, and I am most comfortable with this. I was trying to be fair with everyone, and clear about how I work. I was seen as fair and transparent. Some leaders treated people differently based on personal relationships. I used to be critical of this. I am fair and rigorous, analytical in decisions, and work according to policies and procedures. Coming to Burundi, I kept some of this style, but tried to be softer. The security situation is not good, but if

コネクションによって業務に関わろうとする人々に対応しなければならなかった。私は常に自分の実績に基づいてプロセスを踏むように彼らに勧めた。CAREの決定は、個人的関係ではなく、プロセスに基づいて下されるものなのだ。ポジティブなレビューをという政治的圧力も常にあった。しかし、社会的関係を築くことはできるが、原則は曲げられない。これが私の実績につながった」

マリの実績に基づき、デアワリーはベニン近郊でプロジェクト・マネージャー職に任命され、現地NGOと協力しながら**内部統制**、**透明性**確保、質の高いサービスの提供に取り組んだ。彼はこの新しい役割に合わせて自分のやり方を変えた。「マリでのリーダーシップは技術的スキルに基づくもので、模範を示して指導していた。しかし、ベニンではチームで協力する手法を取らなければならなかったので、チームをリードし、チームプレーヤーになるためのノウハウを学んだ」

デアワリーの取り組みは再び成功をおさめ、ガーナ、トーゴ、ベニンを統括するCAREギニア湾の市民社会セクター・コーディネーターへと昇進した。

デアワリーの次の職務は、ブルンジのアシスタント・カントリー・ディレクターだったが、現地では、中央アフリカの紛争後の民族間緊張がまだ続いていた。新しいリーダーシップの役割において、デアワリーは言う。

「またやり方を変える必要があった。誰に対しても公平に対応し、自分のやり方を明確にしようとしていた。私は公正で厳格、分析的な意思決定、方針や手順に従って業務を進める。ブルンジでもこの姿勢を貫いたが、もっとソフトな対応を心掛けた。治安の悪い地域で、**民族の分裂や紛争**

you are fair, you become respected. People tended to use the **ethnic divisions and conflict** to try to stop what we were doing, claiming that we were favoring one ethnic group or another. So everything had to be transparent, and I had to be more self-aware. The biggest change we made was the food distribution program restructuring—we succeeded where other leadership had failed in aligning this project and reducing staff. I was leading the process, but sometimes I pushed them to make the decision. I had to lead by example and through my experience, by convincing, not by pushing too hard. I tried to make sure that others developed their leadership, working in a team. I learned from colleagues and coached colleagues. I had to give others the chance to prove themselves successful in ways that no one had been successful before, and to utilize their own values and styles to be successful. Timing is critical; it's important not to push too quickly."

In Diawary's recent role in Nepal he faced a new kind of conflict, not ethnic but more social and political. In addition, he had to work in a large operation with experienced staff members, many of whom had probably never met or worked directly with an African in person. "Because of the long history of CARE in Nepal, it was difficult for staff members who had been working there for fifteen or twenty years to accept an African in a leadership position. But I did come to feel accepted, based on CARE Global values and my leadership approach: critical analysis, generating debate, helping them to understand issues. People in Nepal have technical knowledge, so I needed to focus on the strategic level and stay out of the details. If I maintained a strategic approach and challenged the status quo, they felt I was adding value. Also, I recognized the contributions of staff members; I gave them space and a voice because they had been there so long. My role as a leader is to provide room for them to use their skills and make **critical decisions**, and to have CARE demonstrate the values of diversity, respect, excellence, and transparency. This creates ownership and commitment among all staff—these things are critical here."

As in the move to Burundi, Diawary's leadership style in Nepal was again different from the one he had used in West Africa. "If I had pushed in Nepal, I would have been rejected. I had to make a clear distinction between cultures. In Nepal, you have to show your perspective through coaching and mentoring, not pushing. Because of the deeply rooted social, cultural, gender, and caste issues, the existing structures are strong

を利用して、私たちの活動を妨げる動きがあり、どちらかの民族を優遇していると非難する人もいた。全てに透明性が必要とされる。最大の変化は、食糧配給プログラムの改革だった。メンバーに決断を迫ることもあった。無理強いをせず、説得をしながら、模範を示し、経験を通して指導する。チームワークを推進しながら、リーダーシップ力向上にも尽力した。メンバーから学び、メンバーを指導した。タイミングが重要だ。急ぎすぎてはならない」

ネパールでデアワリーが直面した課題は、民族的なものではなく、社会的、政治的なものだった。

「CAREはネパールで長い歴史があり、15年、20年も勤務する職員にとって、アフリカ人を指導者として受け入れることは難しいことだった。批判的分析や討議を行い、問題を理解する手助けをした。ネパールのスタッフは技術的知識が豊富なため、私は戦略的レベルに焦点を当て、技術面での詳細には口出ししないようにした。私が戦略的アプローチを維持し、現状に立ち向かえば、私の付加価値を認めてくれる。また、スタッフの貢献を高く評価し、長年ネパールで活動を続けてきた彼らにむやみに干渉せず、発言の機会を与えた。リーダーとしての私の役割は、彼らが自分のスキルを活用し、**重要な決定**を下し、多様性、敬意、卓越性、透明性の価値をCAREが示せるようにした。これによってスタッフ全員にオーナーシップ(当事者意識)とコミットメントが生まれたのだ」

ネパールにおけるデアワリーのリーダーシップ・スタイルは、西アフリカで用いていたものと異なっていた。

「ネパールで押し付けるような態度を取っていたら、拒否されていただろう。私は文化を明確に区別した。ネパールでは、強要ではなく、コーチングやメンタリングを通して自分の考え方を示す必要があった。社会、

and resistant to change. We are trying to change the power dynamic, to get at the causes of poverty, discrimination, and conflict. We do this by building awareness among marginalized groups like women or the untouchable caste, helping them to analyze the causes of their poverty and empowering them to act. We try to manage within the social context and adapt but question the status quo at the same time, keeping a balance. If you want to create ownership, you need to demonstrate your values and your commitment to a vision. You need to coach the staff to give them confidence. You have to be approachable so that your staff will feel free to come to you for support, but coach in ways that they are not just trying to please you but to be leaders themselves."

The grass-roots development approach that Diawary and his colleagues took at CARE in Nepal has borne results. Rather than bringing in **large sums of aid money** from outside the country, only to have it distributed in ways that reinforce the existing power structures, they have helped numerous communities address the unjust distribution of existing resources as well as better leverage the use of funds from elsewhere. For example, it is common in Nepal for landholders to pay women half the wages they pay to men, even though the women perform the same or greater amounts of work. When the women themselves became ready to demand that this discrepancy be addressed because of its dire consequences for them, the result in some communities has been a one hundred percent increase in women's wages just through bringing them into parity with men's. Likewise, poor communities that had received no government support because they were not favored by government officials have begun to receive money that was supposed to be allocated to them in the first place, thanks to their newfound willingness to challenge the status quo.

Diawary has now returned to West Africa, where he is the country director for Sierra Leone. "I am happy and proud to get the opportunity to serve at the most senior leadership position for CARE operations in Sierra Leone. I am also aware that this represents the biggest challenge for me—to become the first ever African national in the country director position for CARE in this country. My success in fulfilling the overall responsibility associated with the country director position will require a mixed balance of several leadership styles, including adaptive, bureaucratic, and democratic."

文化、ジェンダー、カーストといった問題があり、変化への抵抗は根強い。例えば女性やカースト制度の最下層にいる人など社会から阻害されている人々の間で意識を高め、彼ら自身が貧困の原因を分析し、それに対して行動できるよう支援している。地域の社会的環境に合わせて組織を運営し、バランスを保ちながら現状に疑問を投げかける。オーナーシップを生み出すには、スタッフに自信を持ってもらえるよう指導する必要がある。リーダーは親しみやすい存在である必要があるが、彼ら自身がリーダーとなれるように指導しなければならない」

デアワリーたちがネパールのCAREで行った一般人向けの育成手法は、成果を上げた。国外から**多額の援助資金**を得るよりも、既存の権力構造を変化させる方法で資金を分配し、多くのコミュニティが資金をより有効に活用できるよう支援した。例えば、ネパールでは、女性が男性以上の仕事をこなしていても、雇用主が女性に支払う賃金は、普通男性の半分である。この格差に対して、女性と男性の賃金を同等にすることによって、女性の賃金が100%上昇した。同様に、政府に優遇されず、支援を受けられなかった貧しいコミュニティも、人々が新たな意志を示し、本来自分たちに配分されるべき金銭を受け取れるようになった。

現在、西アフリカに戻ったデアワリーは、シエラレオネのカントリー・ディレクターを務めている。

「シエラレオネにおけるCAREの活動運営のトップ・リーダーシップとして取り組む機会を得たことを誇りに思う。この国で史上初のアフリカ国籍のカントリー・マネージャーになるということは、大きな挑戦でもある。カントリー・ディレクターとして包括的責任を果たすには、適応的、官僚的、民主的といった異なるリーダーシップ・スタイルをバランスよく組み合わせる必要がある」

Expand Ownership

Diawary Bouare is working in the context of a **nongovernmental organization**, which of course differs from the corporate world. However, along the way he has learned to practice a number of the behaviors of successful leaders: seeing the influence of his home environment on his approach to leadership; dealing with unexpected circumstances in new work settings; frame-shifting in terms of his communication and leadership styles from more to less direct, technical to strategic, and so on. Moreover, he speaks about widening the scope of those involved with leadership and decision making to include people who are usually excluded due to **social and organizational barriers**.

The global leadership behavior expand ownership means to create a sense of engagement in a shared process and accountability for setting and achieving targets. Expanding ownership is part of any change effort, whether domestic or global. But working in a global context brings new and sometimes hidden obstacles to involving those who are best informed and able to contribute to decision making, and who will also be crucial to effective implementation.

OBSTACLES TO OWNERSHIP: OUTDATED SYSTEMS

In the corporate arena as well as within the history of many nongovernmental organizations, there is a typical pattern of evolution experienced by organizations: they start with a focus on their national market and then develop an **international presence**. The most complex stage of evolution is the "global" company, which consists of a network of operations exchanging information and expertise. Along the road to globalization, it is necessary to move from a "**mother ship / baby ship**" type of structure to a model that consists of a more interdependent network, in which subsidiaries have freedom while being linked with each other as well as with headquarters.

There is much confusion about the term "global." It is used in several overlapping ways to refer to:

1. An organization that has cultivated its structures, systems, and employee mindset to work effectively on a worldwide basis in a structure where the emphasis is on horizontal collaboration rather than vertical hierarchy.

第五の条件 オーナーシップの拡大

デアワリーは、**非政府組織**で活動している。それは企業の世界とは大きく異なるが、彼はこれまでに、成功したリーダーの行動を実践することを学んできた。新しい職場環境での予期せぬ状況への対応、コミュニケーションやリーダーシップのスタイルにおいて、直接的から間接的へ、技術的から戦略的へといったフレームシフトを実施した。さらに、**社会的、組織的な障壁**によって通常は除外されている人を含めて、リーダーシップや意思決定に関わる人々の範囲を広げた。

グローバルリーダーシップの行動は、共有されたプロセスに取り組むために、関係者すべてにオーナーシップ（当事者意識）を拡大するものである。オーナーシップの拡大というテーマをグローバルな環境に導入するには、新たな、隠れた障害を乗り越える必要がある。

オーナーシップの障害：時代遅れのシステム

多くの場合、組織はまず国内市場に注力し、それから**国際的な存在感**を高めていく。最も複雑な発展プロセスを持つのは、情報と専門知識を交換する事業ネットワークからなる「グローバル」企業である。グローバル化の道のりで「**母船・子船**」タイプの構造から、支社が本社と、また子会社同士で自由につながり、より相互依存的なネットワーク構造へと転換する必要がある。

グローバルという言葉には、混乱がつきものだ。グローバルという言葉は、いくつかの重複した意味で使われる。

1. 上下関係よりも横の連携を重視した構造の中で、ワールドワイドに効果的に働くための仕組みや制度、社員のマインドが醸成されている組織。

2. Central control and authority that are exerted in contrast to local control—there is always a need to balance "global" in this sense with local, even when some aspects of an organization are decentralized.

3. Functions or business units that are designed to achieve their objectives across national boundaries, as in "global business unit," "global IT," or "global" as a term for "headquarters".

Regarding the first meaning of the term "global" as a **horizontal network**, companies globalize in different forms and at different rates based upon their business environment and strategic choices. There is no single formula for success, but the higher the percentage of a firm's revenues that come from outside its home country, the more likely its leaders will perceive an increasing need to evolve in the direction of the **global network model**. Firms experiencing explosive revenue increases in markets abroad, whether through organic growth or as the result of mergers and acquisitions, may find themselves with an **outdated organizational structure** that is closer to the international type; other companies may evolve more gradually.

Whatever path a firm takes, there are common requirements for handling the **complications** that arise from doing business on a global scale. A new level of global understanding and day-to-day collaboration across business units and staff functions becomes essential to handle such things as the **cultural requirements and tastes** of various customers, **fresh competitive threats, supply chain logistics**, and **intellectual property violations**.

Predictable problems tend to occur as an organization moves toward a more globalized business while retaining the systems, mindsets, and behaviors that previously served it well but which have now become obstacles. The **mentality of an international firm** regarding a new product or project is, "We'll develop it here at headquarters and then roll it out to the rest of the world; we can tweak whatever we need to for local markets later." Employees accustomed to designing products or initiatives for their home market and who now need to develop global solutions must change their approach. The following is an example of how this problem **surfaced** in the context of a marketing strategy.

2. ローカル主導のコントロールとは対照的に発揮される中央集約型コントロールと権限—組織の一部が分散化されている場合でも、この意味での「グローバル」とローカルのバランスをとる必要が常にある。
3. 「グローバルビジネスユニット」、「グローバルIT」、または「本部」の用語としての「グローバル」のように、国の境界を越えて目的を達成するように設計されている機能またはビジネスユニット。

まず見たいのは、**水平的ネットワーク**としての「グローバル」化である。それは、企業が事業環境や戦略的選択に応じて、より多様な形態でグローバル化を行うことを指す。成功のための単一の公式は存在しないが、国外からの収益の割合が高い企業ほど、**グローバル・ネットワーク・モデル**の方向に進化する必要性が高い。企業は自らの**時代遅れの国際化構造**の是正が必要だ。

グローバル規模の事業展開による**複雑性**に対応するためには共通の要件がある。様々な顧客の**文化的要件や嗜好**、**新たな競争上の脅威**、**物流**、**知的財産権の侵害**などに対処するためには、事業単位とスタッフ機能全体にわたる新たな基準への国際規模での理解と日々の協力が不可欠である。

新しい製品やプロジェクトに対する**国際企業の標準の考え方**は「本社で開発し、世界中に展開する。現地市場で必要なものは、後から微調整できる」というものである。しかし、グローバルなソリューションを開発しなければならなくなった場合は、そうした手法を変える必要がある。この問題がマーケティング戦略の中でどのように**表面化した**かを以下に示す。

EXAMPLE: **CREATING A GLOBAL MARKETING STRATEGY**

A successful retail firm with a strong brand in its home market was seeking to expand into new markets, including China. The headquarters marketing staff members found themselves and their attempts to enforce company guidelines in conflict with their China-based counterparts, who sought to promote the brand in ways that ran counter to the brand strategy at home. Rather than the traditional emphasis on quality and durability, which had long appealed to the firm's domestic customers, marketing staff in China sought to promote the brand in a more eye-catching way through association with celebrities, special events, and flashy store presentations. As one Chinese marketing employee put it, "Here we're one brand among many, and local consumers don't have any idea who we are. So, we have to reach out and appeal to them by showing them how we are special."

Addressing this kind of marketing challenge will require frame-shifting, with a mindset flexible enough to support both the traditional marketing approach at home and a more flashy strategy in China. But changes are also needed that involve the task of achieving the **optimum global/local balance**. Headquarters must not only revamp the marketing guidelines, but address an outmoded decision-making process that places control and authority for marketing decisions with headquarters, while subsidiary employees on the front lines with customers have to petition for support.

Such a shift in power and control is difficult to achieve because employees in subsidiary locations need to overcome numerous disadvantages, such as physical distance and language barriers, in order for their voices to be taken seriously. Meanwhile, people at headquarters worry about becoming **less important** or **less employable** if they cede responsibility. And yet, persisting with a **centralized approach** can be **self-defeating**.

例：**グローバルなマーケティング戦略を立案する**

国内市場で強力なブランドを展開し成功を収めているある小売企業が、中国を含む新しい市場への進出を模索していた。
本社のマーケティングスタッフは、中国のカウンターパートが、本社の戦略に反する方法でブランドを売り込もうとしていたことに気がついた。本国では顧客に対し品質や耐久性を訴えてきたが、中国のマーケティング担当者は、有名人の起用、特別なイベント、派手な店構えなど目を引く方法でブランドを宣伝しようとした。ある中国のマーケティング担当者はこう述べている。

「ここでは私たちは多くのブランドの中の1つであり知名度も低い。だから、私たちが特別な存在であることを示すことで消費者に訴えなければならない」

このようなマーケティングの問題に取り組むには、自国のマーケティング手法と中国の戦略の両方に対応できる柔軟なマインドセットを持つフレームシフトが必要だ。また、**グローバルとローカルの最適なバランス**を達成する必要もある。本社は、マーケティング・ガイドラインだけではなく、マーケティングの意志決定は本社が主導権を握るという時代遅れな意思決定プロセスも改善する必要があり、顧客と直接接する子会社や支社のスタッフに支援を求めなければならない。

子会社や支社のスタッフの声を真剣に受け止めるためには、物理的距離や言語の壁など多くの不利な要素を克服する必要があり、それは容易ではない。

一方、本社スタッフは、責任を委譲すれば自分たちの**重要性が低下**したり、**雇用機会が減少**したりするのではと心配する。しかし、**中央集権的なアプローチ**に固執すると**自滅する**可能性がある。

OBSTACLES TO OWNERSHIP: LOCAL CUSTOMS

Diawary Bouare has striven to expand **ownership** in each of the locations where he has worked. The greatest obstacles he faced to further enfranchising employees while in Nepal appear to have been local barriers of caste and class; he tried to affect these gradually through demonstrating a commitment to the organizational values of diversity, respect, excellence, and transparency. On the spectrum of central to local control, CARE is a **decentralized organization** relative to most corporations. Its services, such as emergency relief, economic development, education, and health care are customized and delivered to sixty million people in seventy-two countries. In spite of its decentralization and a mission statement that emphasizes self-help, even CARE must struggle with a variety of issues related to **headquarters versus local dynamics**, and headquarters continues to serve a vital role.

For example, Diawary notes he has had to combat pressures to show **favoritism** toward individuals or ethnic groups, and part of his success within the organization is that he has implemented organization-wide CARE principles in his leadership roles despite these pressures. Likewise, CARE must focus on achieving headquarters-driven standards of efficiency and financial reporting in **raising and spending donor money**, while complying with the regulations of donor governments. And there are continuous forms of **knowledge transfer*** between CARE's centers of expertise in developed countries and its local operations around the world.

Complete decentralization should not be the ultimate goal of a globalized organization. Instead, every organization must constantly work to achieve the optimum balance of centralization and decentralized authority.

OWNERSHIP AND PARAMETERS

It is necessary for leaders to scrutinize every segment of their operations to determine the best form of headquarters/subsidiary balance for each business, function, and task. In CARE's case, the proper balance in most locations will probably require compliance with standardized ethical and accounting principles driven by headquarters. Similarly, many companies need to have **uniform solutions** for their IT platforms or financial accounting systems, while functions such as sales, marketing, and human resources must be flexible to accommodate local consumer tastes and labor laws.

オーナーシップ（当事者意識）に対する障壁：現地の習慣

デアワリーは、勤務地ごとに**当事者意識**を拡大しようと努力してきた。

ネパール勤務の時に、従業員の権限を拡大する際の最大の障害は、カースト制や階層性だった。彼は多様性、敬意、卓越性、透明性といった組織的価値へのコミットメントを示すことで徐々に状況を変えていこうとした。

中央集権から地方分権まで、権力分布の多様なあり方において、CAREは一般企業に比べて**分権化された組織**である。緊急援助、経済開発、教育、医療などのサービスが、ニーズに合わせて72カ国、6千万人に提供されている。地方分権と自助を重視しているCAREでさえも、**本部対地域の力関係**についての様々な問題に取り組む必要があり、本部は引き続き重要な役割を担っている。

例えば、デアワリーは、個人や民族グループに対する**えこひいき**の圧力と戦わなければならなかったと述べており、組織内での成功の一部は、こうした圧力にもかかわらず、彼のリーダーの役割において組織全体としてのCARE原則を貫いたことによるものである。同様に、CAREは援助国政府の規制を遵守しながら、**援助資金の調達と支出**について財務報告を行い、本部主導の効率性基準を満たすことにも注力しなければならない。また、先進国のCAREの専門知識センターと世界各地での現地活動との間では継続的な**知識移転**が行われている。

完全な分権化が、グローバル化された組織の最終目標であってはならない。その代わりに、すべての組織は中央集権化と地方分権化の最適なバランスを達成するために常に努力しなければならない。

所有権とパラメータ

つまり、リーダーは、組織の各部門を精査し、事業、機能、業務ごとに最適な本社対支社のバランスを決める必要がある。CAREの場合、本社主導の標準化された倫理および会計原則の遵守が必要となるだろう。また、多くの企業は、ITプラットフォームや財務会計システムに対して**統一されたソリューション**を持つ必要があるが、販売、マーケティング、人事といった機能は、現地消費者の好みや労働法に柔軟に合わせなければならない。

＊すでに知識を持っている人から、知識を必要とする人への知識移転。

The proper balance between centrally and locally driven systems is often a moving target that shifts with the skill level of employees and the growing sophistication of particular markets. Companies are altering the roles of their R&D functions in China and India from the adaptation of products designed elsewhere to more autonomous and demanding roles such as designing new products and finding cutting-edge technologies that originate in those markets. At the same time, the importance of these countries for the success of the company calls for communication and coordination between headquarters and subsidiaries that are still not equal but that exist within a changing balance of power.

Setting the **right parameters** may require an **active process of instruction** along with clarity about the freedom that others have. What does not work well in promoting genuine ownership is pushing an approach formulated elsewhere or talking about empowerment* that does not match the opportunities available.

> "You have to put it out there, teach it, show why and how, help them to understand, give them a choice; let them know that a different answer is okay."

Insights from Global Followers

Our executives often use the word empowerment. But the reality is that we don't have much input regarding our goals. These are set at headquarters by people who are looking at spreadsheets but don't understand our market. Then we are empowered to meet targets that are forced on us and asked to commit to achieving these goals.

When we hear about this kind of "ownership" and "commitment," it is meaningless. If the leader of our business unit asked us, we could provide her with information about what is possible and what is impossible, but maybe she does not want to hear what we have to say because she is listening to her bosses at headquarters, or thinks that we do not have sufficient experience or capability. It feels like she does not trust us even though she talks about building trust.

中央主導型のシステムと地方主導型のシステムの適切なバランスは、従業員のスキルレベルや特定の市場の状況に応じて変化することが多い。

適切なパラメータを設定するには、他の人が持っている自由度を明確にし、**積極的に指示するプロセス**が必要になるかもしれない。真のオーナーシップを推進する上でうまくいかないのは、他の国で作られたアプローチを押し付けたり、機会に合わない権限委譲の話をすることだ。

グローバルフォロワーからの洞察

経営幹部は「エンパワーメント」という語をよく使う。しかし、実際には、私たちは自身の目標について十分な情報を提供されていない。目標を設定しているのは、数字のことばかり気にして、私たちの市場を理解していない本社の方だ。それでいて、課された目標を達成する権限を現地の社員に与え、達成にコミットするよう求めてくる。

このような「オーナーシップ」や「コミットメント」は私たちにとって無意味だ。

＊権限付与、委譲。広くは能力開化、夢や希望を与えること。

OWNERSHIP AND PROCESS

Our interviewees suggested crafting processes for gathering and sharing information, exchanging ideas, and making decisions that are **inclusive rather than exclusive**. Diawary Bouare highlighted the importance of giving local employees a voice, ensuring broad understanding of issues, and creating a format for joint analysis and debate. Others noted the importance of seeking opinions at multiple levels of the organization to avoid being boxed into narrow perspectives due to barriers of hierarchy or language.

> "Listen and do not make quick judgments, but rather take time to get all sides and perspectives, and verify these on different levels. Hold open discussions, not only one-on-one, but with different levels of staff. Some countries are more hierarchical so they have a fear of this; as a leader, don't let the conversation be dominated by a single voice, including yours. Meet with groups at their level. Create a venue and space to share without fear of recrimination. Establish a process for this, and allow for anonymous feedback. Language is also key to this process of gaining input at every level; you will be limited to the senior perspective only if you don't learn the local language and are insulated from employees by a leadership team that speaks your language while other people do not."

The majority of our interviewees expressed a preference for processes that expand **involvement in decision making**. They accomplish this through means such as increasing access to information, providing process instructions, and encouraging inclusive practices.

ACCOUNTABILITY

It is possible to be too **culturally sensitive** and not hold others accountable for their performance, or to fail to act decisively in reprimanding or removing poor performers. Once global leaders have established parameters that provide some freedom and processes that incorporate information sharing, discussion, and involvement in decision making, they can then demand **greater accountability**. Interviewees noted that inclusivity and accountability go together, and that empathy, cultural understanding, and a system open to participation do not exclude an emphasis on performance.

所有権とプロセス

インタビューでは、情報を収集、共有し、アイデアを交換し、**排他的ではなく包括的**な意思決定を行うためのプロセスを構築するべきだという提案があった。デアワリーは、現地スタッフに発言権を与え、共同分析や討論の体制を作ることの重要性を強調している。また、階層や言語の壁によって狭い視野にとらわれないように組織の複数レベルで意見を求めることの重要性を指摘する人もいた。

> 「話を聞いてすぐに判断せず、時間をかけてあらゆる側面と観点を把握し、異なる基準で検証する。1対1だけではなく、様々なレベルのスタッフとオープンな議論を行う。より階層的な国では、各レベルのグループと話し合う。非難し返されることを恐れずに共有する場を確保する。このためのプロセスを確立し、匿名のフィードバックを考慮する。言語はあらゆるレベルで情報を得るためのプロセスの鍵でもある。リーダーが現地の言語を学ばず、自分の母国言語を話すリーダーシップ・チームによって現地スタッフから隔絶された場合、上位の役職者の考えしか知ることができないだろう」

インタビューに応じた人の大半は、**意思決定への関与**を拡大することは好ましいと述べた。彼らは、情報へのアクセスを拡大し、プロセスの指示を与え、包括的取り組みを奨励するといった方法でこれを達成している。

説明責任

文化的に過敏になりすぎると、業績に対する説明責任を負わせなかったり、業績の悪い人に断固とした態度を取らなかったりすることがある。情報の共有、議論、意思決定への関与を含めたプロセスを提供するパラメータを確立したグローバルリーダーは、スタッフに**より大きな責任**を求めることができる。包括性と説明責任は両立するものであり、共感、文化的理解、参加しやすいシステムは、成果重視を排除することにはならないのだ。以下のコメントに注目したい。

"You need to have the same emphasis on accountability as inclusivity. People must be accountable for the results of **inclusive decisions**."

"Don't be afraid to hold people accountable. Our senior manager in Japan did a great job of **adapting to the culture**. But he didn't hold team members accountable, and nothing was accomplished. You need to assess and listen first, understand what they are doing, and utilize their feedback. Three to four months later, come out with a vision, objectives, high standards, and expectations. You get buy-in, give people the support they need, and then you can hold them accountable. If people don't respond, you have to do something about it: get further buy-in, improve the process, or move people out."

"In some cultures, people find it difficult to reprimand or fire someone. There is a risk involved with this, but if there is a poor performer in the office, other staff members know about it. You are seen as a weak leader if you don't do anything about it."

Leaders working in hierarchical and group-oriented cultures sometimes found value in empowering the local management team and holding them accountable for results on a collective as well as an individual basis.

"I have been trying to empower the management team. This group was seen as a rubber stamp, just doing what the country director wanted them to do. The power structure in this country is rigid. There is a tendency to let the senior person make the decision. I am getting the management team to take on a collective leadership role so that I don't have to make all the decisions. I am trying to get this kind of decision-making structure out to all of the staff; trying to make this process more transparent."

Develop Future Leaders

Many of the interview comments regarding expanding ownership referred to leadership development. Beyond widening employees' sense of ownership for projects or initiatives, "opening the system" also means enabling capable people from anywhere in an organization to step into leadership roles over time. For an organization to achieve targets in **growth markets**, it is essential to **develop local talent**. Such development must include the capability to weigh global and local perspectives with the best interests of

「包括性と説明責任を同等に重視する必要がある。スタッフは**包括的決定**の結果に対して責任を持たなければならない」

「人に責任を負わせることを恐れてはいけない。私たちの日本のシニアマネージャーは、現地の**文化にうまく順応**した。しかし、チームメンバーに責任を負わせず、何も達成できなかった。まず、評価して、耳を傾け、彼らが何をしているかを理解し、フィードバックを行う必要がある。3、4カ月後に、ビジョン、目標、高い標準、期待値を提示する。同意を取り付けて、必要なサポートを提供すれば、責任を負わせることができる。もし、反応がなければ、さらなる同意を得るか、プロセスを改善するか、スタッフを異動させるか、何らかの対策を取らなければならない」

「文化によっては、スタッフを叱責したり、解雇したりするのは難しいこともある。リスクはあるが、職場に業績の悪いスタッフがいれば、その存在は他のスタッフにもわかる。それに対して何もしなければ、弱いリーダーだと見なされる」

階層的でグループ指向の文化で業務にあたるリーダーは、現地のマネジメントチームに権限を与え、個人ベースだけでなく、集団ベースで結果への説明責任を負わせることに価値を見出すことがある。

第六の条件 将来のリーダーの育成

オーナーシップ（当事者意識）の拡大についてのコメントの多くは、リーダーシップの開発に関するものだった。「オープンな体制」とは、プロジェクトやイニシアチブに対する当事者意識を広げるだけでなく、組織のどこからでも有能な人材が長期的にリーダーシップの役割を担うことができるようにしなければならない。組織が**成長市場**で目標を達成するには**現地の人材を育成**することが不可欠である。現地の人材開発には、企業の最大利益を念頭に置

the company in mind. Some companies need to complete a massive transfer of knowledge from home-country employees with vital technical and project leadership skills to high-potential individuals in different world regions. In other cases, local employees need an infusion of more generic leadership experience as well as the skills to deal with headquarters.

To develop future leaders, those in global leadership roles must identify and cultivate individuals who can provide the impetus for growth in global markets. Although this sounds straightforward, errors in judgment often occur when working across cultural and linguistic boundaries.

> "It is so easy to arrive in a country with **preconceived ideas**. I stereotyped and was wrong. I judged a person based on a couple of meetings as not right for the role. He turned out to be one of the best people for the job. The problem was my lack of understanding of specific issues. I jumped to conclusions based on asking the wrong questions—people will answer the specific question. I judged that a proposal this person presented was not well thought through. You have to take the time to explore and ask the right questions."

Insights from Global Followers

It is discouraging to see "**apple polishers**" get promoted into leadership roles. By this I mean people whose primary skill is making friends with executives from headquarters. They have the language skills to communicate, but lack technical skills or knowledge of our customers. I think even these apple polishers are surprised when they are promoted, but they like the power, and sometimes to protect their position they will say negative things to foreign executives about the people who are doing the work.

A new global leader who was good at judging people took over our line of business. It was exciting to see him listen to each person on the executive team, speak to other employees, and go on customer visits even when he had to communicate mostly through an interpreter. We began to open up and tell him who is capable, and he has begun to promote these people, including one local sales guy who doesn't speak other languages well but has won a lot of business with customers and is respected by employees.

いて、グローバルな視点とローカルな視点を比較検討できる能力が含まれなければならない。一部の企業では、世界の異なる地域の有望な人材に、知識を大量に移転する必要がある。企業によっては、現地スタッフにより一般的なリーダーシップの経験と、本社に対応するためのスキルの注入が必要となる。グローバルリーダーとしての役割を担っている人は、グローバル市場での成長に勢いを与えることができる人材を特定し育成しなければならない。それには特定の文化に対する先入観をも疑う姿勢が求められる。あるリーダーはこう語る。

> 「**先入観**のある国を訪れることがよくあるが、私の先入観は間違っていた。何度かの打ち合わせの結果をもとに、あるスタッフをその役割にふさわしくないと判断した。が、後に彼はその仕事に最適な人材だったことがわかった。時間をかけて検討してから正しい質問をしなければならない」

グローバルフォロワーからの洞察

ゴマをする人がリーダーに昇進するのを見るとやる気が失せる。これは、本社の経営幹部と親しくなることが第一のスキルであることを意味する。彼らはコミュニケーションを取るための言語スキルを持っているが、技術的スキルや顧客に対する知識は不足している。こうした人は外国人幹部にきちんと仕事をしている人について否定的なことを言うことがある。

中には外国語は得意ではないが、顧客との取引で多くの成功を収め、社員から尊敬されている地元の販売員もいるのだから。

There are a number of reasons why leaders misjudge others who are from different backgrounds. These include:

- A tendency to evaluate most highly those who are most like us
- Incorrect assessment of a candidate's capabilities based upon language skill level
- Evaluation of performance based on activities rather than results

Another factor adding to the complexity of leadership development in a global context is that not only do leaders often misjudge others, but leadership candidates may look at their leaders inaccurately through the lens of cultural stereotypes or the performance of a predecessor.

> "Just as I stereotype others, I am stereotyped based upon the effectiveness or lack thereof of the previous people in my role."

Diawary Bouare noted that change means building the capacity of your core team to be more strategic, while widening the scope of those driving the change. What is challenging is that team members may **accomplish their tasks** using unfamiliar methods. As one interviewee observed, "I had to give others the chance to prove themselves successful in ways no one had been successful before, and to utilize their own values and styles to be successful."

Developmental practices and objectives will probably also require adjustment—for example, a leader accustomed to a consultative style or an extreme task focus might have to help more junior staff cultivate a different leadership style more suitable to the local context. One common denominator recommended by our interviewees for successful leadership development is **accessibility**.

> "You need to coach the staff, to empower and give them confidence. You have to be approachable so that your staff will come to you for support."

A commitment to **being approachable** and to developing employees can produce other dividends, including getting feedback that global leaders

リーダーが、異なるバックグラウンドを持つ人を誤解する理由には以下のことが考えられる。

- 自分に近い人ほど高く評価する傾向
- 言語スキルレベルに基づく候補者能力の評価の誤り
- 結果ではなく活動に基づいた業績評価

グローバルな環境でのリーダーシップ開発を複雑にしている要因のひとつが、文化的先入観や前任者の業績の観点から人材を見誤る傾向なのだ。

デアワリーは、変革とはコアチームの能力をより戦略的に構築しながら、変革を推進するチームの視野を広げることだと言う。難しいのは、チームメンバーが不慣れな方法で**タスクを達成**しなければならないということだ。

開発のための戦略設定や目標設定には調整が必要だろう。リーダーシップ開発に成功のための推奨事項としてインタビューで挙げられた共通の要素の1つは**親しみやすさ**である。

「スタッフを指導し、権限を与え、自信を持たせる必要がある。サポートを求めてスタッフがリーダーのところに来てくれるようにするためには、リーダーは親しみやすくなければならない」

親しみやすさを保ちながら、スタッフを育成するというコミットメントは、他の手段ではなかなか得られないフィードバックを得たり、スタッフのモチ

find difficult to obtain through other means, along with genuine employee motivation and commitment.

> "A tool that I used to keep myself engaged was to work on my direct reports' personal development. I would sit with them on a monthly basis, develop an action plan, and look at their gaps and strengths. I also received **360-degree feedback** that way. This was an excellent tool for building relationships, honesty, and a network. They trust me because they see that I am applying what they say."

The ultimate goal for global leaders is to work themselves out of a job, with new people stepping in who may do things in a different but effective way.

> "I helped other people do things through empowering, giving skills, instruction, and space and time to carry out a task. I have given responsibilities to a local national in all the countries where I have been. I work with national staff to train and coach them to leadership."

ベーションを向上させ、目標達成への責任感を醸成できたりといったメリットがある。

「私が自分の役割を果たすために使った手段は、直属の部下の自己啓発への取り組みだった。私は彼らと月に1度話し合い、アクションプランを作成し、弱点と強みを検討した。私もこの方法で**360度評価**を受けた。これは、人間関係、誠実性、ネットワークを構築するための最適な方法だ。部下たちは、自分たちが言ったことを私が採用しているのを見て、信頼してくれるようになった」

グローバルリーダーの最終目標は、新しいメンバーが加わって今までとは異なるが効果的な方法で仕事をすることによって、自分がいなくても仕事が回るようにすることである。

「任務を遂行するための権限、スキル、指示、場所、時間を与えることでスタッフを支援した。私は、過去に赴任した全ての国で、現地スタッフに責任を与えてきた。現地スタッフと協力してリーダーシップを発揮できるよう指導している」

CHAPTER SIX

Preserving Balance

For decades, the research on **working across borders** has emphasized the **importance of flexibility and adaptation.** While adaptation is essential in a foreign environment, many leaders with whom we spoke were clear that they had to preserve a balance between knowing when to adapt and when not to adapt. They found it necessary both to accommodate local circumstances and to select appropriate moments to contribute their own expertise or exert authority. The behaviors we have labeled adapt and add value and core values and flexibility reflect the kinds of balance these leaders deemed to be most vital.

Global Leader: Gary Ashmore, AMD

Gary Ashmore is the director of AMD's* Shanghai Research and Development Center. Originally from the United States, he has been in China for two years. Gary has been with AMD for fifteen years, has an MBA from Rutgers University, and he served in a previous assignment for the company in Taiwan before moving to China.

Gary's time in the military made him more organized, confident, and better at taking risks, and after starting in a technical support role at AMD, he worked his way up into team leadership roles. However, he discovered, "It was a whole new world to start managing engineering groups in Asia. In Taiwan, I had to adapt my style a lot initially and then recovered my normal self gradually." He brought in a coach to do communication style profiling with his staff and to build awareness of different communication styles.

第6章

バランスを維持する

国境を越えた業務では、**柔軟性と適応性の大切さ**が強調されてきた。適応性は不可欠だが、適応すべき時とそうでない時のバランスも重要だ。現地の環境に適応することと、自分の専門知識を提供し、権限を行使する適切なタイミングを選択することの両方が必要なのである。適応性、付加価値、コアバリュー、柔軟性をバランスよく行使することは、リーダーにとって最も重要な課題である。

ゲイリー・アシュモアの事例

ゲイリー・アシュモアは、AMDの上海研究開発センターのディレクターである。アメリカ出身で、中国に赴任して2年。中国に赴任する前は、台湾で勤務した。

ゲイリーはAMDでテクニカルサポートの仕事を始めた後、チームリーダーの役割を担うようになった。しかし、ゲイリーは気づいた。

「アジアで技術者グループを統率することは未知の世界だった。台湾では、最初は自分のやり方を現地に合わせたが、徐々にいつもの自分のやり方に戻った」

ゲイリーは、スタッフとの研修を通して地域ごとに異なるコミュニケーション・スタイルがあることに気がついた。台湾と中国の差はさらに大きかった。

＊ Advanced Micro Divices、アメリカで設立された半導体製造メーカー。

Gary describes himself as a very outgoing person compared with his engineering colleagues in the United States. In Taiwan and then in China the differences were even greater. "I always had to watch my style, as engineering folks are quieter and analytical. When I came to Asia, I was dealing with engineers who were also **culturally shy and reserved**, and not very good at giving feedback, criticizing, or challenging management. I had to completely quiet down. I had to take time to understand the local culture better. And there was a whole new level of organizational politics to learn. There is a lot of **not-so-obvious power**, and it takes a lot longer to understand this and to influence things in the right ways."

There were many standard local practices that were unfamiliar to Gary, and he found it necessary to adapt. "I became more open-minded to the HR side of things. For example, everyone comes to work around 10 a.m., catches up socially, checks email, and then breaks for lunch. After lunch, they may take a nap, but they stay and work until 10 p.m. to get things done. You have to choose your battles. I also had to be more open about special seating arrangements in meetings, whom to give business cards to, the protocol. I had to push to get more feedback, because people won't always give you the information on protocol or what is offensive, so you have to learn to ask. I started to read and learn the body language and stop and ask more, while slowing down a bit and taking more of a listening posture."

It took time for him to establish his own credibility with his Chinese colleagues. "I had to earn respect through work, coming out with ideas and then relaxing and letting them come up with specific details and questions in their own time—then listening to them and explaining things to them. Once the team gets used to you, they start to understand what needs to happen."

A major step forward for Gary was "getting a local person to be my business manager... It was good to have someone who had worked for a multinational corporation before, who understood how the local people see things. I used that person to seek out advice... Local managers can be trained to fill that role as well. It is important to have someone you can trust with all aspects of the business."

Gary describes himself as a kind of cheerleader in his current leadership role. "Everyone at work has a job to do, and when they are here, I

「技術者たちはより静かで分析的だった。アジアに赴任した当初、**文化的に内気で控えめ**で、幹部にフィードバックを与えたり、批判したり、異議を唱えたりすることがあまり得意ではない技術者と仕事をする機会があった。私はずっと口をつぐみながら、時間をかけて現地の文化をよく理解しなければならなかった。また、全く新しい政策や基準も学ぶ必要があった。**わかりにくい力関係**も多くあり、これを理解し、適切な方法で物事に影響を与えるには時間がかかる」

「私は寛容になった。例えば、誰もが午前10時頃出社して、おしゃべりをしながら情報交換し、メールをチェックし、昼休みを取る。昼食後は、仮眠を取ることもあるが、皆午後10時まで残って働く。会議中の席順についても同様だった。そこで名刺を交換する習慣があったためだ。より多くのフィードバックを得るために努力をした。習慣や礼儀について現地スタッフが常に教えてくれるわけではないので、自分から質問をして学ぶ。ボディランゲージも覚えた。また、ペースを少し落として耳を傾ける姿勢を貫き、多くの質問を投げかけた」

中国人スタッフと信頼関係を築くのは時間がかかったようだ。
「仕事を通じて尊敬を得るしか方法はない。アイデアを出し、リラックスさせ、具体的な情報や質問を彼らのペースで考え出してもらい、それを聞いてから、説明した。リーダーに慣れれば、チームはやるべきことは何かを理解し始める」

ゲイリーにとっての大きな前進は、地元出身者をビジネスマネージャーにしたことだった。多国籍企業で勤務経験があり、かつ現地の人々の考え方を理解してくれる人がいたことは幸いだ。ゲイリーはその人に助言を求め訓練してもらった。

ゲイリーは、自分の現在の役割は、チアリーダーのようなものだと言う。
「職場では、誰もがすべき仕事がある。悩まず、やりがいを持って取り組

want them not to be suffering but excited, with lots of teambuilding activities including things like a barbecue on the roof, and pictures on the wall from every fun activity we do so they can call us a 'family'." At the same time, he is **demanding**. "I take a very hard line at a certain point. When people don't meet their goals, we have a hard meeting. The health and mind of each person comes first, their families are second, and work is third. But I don't mind calling someone at 2 o'clock in the morning if they don't have their deliverables."

Gary's business objectives for the Shanghai Research and Development Center included transforming the team into a more innovative unit that would be able to go beyond its prior role. Ultimately this task involved making difficult changes in personnel. "About ten percent of the people couldn't adapt to the new dynamics of the team, which sometimes meant multitasking or changing directions on a day's notice. The new setup requires different thinking. There were people who could not get their mind around this so they couldn't stay. This doesn't happen with new graduates, but it can happen with managers from local companies—the old guard is sometimes not able to adapt.

Gary's leadership style seems to work well in the competitive Chinese business environment, where keeping employees is a constant challenge. "I have had to fire twenty people in my lifetime and have managed several hundred, but have had just one staff member resign on me."

Gary notes that over time his role has broadened beyond R&D. "You are an ambassador, representing the company. Everyone is looking at me to see what it is like to work for this company, so you are representing the company both internally and externally. I'm also an ambassador back to the U.S., where there are preconceptions about losing jobs to China, or that the Chinese engineers don't get paid as much so they must not be as valuable."

Gary has come to value some of the behaviors he sees in his Chinese team members. "I'm sometimes disappointed with teams in the U.S., which tend to think by the fiscal quarter. Here, we need to think by the year, or three to five years. People don't get as excited in China about not meeting quarterly goals perfectly, and this makes for a much calmer business environment."

んでもらいたい。屋上でのバーベキューなどチームビルディング活動も積極的に行い、その写真を壁に貼ったりして、みんなが『家族』と呼べるようなチームにしたい」。とはいえ、彼がチームに要求するものも多い。

「**厳しく要求する**こともある。目標を達成できない時は厳しい会議を行う。一番大切なのは各自の健康と精神、次は家族、仕事は3番目だ。が、成果が出ないスタッフには、午前2時に電話することもいとわない」

上海研究開発センターでのゲイリーの事業目標には、チームを革新的な組織に転換することが含まれ、そのための人事異動も行なった。

「複数の業務を1度に行うことや、1日前の通知で方向を変えることもあったので、スタッフの1割は変化に適応できなかった。新しいことに取り組むには、今までとは異なる考え方が必要だが、それを理解できない人はチームにとどまることができなかった。新卒者にそのような人はいないが、地元企業の管理職者の中にはいる。保守的な人は適応できないことがある」

ゲイリーのリーダーシップ・スタイルは、競争が激しく従業員の維持が継続的課題である中国のビジネス環境でうまく機能しているようにみえる。「私は20人を解雇し、数百人を管理してきたが、辞職したのは1人だけだ」

ゲイリーは、徐々に自分の役割が研究開発センターを超えて広がったと言う。「グローバルリーダーは、会社を象徴するアンバサダーだ。この会社で仕事をすることがどういうことなのか誰もが私を見て判断する。リーダーは社内的にも社外的にも会社を象徴している。例えば中国の技術者はそれほど給料をもらっていないから価値があるはずはないなどという偏見がアメリカの人々にはあり、私には、アメリカに戻ってもアンバサダーの役割が残った」

ゲイリーは、中国のチームメンバーのある行動を高く評価するようになった。「四半期単位での成果を重視するアメリカのチームに対して失望する時がある。中国では、1年、あるいは3年、5年単位で業績をとらえる必要がある。中国では、四半期の目標を完全に達成できなくても構わない。事業環境はずっと穏やかだ」

Adapt and Add Value

To adapt and add value means to balance adaptation to local practices with finding the best places to contribute a different perspective. Leaders' tasks often include pushing a change agenda, which calls for **setting a new direction and a fresh set of objectives.** Change agentry and action orientation are the **hallmarks of great leaders.** However, global leaders must learn, through **self-awareness,** a heightened sense of **judgment and restraint.** At the same time, they must demonstrate their ability to make a contribution to employees who may question their authority. It is sometimes necessary to teach as well as to learn. Getting this balance right is crucial to long-term success.

WAYS OF ACHIEVING BALANCE

Our interviewees suggested numerous ways of trying to achieve the proper balance between adjusting and contributing. These include building a **foundation of mutual respect** and inquiry, and patiently investing the time to learn about the new environment before initiating something new. They also stressed the importance of asking questions, challenging the **status quo,** and introducing different perspectives.

> "You're only in your role for a short time. Don't march in and make decisions or kick off projects too quickly. It's good to learn a broader perspective on everything."

> "I am very results- and performance-oriented and we should not give up those points or we would be ineffective, but being aware of the planning and time needed to get the correct understanding and answers the first time is essential."

POSITIONING THE LEADER'S ROLE

An important consideration for global leaders is how they **position themselves.** The role that a leader will take depends upon the nature of the initiative and the capabilities of the people in the organization. However, our interviewees generally favored an approach in which they contributed expertise without forcing it. They were positioned in a strategic role to structure and guide processes while incorporating local knowledge. This does not mean avoiding problems that must be addressed in favor of getting along

第七の条件 適応と価値を付加する能力

リーダーの任務の一つには、**新しい方向性と目標の設定**を行い、そのための変革を推進することがある。変革に取り組み、自ら行動で示すことは偉大な**リーダーの証し**である。しかし、グローバルリーダーは、**自己認識**を通じて、**決断力と自制心**を向上させなければならない。教えることと学ぶことも同時に必要だ。このバランスを適切に取ることが長期的な成功に不可欠である。

バランスをとる方法

インタビューでは、新しい環境への適応と、そこでの業務への貢献との間の適切なバランスを実現するための方法についてコメントが集まった。その中には、**お互いが尊敬の念を持ち**質問し合える環境を築くことや、新しいことを始める前に、忍耐強く時間をかけてそれについて学ぶことが含まれる。また、質問を投げかけ、**現状に**異議を唱え、異なる考え方を取り入れることの重要性も強調した。

> 「駐在の任務は短期間だ。いきなり決断を下したり、プロジェクトを開始したりしてはならない。あらゆることに関して広い視野を持つことが大切だ」

> 「結果と実績を重視すべきで、これを放棄してはならない。しかし、そのために必要な計画と時間を前もって把握することは重要だ」

リーダーの役割の位置付け

グローバルリーダーが考慮すべき要素の1つは、**自分自身の位置づけ**だ。リーダーの役割は、イニシアチブの種類と組織内の人々の能力の度合いによって異なる。しかし、インタビューに応じたほとんどの人は、相手に押し付けずに専門知識を提供するアプローチを好み、現地の知識を吸収しながら、手順を策定し導く役割を担っていた。これは、人間関係を円滑にするために、意図的に問題を避けるという意味ではない。時差を超えて業務を支援し、必

well with others. They supported efforts across many time zones and made difficult choices when necessary. In some cases, a leader may need to move faster rather than slower.

> "You have to be able to educate and share your knowledge **without imposing.**"

> "My advice is to not come across as if you know everything, but you have to prove you can add value."

> "You must **deliver results**. I had a 'hundred-day plan' with results visible to everyone. If you don't know the environment, on the other hand, you need to practice patience—plan realistically considering the local culture."

Core Values and Flexibility

Learning the values of a different culture is an important part of building meaningful relationships. Another step involves learning to "**style-switch**;" to change one's behavior in order to function better in the local environment. However, the leaders we interviewed have gone beyond style-switching. Most of them have incorporated other ways of approaching the world into their own personal belief systems. Taking a long-term approach, being careful in the use of resources, or avoiding **nonessential information exchange and discussion** have now become a part of their expanded world view.

> "Even if you know about the other culture, you still need to be flexible enough to embrace some of the true values of the culture. Understanding and being flexible are two different things. The ability to adjust at the level of personal values is more challenging."

There is another side to this equation. Many of our interviewees, especially those with experience in the developing world, insisted that it is essential for leaders to identify their own values and to know clearly which have the highest priority. "**Core values**" signifies a few items that the leader is prepared to defend at all costs, even when they go against local business practices.

要な際は難しい選択も行う。時には、ペースを落とすだけではなく、より迅速に行動する必要もある。

「**押し付けずに**スタッフを教育し、知識を共有する必要がある」

「自分はすべてわかっているなどと思わず、価値を付加しているのだということを理解してもらわなければならない」

「**結果を出す**必要がある。一方で、未知の環境では、忍耐強く、その地域の現実を考慮し、計画を立てなければならない」

第八の条件 コアバリューと柔軟性

文化ごとの異なる価値観を知ることは、有意義な関係を築く上で重要だが、同時に現地の環境でより適切に機能できるように自分の行動様式を変える「**スタイルの切り替え**」を学ぶのも1つの方法だ。しかし、インタビューに応じたリーダーたちは、スタイルの切り替え以上のことを実践していた。長期的な取り組みを行うこと、資源の利用に慎重になること、**不要な情報交換や議論**を避けることなどは、今やリーダーたちの広い世界観の一部となっている。

「たとえ現地の文化を知っていたとしても、その真の価値観を受け入れるためには十分な柔軟性が必要だ。理解することと柔軟であることは別のものだ。個人の価値観のレベルで調整するのは、もっと難しい」

この方程式には別の側面がある。特に途上国での経験を持つ人から、リーダーは自分の価値観を把握し、最優先事項は何かを明確にすることが不可欠だという意見が多く聞かれた。「**コアバリュー**」とは、地域のビジネス慣行に反していても、リーダーが何としても守らなければならない概念となる。慣れない環境で必要なのは、自分の価値観と、その中で妥協の余地がないものは何かを理解することだ。そうでなければ自分自身を見失うかもしれないと

"When you are in someplace different, you need to understand your own values, including which ones are nonnegotiable. Otherwise, you can lose yourself."

Inflexibility is a recipe for disaster in a global leadership role, but our interviewees reported that upholding a few closely held values tended to gain them respect from foreign colleagues. In the meantime, leaders in a global context must learn to exercise flexibility with nearly everything else.

"I try to tackle problems from a variety of angles while sticking to core values."

"You can develop social relationships, but don't compromise basic principles."

DEALING WITH CORRUPTION

Among the challenges that global leaders face are **bribery, corruption,** forms of **exploitation,** and **basic human rights** issues. Resisting such practices is neither popular nor easy, but some of the leaders we interviewed said that they had to take a stand due to deep conflicts between their values and the circumstances in which they found themselves. Having a precise understanding of company policies and national laws is also advisable.

"We have to learn to respect and work with **cultural norms**. Yet as leaders of international organizations, we are often pushing those norms. An example is our policy of **zero tolerance** for sexual exploitation. In an African setting, the understanding of sexual exploitation is not the same as in the West. Even if such exploitation is acceptable by local cultural standards, we have to be clear and demonstrate the organization's policy in our behavior. If an employee in this country engages in inappropriate behavior, you have to call him on it even if it is **within his cultural norm**. I have to spend time with the staff to explain and then give them the chance to develop trust."

いうコメントがあった。

グローバルリーダーの役割において、**柔軟性の欠如**は失敗につながる。しかし、インタビューでは、確固とした価値観を維持することは外国人の同僚からの尊敬につながるという指摘もあった。グローバルな環境で、リーダーは、コアバリュー以外ほとんど全てのことには柔軟に対応できなければならない。

「コアバリューを守り続けながら、様々な角度から問題に取り組んでいる」

「社会的関係を築いてもよいが、基本理念を曲げてはいけない」

不祥事への対応

グローバルリーダーが直面する不祥事についてここで触れてみたい。不祥事には**贈収賄**、**背徳行為**、様々な**搾取**、**基本的人権**の侵害などがある。このような事態を阻止することは容易ではないが、リーダーの中には、自分の価値観と現実の状況との間に深い溝があり、それに立ち向かわなければならないという人もいた。また、企業の方針や国の法令を正しく理解する必要もある。

「**文化的規範**を尊重し業務に取り組まなければならない一方で、国際的な組織のリーダーとして、厳しい規範が必要となることも多い。一例が、性的搾取の問題で、アフリカでの性的搾取に対する理解は、欧米の**いかなる違反も許さない**という点と異なっている。このような搾取が地域の文化的基準で受け入れられているとしても、私たちは組織の方針を明確に示さなければならない。この国で従業員が不適切な行動を取った場合、たとえそれが本人の**文化的規範内**であったとしても、忠告する。時間をかけて当事者に説明し、信頼関係を築くチャンスを与えなければならない」

Insights from Global Followers

One of the principles that the leader of our business has been very firm on is what she calls "**integrity**"—for her this means no bribery in any form. Although at first we didn't understand what she meant, this is a big issue for her, and she fired or reprimanded several senior employees who were giving gifts to government bureaucrats.

Actually, in my country bribery is not seen as an ethical issue, especially when you are providing gifts to officials to build relationships and to encourage them to help our company's business. Although our legal system officially prohibits bribery for some purposes, in practice there are many gray areas and the laws are broken by everyone. For ordinary people here, **integrity and ethics** have more to do with social relationships: how loyal and generous you are to your own family and friends; whether you respect and care for seniors and elderly parents.

When our leader began to enforce her new policy, at first everything took longer and it was difficult for us to get even standard permits approved. However, the government officials eventually accepted that things are different with our company, especially because we worked out ways to donate equipment and training classes to local schools that are a priority for each province.

Our employees are gradually becoming proud of this policy. They also like to work here because they know that within the company you aren't going to be promoted just because you are a friend of the boss and have given your superiors nice gifts.

CORE VALUES: EXAMPLES

Core values come in many forms. Interviewees brought up examples such as fairness, integrity, respect, honesty, effective feedback, openness, loyalty to common goals, rational allocation of organizational resources, and obeying the law.

グローバルフォロワーからの洞察

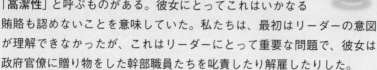

私たちの部門のリーダーが持つ確固とした原則の１つに「**高潔性**」と呼ぶものがある。彼女にとってこれはいかなる賄賂も認めないことを意味していた。私たちは、最初はリーダーの意図が理解できなかったが、これはリーダーにとって重要な問題で、彼女は政府官僚に贈り物をした幹部職員たちを叱責したり解雇したりした。

実際、贈賄は倫理的問題とみなさない国がある。特に、関係を構築して会社の事業を支援してもらうために、公務員に贈り物をする場合は問題にならない。私たちの法制度では、目的によっては贈収賄を禁じているが、実際には多くのグレーゾーンがあり法は守られていない。この地域の一般的な人々にとって、**高潔性と倫理性**とは社会的関係上の指標である。自分の家族や友人に対してどれだけ誠実で寛大か、年配者や高齢の両親を尊敬し大切にしているかを問うものである。

「私たちのリーダーが、自分の新しい方針を実行し始めた当初は、すべてに時間がかかり、定型的な承認を得ることさえ難しかった。しかし、行政区分ごとに優先度の高い地元の学校に備品を寄贈したり研修を支援したりする施策を講じたことなどから、政府関係者も私たちの会社が他社とは違うことを受け入れた」

私たちも徐々にこの企業姿勢を誇りに思うようになった。上司と仲がいいから、上司に贈り物をしたからという理由が昇進につながらない会社だとわかって、ここで働くことが好きになった。

コアバリューの例

コアバリューには様々な形がある。インタビューでは、公正性、高潔性、誠実性、尊敬の念を持つこと、効果的なフィードバック、開放性、共通目標に対する忠誠心、組織資源の合理的配分、法律遵守などの価値がそれに該当するという意見が多かった。以下は、グローバルリーダーのコメントである。

"When I was in Sri Lanka, there were many ethnic tensions. Although this happens in the external social context, it manifested itself internally as well. I couldn't be seen as biased; I had to give equal time to all perspectives."

"My values are honesty, effective feedback, and openness. Feedback was initially very difficult."

"In this part of the world, laws don't exist. You can be surprised. People won't say anything but will try to do what they want anyway, whereas in other countries if you break the law you go to jail. Our corporate culture has very strong values related to following the law."

The core values of a **skillful leader** can become a key point for the team as a whole, even when the values are not entirely consistent with local norms. At the same time, for general values such as "**respect**" or "**honesty**," it is useful to discuss what each value means in terms of specific behavior. What appears to be a demonstration of respect in one location may be regarded as offensive in another. Leaders who immerse themselves in the countries where they work will probably find that their personal values and their understanding of how these are best defined and demonstrated gradually evolve over time.

「スリランカ勤務だった時、現地では民族間の緊張が続いていた。これは外部の社会的状況のみならず、社内でもその兆候が現れる。私は偏見を持っているとは思われないよう、あらゆる考え方に対し同じ時間を割いて向き合った」

「私は、誠実性、効果的なフィードバック、開放性を重視している。当初フィードバックの実施は非常に難しかった」

「驚くべきことにこの地域では、法は存在しない。他の国では法を犯せば刑務所に送られる。誰も何も言わないが、ここでは自分がやりたいことをしようとする。私たちの企業文化は、法律の遵守に対して非常に強い価値観を持っている」

優れたリーダーのコアバリューは、たとえ現地の規範と完全に一致していなくても、全体としてチームにとって重要な規範となることがある。同時に「**尊敬の念を持つこと**」や「**誠実性**」といった一般的な価値観を、具体的な行動におきかえて協議することは有益である。ある地域では敬意を表しているように見えるものが、他の地域では無礼だと見なされることもある。赴任した国に溶け込んでいるリーダーは、個人的価値観を、どのように定義し実施しているかを現地スタッフが時間とともに理解してゆくことに気づくだろう。

CHAPTER SEVEN

Establishing Solutions

However wide the gaps might be between their home context and the global business environment, leaders must **produce results**. In this chapter, we will focus on the process of creating solutions. Influence across boundaries and third-way solutions represent essential aspects of this process.

Global Leader: Khalid al-Faddagh, Saudi Aramco

Khalid al-Faddagh is from Saudi Arabia. Saudi Aramco, his employer, is the national oil company of Saudi Arabia. Starting in 2003, Khalid was assigned for four years in the Philippines as the president and CEO of his company's joint venture operations there. Upon his return to Saudi Arabia, Khalid was assigned to corporate planning to lead the team responsible for strategy development and the five-year business plan for this global giant. Subsequently, he was again promoted to become the company's general auditor.

During his more than twenty-five years with Saudi Aramco, Khalid has served in various roles. Khalid describes his leadership style as one that balances **people skills**[*1] and **technical skills**.[*2] "Technical knowledge is important, but people skills have also been quite critical when dealing with the many people reporting to me during my different assignments. I have an **open-door policy**, with not much formality. When working in the **technical arena**, I use a different style than with a more **field-oriented assignment**, where setting certain targets and tasks, checking on progress, and assessing the implications of recommendations become more critical. When I had a chance to manage the maintenance programs at a major oil facility, I had to be clear with the superintendents reporting

第7章

ソリューションの確立

自国の環境とグローバルな事業環境との差がどれほど大きくても、リーダーは結果を出さなければならない。本章では、そんなリーダーのためのソリューションの構築プロセスに焦点を当てる。国境を越えた影響力と第3のソリューションと呼ばれるアプローチについて解説する。

カリッド・アル・ファダの例

サウジアラビアのカリッドは、国営の石油会社サウジアラムコに勤務している。カリッドは2003年から4年間、同社のフィリピンのジョイントベンチャー事業の社長兼CEOを務めた。本国に戻った後は、戦略開発と5カ年事業計画を担当するチームを率いる経営企画担当に任命され、同社の監査役に昇進した。

カリッドは、自分のリーダーシップ・スタイルについて、**ヒューマンスキル**と**テクニカルスキル**のバランスを重んじていると自認する。

「技術的知識は重要だが、多くの部下に対応するにはヒューマンスキルも非常に大切だ。形式にとらわれない**オープンな姿勢**でスタッフと接してきた。**現場志向の業務**では、特定の目標を設定し、職務を分担し、進捗を確認し、推奨事項の影響評価をすることが重要だが、**技術系の業務**では異なる手法を使う。大規模な石油施設でメンテナンスプログラムを

＊1 対人関係能力。他者と良い人間関係を築き、維持するためのスキル。
＊2 業務遂行能力。具体的に知識や技術を用いて業務を実行するスキル。

to me about the objectives, and more assertive and clear about expectations, because we don't want any interruption to oil production."

The best preparation that Khalid had for his leadership role abroad turned out to be special projects to which he was assigned. "Not only the standard assignments but special projects I got involved with developed competencies and skills that helped in later assignments. I led one special project with highly technical people to conduct plant integrity and safety assessments of five major Saudi Aramco refineries. I formed a team of thirty-plus specialists to assess the integrity of the plants in question. This leadership role required me to go into ambiguous but exciting situations to try to find the right answers. You have to rely on your people skills, motivating your counterparts with conversation and charm, and not just telling people what to do. In the international arena you need a different approach and competencies."

In the Philippines, Khalid found that he was challenged in very different ways than he had been accustomed to in Saudi Arabia. He had to use all of his prior experience. For the two years before his assignment to Manila, Khalid served on the board of directors of the joint venture, traveling there four times a year. This allowed him to get to know the people, to go out into the city, and to begin to understand **local sensitivities and culture**.

Khalid comments that all of these experiences were very helpful, and that after arriving in Manila as an expatriate, "I discovered I had things in me I had developed and could actually display and use in this different environment. People are people, with the same basic aspirations, and the simple things that humans want—family, a decent living, good schooling, etc. But you also have to learn cultural sensitivity quickly. I tuned in to the fact that everything you say or do as a leader has an impact.

"The perception in Saudi Arabia is that most Filipinos work in the service industry as skilled labor and domestic helpers. However, when you live in that country you realize how intelligent they are, like in any other nation in the world. If you go there with the wrong perception, then you can expect to have huge problems. Family ties are very strong in the Philippines. It is best to **talk with people one-on-one**, to eat with them without an aloof attitude. You can appreciate the culture without compromising your leadership."

He also points out communication style differences between the

管理した際、石油生産を中断させないように、監督者たちに目的を確認し、期待値をより明確にする必要があった」

海外赴任の準備としては、特別なプロジェクトを任されたことが役に立った。「特別なプロジェクトに携わったことで、その後の職務に役立つ能力やスキルを磨くことができた。サウジアラムコの5つの主要精油所でプラントの完全性と安全性を評価するために非常に高度な技術を持つ30人を超える専門家からなるチームを結成して、対象となっているプラントで活動した。リーダーとしては、正しいソリューションを見つけるために、不透明な状況に対応することが求められた。やるべきことを指示するだけでなく、スタッフの能力を信頼し、会話や態度で相手をやる気にさせた。そのことがグローバルな環境でも役に立った」

フィリピンでは、サウジアラビアと全く違う対応を迫られた。マニラに赴任するまでの2年間、カリッドはジョイントベンチャーの取締役として、年に4回現地を訪れていた。その間、現地の人々と知り合い、街を歩き、**土地の感性や文化**を理解し始めることができた。カリッドは、この経験を活かすことができたのだ。

「自分で培ってきたものを、この異なる環境で実際に活用できた。海外に赴任するときは、現地の文化的感性を早く学ぶ必要もある。フィリピンではリーダーとしてのあらゆる言動が影響力を持つという事実に気づいた」

「フィリピンでは家族の絆が非常に強い。最善の方法は、**一対一で人と話して**、うちとけた態度で一緒に食事をすることだ。リーダーシップを損なうことなく文化を理解することができる」

フィリピンと他の国とのコミュニケーションスタイルの違いについて

Philippines and other locations. "In the U.S., you **go straight to the point**, but in the Philippines people don't like to confront; they will tell someone off to a third party or do it in private. You will have the whole organization against you if you **embarrass someone** in public. When there is a conflict, you can disagree but do it tactfully without showing disrespect. My advice is not to come across as if you know everything, but to look for ways to show that you can add value. For the first four to six months it would be advisable to listen and engage people, to understand the cultural sensitivities, and adjust your style." Over time, a global leader can emerge from this listening profile and begin to reach out to talk about strategic direction, **both internally and externally**.

Khalid emphasizes the importance of relationships and a personal touch. "You have to pay attention to the details, such as sending a note to someone whose mother died. We had six or seven thousand dealers who operate gas stations. Can you make yourself visible and show sincerity and appreciation even to the dealers in remote locations? These people are your face to the public. Go there and have your picture taken with them; this sends a good message. While communicating a clear message regarding the company's strategic direction is important, it is equally important to use your soft skills to send a clear message about who you are as a person by appreciating people who are doing a great job. Show up for ceremonial occasions, including funerals. This goes a long way with the families, and matters at all levels of the organization."

Another thing that is important is facing the media. You need to be articulate, show passion and sincerity, and attend functions. You are often put in public situations where you have to make a speech on the spot in front of smart and influential people. We are protected from the media in Saudi Arabia, but in the Philippines if the public gets upset with the rising gas prices and you have a poor company image, there may be protests in front of your building, and you get all sorts of threats. A lack of the right public relations skills could ruin your reputation and the company's. Such awareness and skills are essential, as you could easily end up in jail through ignorance."

Khalid's greatest test in the Philippines was leading the joint venture company through a crisis. "There was a major oil spill while I was there, polluting the sea and the beaches. We had to face the **hostility of the media and citizens**. I had to apologize publicly, and make clear commitments

も実感した。「アメリカでは、**単刀直入に要点を述べる**が、フィリピンの人々は対立を好まず、叱責する時は第三者を通すか当事者だけに伝える。人前で**恥をかかせたりする**と、組織全体を敵に回しかねない。対立している場合、異議を唱えることもできるが、無礼な態度は見せずにそつなくやるほうがいい。私がアドバイスしたいのは、すべてを知っているかのような印象を与えるのではなく、価値を付加できることを示す方法を見つけることだ」。時間の経過とともに、ただ人の話に耳を傾けることから抜け出して、**社内外を問わず**戦略的方向性について語り始めることができるようになると彼はいう。

カリッドは、人間関係と人間味の重要性を強調する。「母親を亡くした人に手紙を送るなど、細部に気を配った。ガソリンスタンドを運営しているディーラーは、6、7千人もいる。ディーラーたちは会社の顔だ。ディーラーを訪問し、一緒に写真を撮る。これはいいメッセージになる。企業の戦略的方向性を明確に伝えることは大切だが、優れた仕事をしている人々に感謝することによって自分がどんな人間であるかというメッセージを明確に伝えられる。葬式など冠婚葬祭にも足を運ぶ。これはスタッフの家族を大切にしていることを意味し、組織のあらゆるレベルで重要な効果がある」

メディア対応も重要だ。意見を明確に伝え、情熱と誠実さを示さなければならない。正式な会合や行事にも出席する。公共の場で影響力を持つ人々の前でスピーチをしなければならないことも多々ある。サウジアラビアではメディアから守られているが、フィリピンでは、ガソリン価格の高騰に大衆が怒り、会社のイメージが悪くなると、会社の前で抗議行動が起こったり、様々な脅迫を受けたりする。無知であったがために刑務所に送られる可能性もあるので、自分自身と会社の評判を守るために渉外に対する意識とスキルは不可欠だ。

カリッドはフィリピンでの最大の試練に直面したときのことを語る。

「赴任中に大規模な石油流出があり海が汚染され、**メディアと市民の敵意**に直面しなければならなかった。公式に謝罪し、ダメージを修復する

to repair the damage."

In retrospect, Khalid remarks, "I learned a lot about myself. I didn't know that I could deal with the media, and learned I could do a good job at handling a crisis and with public relations. I had to display these skills or fail and disappoint many people around me. At home, I don't need these skills."

Influence Across Boundaries

Khalid al-Faddagh underwent a role expansion in a crisis situation. Suddenly he was the face of his company toward the Filipino public, and he had to use all of his experiences and inner resources to handle the crisis. Although his story might seem unusual, many of our interviewees told similar stories. Some tales were less dramatic, but the consistent theme was that these leaders stepped into wider responsibilities in roles where they had to find new ways to exert influence.

Role expansion while working in a global context was a persistent theme in nearly every interview. Global leaders must often contend with a lack of support systems that are available within a company's home market, and yet they face constant pressure to get things done across internal and external boundaries. In many cases, they need to create solutions without having direct authority, finding ways to influence others across the organization.

A person who has worked in a global role can return home and be promoted to a domestic job that appears to be at a higher point in the leadership pipeline yet turns out to be **less challenging**. In fact, some of our interviewees who had already completed their assignments abroad and had returned to headquarters reported with regret that even though their new jobs at home involved promotions to a higher rank within the organization, the scope of their job responsibilities was narrower. This may be one of several factors behind the **poor retention record** that many companies have with employees who have completed global assignments.

THE AMBASSADOR ROLE

Many interviewees used words like **ambassador and diplomat** to describe their role, both externally as well as within their organizations. They often had to represent their enterprise to the government, the media, or to

ための明確なコミットメントを示さなければならなかった。本国にいたときは必要とされなかったメディア対応能力を発揮しなければならないとき、意外とそうしたことに自分が向いていることがわかった。このような能力を発揮できなければ、職務を果たせず、周囲の多くの人々を失望させていただろう」

第九の条件　境界を越えた影響力の発揮

危機的状況に立ち向かったカリッドは、たちまちフィリピン人に対する会社の顔となり、自分のあらゆる経験と能力を使って危機に対処しなければならなくなった。カリッドの例は決して特殊なものではない。それほど大げさではない事例もあったが、一貫したテーマは、これらのリーダーたちが、影響力を行使する新しい方法を模索しなければならない任務に、より大きな責任を負うようになったということだ。

グローバルな業務における役割の拡大は、ほぼ全てのインタビューで取り上げられたテーマだった。グローバルリーダーは、本社で利用できるサポート体制の欠如に対応しなければならないことが多く、社内外の境界を越えて業務を遂行するというプレッシャーを常に抱えている。多くの場合、直接的権限を持たないままにソリューションを見いだし、組織全体に影響を与える方法を見つける必要がある。

グローバルな役割を担った人は、帰国して国内の業務で昇進する可能性があるものの、帰国後の業務を**物足りなく感じる**こともある。実際、インタビューに応じた人の中には、帰国後、組織内で昇進して新しい職務を与えられたにもかかわらず、責任範囲が狭くなったことを残念に思っている人もいた。これは、多くの企業において、海外勤務を終えた社員の**定着率が低い**原因の1つかもしれない。

アンバサダーとしての役割

インタビューでは、海外勤務のことを**アンバサダー（大使）**や**ディプロマット（外交官）**といったことばで組織内外における自分の役割を語る人が多かった。政府、メディア、業界団体に対して企業を代表しなければならないこと

industry associations.

> "As a leader, you are likely to find yourself working in community and public relations activities that may not have been involved in your home-country role. I meet with the government here in Australia, whereas I would never do that in my same role at home."

These leaders were also analyzed by employees who had never been to headquarters and who viewed them as an example of what it is like to work for this particular firm: "Everything you do is seen as what everyone in the company does."

> "You need self-confidence because you represent something unknown to the people you are living and working with. They see everything through the lens of you. The company is viewed through your behavior; this is a tremendous responsibility. You need to be the first one in, last one out—a real role model."

INFLUENCING ACROSS FUNCTIONS

Global leaders must be able to **drive collaboration** across organizational boundaries in order to create solutions. People who are based in R&D will soon find themselves working with manufacturing; if their particular expertise is in marketing, it is likely that they will soon need to learn about sales and product development as well. Going back to the **concepts of adding value and frame-shifting,** some roles may require leaders to demonstrate that they have the expertise to make **effective contributions** in several functions; other roles may require the leader to step back and organize collaboration in a more strategic manner.

> "You have to work outside your functional area, and have a greater breadth of communication within the organization and across functions."

> "In a foreign assignment, you cannot work in a silo. You have to **communicate cross-functionally** as a team."

が多かったというのだ。

「リーダーとして、母国では関与していなかったかもしれないコミュニティやPR活動に携わっていることに気づくだろう。海外では政府関係者と会うことがあるが、自国でそのような役割を担うことは決してないだろう」

また、リーダーは、本社へ行ったことがないスタッフから、その企業の模範として注目されることも指摘したい。

「現地のスタッフはリーダーの視点を通して物事を見ている。リーダーの行動を通して会社が評価されることになる。これは非常に大きな責任だ。一番早く職場に来て、最後に職場を出る真のロールモデルとなる必要がある」

組織を越えた影響力

グローバルリーダーは、ソリューション構築のために、組織の境界を越えた**コラボレーションを推進**できなければならない。**付加価値とフレームシフトの概念**に話を戻すと、リーダーは、役割によっては、複数の業務で**効果的な貢献**を果たせる専門知識があることを示したり、あるいは一歩下がってより戦略的な方法でコラボレーションを進めたりしなければならない。

「自分の職務領域以外の業務もあるため、組織内や部門間のコミュニケーションを拡大しなければならない」

「海外勤務では孤立した組織内だけで業務を遂行することはできない。チームとして**部門の枠を超えたコミュニケーション**を取らなければならない」

Insights from Global Followers

Our current country director is from headquarters, and has been here now for two years. We see her as a kind of model, and listen carefully when she is talking on conference calls or holding a meeting with employees. As a woman, I find it inspiring to have her here as a leader because it is rare for women to rise to such a high rank in my country. The country director's leadership style is different from most of the local leaders here. Even though she does her best to fit into the local culture, she is still more direct in her communication style in a way that people sometimes find surprising, and she stays very focused on the business tasks. It is hard for me to imagine a whole building at headquarters filled with people like her.

FREEDOM TO EXPERIMENT

With the responsibility for driving solutions comes a measure of freedom, too. Global leaders who are working away from headquarters frequently discover that they have opportunities to make decisions and try out new ideas or products. A significant degree of anticipation, analysis, and advance planning are required to set the right course.

> "You need to be able to read situations and predict scenarios, to think ahead—**forethought** is very useful. You play a lot of roles. No one will tell you what will happen tomorrow so you have to look at trends, analyze the situation, and get a good sense for what is going on around you. I have to have acumen in terms of feelings and undercurrents in the organization, and need to keep my finger on how things are changing in society and in the office."

CREATIVE RESOURCEFULNESS

Our interviewees also noted that they encountered many dead ends—and still had to find another way. The experiences they described are not for the faint of heart, and the situations demanded a rapid learning curve along with tolerance not only for ambiguity but for failures along the way. These

グローバルフォロワーからの洞察

ある会社では、現地スタッフが、本社から来たディレクターを一種の手本と見なしていると証言する。彼女が電話会議やスタッフとのミーティングで話している時は注意深く耳を傾けるようにしている。この国では女性がこれほど高い職位に就くことは珍しいので、ここで彼女をリーダーとして迎え仕事ができるのは刺激になる。この会社でのカントリー・ディレクターのリーダーシップ・スタイルは、ほかのローカル・リーダーとは異なっていた。彼女は最善を尽くして現地の文化に合わせているが、それでも時にはスタッフが驚くような直接的なコミュニケーションスタイルを貫き、業務に集中していると彼らはいう。

試す自由

ソリューションを推進する任務には、ある程度の自由が必要だ。本社を離れて業務を遂行しているグローバルリーダーには、意思決定や新しいアイデアや製品を試す機会があることに気づく。正しい方向に進むためには、本社に頼らず事前に十分な予測や分析を実施し、計画を策定しなければならない。

> 「先のことを考えるためには、状況を読み取り、シナリオを予測できなければならない。**事前の検討**は非常に有用だ。リーダーは多くの役割を担う。明日何が起こるか誰も教えてくれない。動向を読み、状況を分析し、自分の周りで何が起こっているかを感じ取らなければならない。組織内の感情やその背後にあるものについて洞察力を持ち、社会や職場での変化や実情を把握する必要がある」

利用可能な資産

インタビューでは、行き詰まりを感じ、別の方法を探さなければならなかったと述べた人もいた。彼らには、あいまいな場合や途中で失敗した場合にも持ちこたえられる耐性が求められるが、気の弱い人には難しいだろう。こ

global leaders went through a **process of toughening** or tempering that made them more resourceful and better able to find solutions using the assets available to them.

> "There is no better experience than international, but you have to walk in with your eyes open. You won't be afloat the whole time; this experience is not for everyone. There is risk, without much time to learn to swim. You will swallow water."

Third-Way Solutions

Third-way solutions draw upon all of the behaviors that have been outlined already, and therefore in a sense this term signifies the ability to put everything together to generate solutions.

> **Neuroscience and Culture: Multiculturalism and Creativity**
>
> A study published in the American Psychologist demonstrates that **exposure to multiple cultures** enhances creativity. The research found that one's degree of exposure to multicultural experiences was positively related to both creative performance, such as insight learning and idea generation, and to creativity-supported cognitive processes, such as retrieval of unconventional knowledge for idea expansion. Individuals with significant multicultural exposure are more likely to come up with novel combinations, see the same form as having multiple possible meanings, have access to alternative forms of knowledge, and seek ideas from diverse sources. Significantly, an individual who has been exposed to different cultures is more able to take ideas from two cultures and integrate those ideas in a new way.

In the more micro, **problem-solving context** in which a leader seeks to address a specific issue, there is also an application for many of the behaviors we have described. Other behaviors, such as developing future leaders or core values and flexibility, shape the overall climate in which viable solutions can be reached.

れらのグローバルリーダーは、**強化プロセス**を経て、より臨機応変に、利用可能な資産を用いてソリューションを見られるようにしなければならない。

「周りをよく見ながら業務を遂行しなければならない。ずっと楽な状態が続くわけではないため、海外勤務の経験は万人向けではない。対応方法を学ぶ十分な時間がない場合、リスクと困難を伴うことになるだろう」

第十の条件　第三のソリューションの提供

第三のソリューションとは、前述のあらゆる行動を手段とし、ソリューションを生み出すためにすべてを統合する能力を意味する。

脳科学と文化：多文化と創造性

複数の文化に触れることは、人間の創造力を高める上で役に立つ。多文化を経験している人は、新しい組み合わせを考え出し、同じ形式を複数の意味を持つ可能性があるものと見なし、それ以外の形式の知識を取り入れ、多様な情報源からアイデアを求めようとする傾向が強い。異文化に触れた経験を持つ人は、2つの文化からアイデアを得て、それを新しい方法で統合することができる。

リーダーが特定の問題に対処する際、よりミクロな**問題解決**において前述の多くの行動を適用することもできる。将来のリーダー、コアバリュー、柔軟性を育てるといった取り組みによって、ソリューションへの環境が形成される。

An easy way to remember this sequence is with the label BRIC(C): Bracket, Relate, Inquire, Cocreate, and Commit. Although the steps follow a logical sequence, they can all occur at the same time with the exception of the final one: commit to implementation.

Leaders who seek to be effective should consider the following short checklist of questions related to each element of the BRIC(C) model:

1. **Bracket:** What would I normally recommend in this situation based upon my cultural background and experience, and am I willing to set it aside for the moment?
2. **Relate:** Does everyone involved in this process know each other, and how can we develop a foundation of **personal trust** and **mutual understanding** across cultural differences?
3. **Inquire:** What does each of us not know about this situation that we need to know, and how can we work together to find out? Are there aspects of my strategic approach that I should consider changing to better support our global work?
4. **Cocreate:** Who are likely to be key global players influencing the decision and implementing the outcome—even those who haven't previously been decision makers—and how can I involve them in creating the solution? How can I both learn and contribute?
5. **Commit:** Does each person who participated in the process feel that the final outcome is their own, with some pride of authorship? Have we fully utilized the global, local, and functional resources available to us and our freedom to experiment in this location?

TRANSPARENCY

Our interviewees stressed a couple of additional features of their role in creating shared solutions. One was to be transparent about their assumptions and expectations as well as consistent in their actions. Leaders may **set the ground rules** for a discussion or define a result that is nonnegotiable, but they also need to make their own preconceptions clear enough to themselves and to other team members so that these can be called into question.

"I had to become more articulate. When working with shared implicit meanings, you don't need to be so specific. But the minute you shift out

このプロセスを、Bracket（除外する）、Relate（関係を構築する）、Inquire（問いかける）、Concreate（協働する）、Commit（コミットする）を総称してBRIC（C）と呼ぶ。BRIC（C）は論理的順序に基づくものだが、最後のステップ「Commit to implementation（実施をコミットする）」を除き同時に実行できる。

成果達成を目指すリーダーが検討すべきBRIC（C）モデルの各要素に対する質問事項を以下に示す。

1. **Bracket（除外する）：** 自分の文化的背景と経験に基づいてこの状況で通常何をすべきか？　差し当たって何を放置してもよいか？
2. **Relate（関係を構築する）：** このプロセスに関わる全員がお互いを知っているか？　どうやって文化の違いを超えて**個人的信頼**と**相互理解**の基盤を築くか？
3. **Inquire（問いかける）：** この状況について各自が知らないことは何か？それを知るためにどのように協力できるのか？　グローバルな業務をより適切に支援するために変更を検討すべき戦略的アプローチはあるか？
4. **Concreate（協働する）：** 意思決定に影響を与え、その決定を実行する鍵となるグローバルプレーヤーは、以前に意思決定を行ったことがない人も含めて誰なのか？ そのグローバルプレーヤーをどのようにしてソリューション構築に関与させることができるか？　どうすれば学ぶことと貢献することを両立できるか？
5. **Commit（コミットする）：** プロセスに関わった人は、各自最終的な成果が自分のものであることを自負し、それに対する誇りを感じているか？自分たちが利用できるグローバル、ローカル、部門の資源と、この地域で自由に挑戦するための環境を十分に活用しているか？

透明性

ソリューションを構築するためにはいくつかの特徴がある。1つは、仮説と期待値の透明性と行動の一貫性である。リーダーは**基本原則を設定**したり、結果を定義したりできるが、異なる文化の中にいるときは、そんな自分の先入観を自分自身や他のチームメンバーに対して十分に表明し、疑問を投げかけられるようにしなければならない。

of your home context, you cannot do this anymore. You have to be explicit about your expectations."

ACTING AS A BRIDGE

The diplomatic skills described earlier in this chapter for influencing across boundaries are vital for generating solutions. At times, there is even a kind of "**shuttle diplomacy**" that the global leader must engage in back and forth between headquarters and other locations to increase understanding and collaboration from all sides. Setting expectations, providing information, coaching, explaining, linking corporate and local objectives, introducing new players, obtaining resources, resolving misunderstandings, solving cultural conflicts, **gaining buy-in**—all of these are aspects of the global leader's bridge role.

"Don't lose sight of corporate and local objectives and how to weave those two together."

"A person from headquarters turned to a person from another country at the break and said, 'I hope this will open your eyes up to doing it our way...' I ended up chatting with the department head about making everyone feel like part of the company."

CREATING VIABLE SOLUTIONS

Overall, our interviewees were less attached to the specific form that solutions took than to the process of getting there and the fact that the solution was ultimately achieved. Their focus was on integrating the various parties involved to discover common ground and to generate solutions, without being so concerned about where the solution ultimately came from.

"Sometimes I end up with a different solution because I listen to all players, a solution not even related to what I originally thought. Sometimes I push through my thought process and get them to adapt... but generally I end up with something different."

橋渡しとしての役割

当然、国境を越えて影響力を行使するための外交スキルも必要だ。グローバルリーダーには、あらゆる方面から理解と協力を得るために、本社と他拠点の間を行き来する一種の「**シャトル外交**」を求められることもある。期待値の設定、情報の提供、指導、説明、企業と地域の目標の連携、新しいプレーヤーの採用、リソースの獲得、誤解の解消、文化的対立の解決、**同意の獲得**などにおいて、グローバルリーダーはブリッジとしての役割を担っている。

実行可能なソリューション

全般的にインタビューに応じたリーダーたちは、ソリューションの具体的な形よりも、そこに至るまでのプロセスとソリューションが最終的に達成されたという事実を重視している。ソリューションが最終的にどこから来たかはそれほど気にすることなく、共通の基盤を見出し、ソリューションを構築するために様々な関係者を取りまとめることが大切だ。彼らは次のようにいう。

> 「関係者全員の話を聞いた上で検討するため、当初自分が考えもしなかったソリューションに行き着くこともある。また、自分の思考プロセスを押し通して彼らを適応させることもあるが、結局は違うものになってしまうこともある」

Third-way solutions can assume a number of possible forms. Global leaders who have demonstrated the other behaviors described in this book will find that they have a reservoir of trust to draw upon, and that employees around the world understand and expect that their leaders will want to explore a full range of solution options. A viable process for creating third-way solutions always places the needs of the organization and its customers first while welcoming and building upon worthwhile input from any source. Options for third-way solutions include the following:

- **Standardize:** Establish a single policy at corporate headquarters that is applied uniformly worldwide.
- **Select:** Work with local managers in each country to choose and apply the elements of a corporate-wide initiative that have the most relevance for their operations.
- **Adapt:** Alter the form or packaging of a particular change to make it more readily acceptable to local employees or customers.
- **Combine:** Seek a combination of ideas from headquarters and local sources that will work better than a one-sided approach.
- **Integrate:** Fuse different contributions from diverse participants into a synergistic result that exceeds the sum of the parts.
- **Adopt:** Identify an idea from a subsidiary location and apply it in other markets where it offers potential benefits.

このように、第三のソリューションは、様々な形式を想定できる。第三のソリューションを構築するプロセスでは、常に組織と顧客のニーズを最優先し、あらゆる情報源から価値のある情報を取り入れて活用している。第三のソリューションには以下の選択肢がある。

- **標準化する：**本社の方針を統一し、それを世界で一様に適用する。
- **選択する：**各国の地域マネージャーと協力して、全社的な取り組みの中から、自社の業務に最も関連するものを選び適用する。
- **適応する：**特定の変更のパッケージや形式を部分的に変えて、現地のスタッフや顧客にスムーズに受け入れられるようにする。
- **組み合わせる：**一方的なアプローチよりも効果的な、本社と現地からのアイデアの組み合わせを模索する。
- **統合する：**多様な関係者からの異なる貢献を融合し、それらを合計したものを上回る相乗効果を実現する。
- **採用する：**ある子会社の地域からのアイデアを特定し、潜在的メリットがある他の市場に適用する。

CHAPTER EIGHT

Training the Ten Behaviors

Global leadership training programs perform important functions. In particular, the face-to-face connections and network-building that take place between **high-potential leaders** from around the world are usually worth the investment.

Program Design: Going Global?

Contemporary leadership program designs typically involve anywhere from twenty to forty participants, and their content includes elements such as:

- Invitation and messages from top executive(s)
- Dialogue with customers and/or community members
- Presentations from experts on national culture and the local marketplace
- Cultural experiences such as visits to historical or religious sites and art exhibits
- Personal career planning

Although this kind of program design has many virtues, it usually contains flaws as well. Most of the leadership models shared by executives, academics, and consultants—even those explicitly labeled as "global"—are shaped in unacknowledged ways by Western and largely U.S. cultural perspectives. But what about, for example, considering Chinese approaches to leadership that have a history of more than 2,500 years?

There is a potential danger that leadership development programs, although **global in name**, will repeat and reinforce the limitations of an

第8章

「10の行動」へのトレーニング

グローバルリーダーシップを育成するためのトレーニング・プログラムは重要だ。これは、世界中の**有望なリーダー**たちとの直接的な連携やネットワーク構築のためにも、企業が投資しなければならないテーマである。

プログラム設計

リーダーシップ・プログラムの設計には、以下の項目が含まれる。

- 経営トップからの招待とメッセージ
- 顧客や地域のメンバーとの意見交換
- 国の文化や地域の市場に関する専門家のプレゼンテーション
- 歴史的、宗教的な場所の訪問や芸術鑑賞などの文化体験
- 個人のキャリアプラン策定

ただ、この種のプログラムには課題も存在する。というのも、リーダーシップモデルの多くは、たとえ「グローバル」と名付けられていても、西欧、特にアメリカの文化的観点によって作り上げられたものなのだ。であれば、例えば2500年以上の歴史を持つ中国のリーダーシップへはアプローチできるのだろうか。

そのことから、リーダーシップ開発プログラムには、**グローバルと名乗っていても**、将来に向けた組織の能力を育成するのではなく、組織の現状をた

organization's current state rather than cultivate behaviors that can take it into the future. For companies trying to grow in emerging markets, having a large number of Western participants doing most of the talking and referring to models that derive from their own cultural background is not the best way to challenge participants to think and act differently.

Often there are participants with firsthand knowledge of emerging markets whose voices have the potential to transform the dialogue and to create a fresh sense of mutual learning. The following are examples of comments made by leadership program participants from emerging markets that have set off serious reflection and intense debate.

> "Customers like us because we are foreign."
>
> "Our prices are too high by a factor of ten for this market segment."
>
> "The average monthly wage for workers in our factory is around $200."
>
> "Our largest competitor is based in this market, and their revenue is growing by about thirty percent per year."

One means of generating a learning environment is to introduce some of the key global leadership behaviors described in this book and to craft a venue that enables participants to begin to apply them.

Training for Results Through Relationships

The global participants represent the program's greatest asset, and it takes a major investment to bring them all together. Years after a leadership program is complete, what lives on most vividly are the recollections participants have of each other, along with the personal networks they have created. It is a good idea, early in the program, to get participants focused on regularly reaching across their own mental boundaries to get to know people they would otherwise be unlikely to meet.

RELATIONSHIP-BUILDING EXERCISES

There are various techniques for accelerating the growth of interest, interaction, and conversation among program participants. Members of a leadership development group usually have bios of the others in the program, but

だ強化する目的でデザインされるという潜在的な危険性がある。新興市場で成長しようとしている企業にとって、その市場への知識が薄い欧米からの参加者が中心となって自分たちの文化的背景から派生した様式を引き合いに出すことは、参加者の考え方や行動を変えることを促す最善の方法ではない。

新興市場を知っている参加者の声は、プログラム内で対話を変え、お互いに学び合おうとする感覚を生み出すことがある。

人間関係で成果を出すトレーニング

グローバルな参加者は、このプログラムの最大の資産であり、彼らをひとつにまとめるためには大規模な投資が必要である。リーダーシップ・プログラムが終了して数年経って、最もはっきりと残るのは、参加者のお互いの思い出と個人的なネットワークである。プログラムの初期段階では、参加者は自分の精神的な境界をいつも越えることに集中したほうがよい。そして、プログラムがなければ出会う機会がなかった人たちと知り合うことも大切だ。

関係構築とフレームシフトの演習

プログラム参加者間の関心、交流、会話を促すためには様々な手法がある。リーダーシップ開発グループのメンバーは、通常はプログラムの他のメンバーの略歴を知っている。他のメンバーが自分に何を提供すべきか、他のメン

they can benefit from knowing more specifically what others have to offer to them, and what they bring that others find valuable. One simple warm-up exercise called "Give and Get" can be facilitated using the instructions offered here.

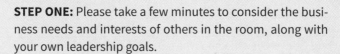

RELATIONSHIP BUILDING EXERCISE:
GIVE and GET

STEP ONE: Please take a few minutes to consider the business needs and interests of others in the room, along with your own leadership goals.

- Identify one thing you can give to others that will help them achieve their objectives. Write it on a Post-it note and place it on the world map in a location that seems appropriate. Be sure to include your name.
- Identify one thing that you would like to get, or to receive from others in order to achieve your own objectives. Write it on a Post-it note and place it on the map in a location that seems appropriate. Be sure to include your name.
- After you have finished writing your own notes, spend ten minutes looking at all of the notes on the map.

STEP TWO: Find a person with whom you may have something to exchange (either give or get) and initiate a conversation with that person. After ten minutes, change partners and repeat.

"Give" and "get" examples: A local contact, a best practice, a technical application, market knowledge, a suggestion, or an idea.

Training for Frame-Shifting

There are many ways within a training context to approach the behavior called frame-shifting. With respect to communication style, for instance, there are video resources and role-playing exercises that demonstrate common differences and teach new skills. Most effective of all is the structured sharing of stories and examples among leadership program participants from different cultural backgrounds.

バーが自分に対して認める価値は何かをより具体的に知ることによってメリットを受けることができる。その前提で「ギブ・アンド・ゲット」と呼ばれる以下のような簡単なウォーミングアップを行うことができる。

関係構築の方法
与える＆得る

ステップ1

自分のリーダーシップの目標に沿って、他の参加者たちのビジネスニーズと関心を数分間話し合う。

- 自分が提供できるもので他の人の目標達成に役立つ可能性のあるものを特定し、それを付箋に書いて世界地図の適切な箇所に貼り、自分の名前を書く。
- 自分自身の目的を達成するために、他の人から得たいものを１つ特定する。これを付箋に記入して、地図の適切な箇所に貼り、自分の名前を書く。
- 書き終えたら、10分間地図上に貼られたすべての付箋を確認する。

ステップ2

交換相手（与えるまたは得る）を見つけ、その相手と会話を始める。10分後、別の交換相手と同じことをする。

フレームシフト力を育成する

フレームシフトの能力を育成するには、様々な方法がある。コミュニケーションスタイルに関しては、例えば、一般的な相違点を示し、新しいスキルを教えるビデオ教材やロールプレイ演習を活用することができる。最も効果的なのは、様々な文化的背景を持つリーダーシップ・プログラムの参加者の間で経験や事例を体系的に共有することである。

Global Leader: Gina Qiao, Lenovo

Gina Qiao is the chief financial officer for Lenovo in Beijing. Before this job she was based in the United States and was director of Human Resources for her employer's global computer business.

Gina's early roles with Lenovo were in marketing, and these experiences have strongly influenced her leadership style. "This time really trained me. I broadened my writing skills, communication ability, and organizational skills, and learned how to inspire my own team. I started out with a small team and then developed it into a very large team, working with a number of different products. We did a lot of big product launches, so this time taught me a lot about team motivation and nurturing a team."

She did receive some global management and leadership skills training while in China. However, she notes, "The focus was on how to manage within a Chinese organization; how to communicate effectively with those above you, below you, on the same level as you; how to navigate the different layers [above and below]; how to create team cooperation; how to work towards goals and to motivate others. I received training on all of this in a Chinese context."

Gina's initial experiences abroad were challenging, but she learned a great deal from them, including how to prepare. "The assignment that I had in Singapore for one year, and then before that for a half-year in New York—these were very tough assignments. I think an important reason that Singapore and New York were so difficult was because I never received any kind of preparation, no basic training. I just went. So during those first two assignments I felt uncomfortable in many ways: getting off the airplane and trying to find the location, with no one picking me up; trying to use a credit card and not knowing how it worked; showing up at a meeting and not understanding anything or being able to express myself. But after these assignments, in preparation for moving to North Carolina and because of these past two experiences on assignment, I arranged a lot of training before moving. This training included information about my assignment country's religion, history, working style, culture, and so on. We also included a daily life section in the training, covering what is important in daily living in addition to what is important at work. The three-year assignment to North Carolina allowed me to improve a lot

ジーナ・チャオの例

ジーナは北京のレノボのCFOである。

ジーナのレノボでの最初の役割はマーケティングで、この経験が彼女のリーダーシップ・スタイルに強く影響を与えた。

「今回の経験は私を本当に鍛えてくれた。文章を書くスキル、コミュニケーション能力、組織化のスキルを広げ、自分のチームを鼓舞する方法を学んだ。最初は小さなチームでスタートしたが、その後、大きなチームに成長し、様々な製品を扱うようになった。大規模な製品の立ち上げを数多く手がけたので、チームのモチベーションとチームの育成について多くのことを学んだ。中国では、グローバルマネジメントとリーダーシップ・スキルのトレーニングを受けた。中国の組織内でのマネジメント方法、上下、同じレベルの人たちと効果的にコミュニケーションをとる方法、(上と下の) 異なるレベルをうまく調整する方法、チームの協力関係を築く方法、目標に向かって仕事をする方法、他の人のモチベーションを高める方法などに焦点が当てられていた。私はこれらすべてについて、中国語の文脈でトレーニングを受けた」

しかし、ジーナの最初の海外勤務は困難を伴ったものだった。

「シンガポールで1年間、その前のニューヨークで半年間の任務は大変だった。それは、何の準備もせず、何の基礎研修も受けずに現地に赴いたためだった。飛行機から降りても誰も迎えに来ておらず、どこへ行ったらいいかわからない、クレジットカードの使い方がわからない、会議に参加しても何も理解できず、自分の意見も言えないといった多くの点で居心地の悪い思いをした。しかし、その経験を踏まえて、その後、ノースカロライナへ異動する際には、事前に多くの研修を受けて準備した。研修では、赴任地の宗教、歴史、ワークスタイル、文化に関する情報も提供された。また、仕事上や日常生活での重要なことについても研修で学んだ。3年間のノースカロライナ勤務では、多くのことを改善し、以前のような失敗はなくなった」

and to correct my previous mistakes."

In terms of her communication style as a leader, a key learning experience for Gina was to be more open. "I have learned to **become more direct**. Before, in China, if I was in a meeting and had a conflicting idea, I would like to agree. We like to quickly agree for agreement's sake. But while on assignment, I saw that in meetings you could say directly that you disagreed and no one minded. In a meeting in China, if you want to say something or express a thought, you have to consider the system, the organization. In the States, I saw that people spoke without any hesitation, just spoke their thoughts. In the U.S., hearing everyone's voices is how they measure if people are engaged or not. Are you willing to participate in this meeting, are you adding value? You always have to prove this."

Gina also reports discovering different approaches to risk-taking, particularly **risks related to strategy**. "Another area where I learned a lot from the different working styles that I found in the U.S. and China was in attitudes towards risk. In China, people like to consider for a long time, thinking things through and getting a lot of clarity before they can start doing something. But in the U.S., I realized that from small things like creating a PowerPoint presentation or planning a meeting, to big things like creating a strategy, they would first just do it and then if it didn't work, they would change things."

Gina also encountered major contrasts in **attitudes toward authority**. "In China, there is always a head and he is always the one with the authority. For example, if there are three department heads working together, there is always one head with the authority among these three, and everyone recognizes this; he is the one whose position is highest.

But in the U.S., the authority or the head isn't always the person with the highest position. It could be that within the organization, there is just an average person who is given the task of being the facilitator, and this person has the authority in a certain situation."

Contrasting approaches to authority are linked with methods for resolving conflicts, as Gina discovered. "When I was working in North Carolina, I would go to my boss with any issue that I had because this is what you do in China. According to the American way of thinking, this was a major insult from the standpoint of my team members. Their reaction was, 'Why would you go to the boss and tell on me?' I had difficult relations with a lot of people because of this."

リーダーとしてのコミュニケーションスタイルに関しては、ジーナは学習経験に基づきよりオープンなものを目指した。

「**もっと率直になること**を学んだ。以前、中国では、会議で出された意見が自分の意見と相反するものであっても同意していた。中国では皆、合意に達するために早く同意したがる。一方、ノースカロライナでは、会議で、反対意見を率直に述べることができ、それを誰も気にしていない。中国の会議では、発言したり、考えを示したりする際には制度や組織のことを考慮しなければならない。アメリカでは、ためらうことなく自分の考えを述べることを知った。彼らは、発言を聞いてその人が本当に参加しているかを判断するのだ。会議に参加する気があるのか？　付加価値を与えられるか？　常にこれを証明しなければならない」

また、ジーナはリスク、特に**戦略に関するリスク**を冒すことへの異なるアプローチを見つけたと述べている。

「アメリカと中国では、リスクに対する姿勢も異なる。中国では、何かを始める前に時間をかけて考えて、様々なことを明確にしようとする。アメリカでは事の大小を問わずまず実行し、もしうまくいかないことがあれば都度戦略を変更して前に進む」

また、ジーナは**権威に対する態度**が中国とは大きく異なることに気づいた。

「中国では常にトップが権力を持つ。３人の部門長がいるとしたら、必ずその3人の中の一人が権力を持ち、一番地位が高い人と見なされる。しかし、アメリカではトップが必ずしも絶対ではない。組織内で、ファシリテーターの役割を担うのは平均的な人で、特定の状況ではその人が権力を持っていることがある」

権威に対する対照的なアプローチは、ジーナが発見したように対立を解決する方法と結びついている。

「ノースカロライナ赴任中、何か問題があると、中国でしていたように上司のところへ行こうとした。アメリカ的な見方では、チームメンバーにとってそれは大きな屈辱であり『なぜ上司のところへ行って告げ口をするの？』と反応される。このため、多くの人との関係構築が難しくなった」

Gina points to deep-rooted **social causes** for such cultural differences, and notes that her time abroad has caused her to incorporate different values, and to change her own approach in some cases. "In China, if as children we have a fight, we always seek an adult to sort it out for us. But my U.S. colleague told me during our training program that he sends his kids into another room and says, 'You work it out yourselves!' In the States, the boss is more like the parent telling kids to go work it out themselves.

It's funny because now I have adjusted so much to the American way of resolving things that I no longer take a problem to a superior for resolution, but I haven't yet been able to adjust back to the Chinese way. I am shocked now in China when people come to me to resolve an issue, and I tell them to go resolve it themselves."

Gina emphasizes the importance of being able to adjust leadership styles to accommodate new circumstances. "The most vital skill for leaders is the ability to style-switch, to use different language with different people, to be able to use a different style that matches with the style of the people you are with and to have flexibility as a leader."

She provides examples related to a variety of activities from decision making to workplace hours in which leaders may need to either shift their own established patterns or recognize that others have equally effective ways of getting things done. "I think that some differences lie in a leader's policies. For example, in America, everyone is very results oriented, but flexible. So maybe you have a private phone conversation here and there during the day but if in the end you get things done, then everything is okay. But if you go to China, the value system is about working very hard and being seen as working very hard during the workday, not leaving to go home right on the dot."

Gina observes that both she and Lenovo have changed substantially as a result of their global experiences. "Lenovo is now a **merged entity**, so these differences have become important to us, and it is important for me to spend time thinking about them. If I could describe our style, it is half thinking and half doing. Before going on assignment, I wasn't aware of these differences and had not run into them before or understood them. But now I feel I can understand all these approaches.

"These were all things I learned, ways that I changed, and this was also a time when I improved my understanding of different people. My colleagues feel that my working style has grown a bit, and I have more

ジーナは、このような文化的な違いには根深い**社会的要因**があると指摘する。彼女は海外生活を通じて異なる価値観を取り入れたり、場合によっては自分のアプローチを変えたりするようになった。

「中国では子が喧嘩をすれば、必ず大人に解決を求める。アメリカ人の同僚によれば、アメリカでは、子どもたちを別の部屋に行かせ自分たちで解決させる。同じように、上司も部下に自分で解決させる。

おもしろいことに、私はアメリカ式の解決方法に慣れすぎてしまい、中国式の解決方法にいまだに戻れない。今では、中国で問題を解決しようと私のところに誰かが相談に来ることにショックを受けるようになった。そういう人に対しては自分で解決するように言っている」

ジーナは新しい状況に適応するためにリーダーシップ・スタイルを調整することの重要性を強調する。

「リーダーに必要なスキルは、スタイルを変える能力、異なる人々と異なる言語でコミュニケーションする能力、一緒に働く人のスタイルに合わせて自分とは異なるスタイルを使える能力、そしてリーダーとしての柔軟性だ」

ジーナは、その他にもアメリカと中国との違いを指摘する。

「例えば、アメリカでは誰もが結果重視だが柔軟性があり、仕事中にプライベートな電話をしても、最終的に結果を出せれば構わない。中国では、熱心に働くことに価値がおかれ、勤務時間中は懸命に働いていることをアピールし、終業時間通りに帰ったりしない」

ジーナのグローバルな経験は、自身と会社の双方の変化に貢献した。

「**合弁企業**となった今のレノボにとって、このような異文化の認識は欠かせない。海外赴任する前はこの相違点に気づかなかった。直面したことも、理解したこともなかった。今ではこういったアプローチを全て理解できるようになった」

thoughts or resources for how to do things. I have also become a bridge between Americans and Chinese. If we are having a meeting, I know the points at which my Chinese colleagues must have thoughts or opinions on an issue and are not saying anything, and I will urge them to speak. So these are the new leadership methods I have learned and taken with me."

A leadership development program that taps into the experiences of participants such as Gina Qiao has the potential to induce deep insights and to initiate behavioral changes on the spot. It is not easy to bring such voices into the discussion for reasons that Gina herself describes: culturally based communication standards for carefully considered and eloquent expression, or concern about hierarchical factors that may be present in the group. But those who design and deliver global leadership programs need to seek out, model, and cultivate channels of mutual inquiry and exchange that draw upon participants like her.

Training to Expand Ownership

Companies seeking to enhance their global leadership strength normally have positive examples within their own operations that are not widely known or recognized. Leadership programs can serve a useful purpose by identifying and promoting such **best practices**.*

A Kohler VP and his team have enhanced the responsibilities of their global counterparts through process adjustments, face-to-face interactions, and **altering the organizational structure** of the project to give greater responsibility to a manager who is closer to the new facility's site. Most importantly, instead of handing off projects that are mostly complete, his team has increasingly taken the approach that is "global from the start."

ジーナのような経験を活用したリーダーシッププログラムは重要だ。文化ごとのコミュニケーションの基準の違いや、グループ内に存在するかもしれない階層に対する懸念は地域によって異なってくる。しかし、グローバルリーダーシップ・プログラムを企画し実施する人は、ジーナのような参加者を活用して相互に質疑応答をし、交流チャネルを探し、モデル化し、育成する必要がある。

オーナーシップ拡大の研修

グローバルリーダーシップの強化を目指す企業は、通常、自社の中にあまり知られていない有効なリソースを持っている。リーダーシップ・プログラムはそのような**ベストプラクティス**を特定し、広めることを目的とする。

アメリカのコーラー社のチームは、プロセスの調整、直接のやり取り、**組織体制の変更**を通じて、施設のある場所の近くにいるマネージャーにより大きな責任を与えることで、グローバルなカウンターパートの責任を強化した。最も重要なのは、ほとんど完了したプロジェクトを引き渡す代わりに、チームが「最初からグローバル」なアプローチをより多く採用していることだ。

＊結果を得るために最も効率のよい手法のこと。

BEST PRACTICE EXAMPLE: **KOHLER FACILITIES CONSTRUCTION**

Kohler is a famous manufacturer in the midwestern region of the United States. Founded in 1873, the company is best known for the products of its Kitchen & Bath Group; other business units include Interiors (furniture, tiles), Global Power (engines, generators), and Hospitality (luxury resorts). Kohler has gone through a remarkable process of globalization in the past decade, with more than fifty manufacturing locations worldwide.

As the company's employees and business reach have become more global, it has also needed to reevaluate and revise systems that have traditionally been centralized at headquarters. One of these is the system for new site development. Kohler is now building manufacturing facilities in places like India and China. The company's vice president for Corporate Operations Support describes the work of his site development team along with the significant changes it has made to work more efficiently on a global scale.

"Construction Engineering Management is the group that goes out and works with the business to find the site, and then, depending on the manufacturing process, we design a building to fit that process and do the construction. There are three different phases in the design: first is the concept design, then the detail design, and the last is the finished design, including the construction drawings.

"Historically, we've had a large group of facility engineers who reside here in Wisconsin. These engineers would do the concept design through the detail design, which meant the building design would be seventy to eighty percent complete. Once that design work was complete, we would send it overseas and our counterparts there would work with their local design institute to finish the design and do the construction drawings.

"It is understood that in the product design process, once a product is designed, eighty percent of the cost and eighty percent of the quality are locked in. So when we talk about manufacturing process improvement of existing products, we are working on a twenty percent window. To improve quality, we've worked a lot on moving our

ベストプラクティスの例

コーラー社の事例

コーラーはアメリカ中西部を拠点とするメーカーである。1873年設立の同社は、キッチンとバスルーム製品で知られていたが、他にもインテリア（家具、タイル）、グローバルパワー（エンジン、発電機）、ホスピタリティ（高級リゾート）などの事業を展開している。コーラーは、過去10年間に驚くような速さでグローバル化を推進し、今では世界に50箇所を超える製造拠点を持つ。

事業範囲がグローバル化するにつれて、本社に集中していた体制を再評価する必要がでてきた。そのひとつが新しい拠点開発の体制である。コーラーは現在インドや中国などに製造施設を建設中だ。同社の担当副社長は以下のように語る。

「コンストラクション・エンジニアリング・マネジメントは、適切な場所を見つけるために外に出て事業部門と協力し、製造プロセスに合わせた施設を設計し、建設するグループだ。設計には3つのフェーズがある。1つ目は概念設計、2つ目が詳細設計、3つ目が施工図作成を含む最終設計だ」

「従来、ここウィスコンシンには施設技術者の大きなグループがいた。技術者たちは、概念設計から詳細設計まで行う。つまり、設計フェーズの70%から80%を完了させる。設計が完了したらこれを海外に送り、現地のカウンターパートが現地の設計事務所と協力して、設計を完成させ、施工図を作成する」

improvement activities up into the process so we have input from all parties before we get that design locked in. We're doing the same thing with buildings now.

"India was a great learning experience for us. One of my sayings to my organization is, 'We don't know what we don't know.' In the area of working cross-culturally, most of the time, **we don't know what we don't know**. India was a very tough project to complete on schedule, at the right quality, and at the right cost. What we found is that the way we had always done the design and construction management process wasn't working. Fortunately, we dramatically changed not only our approach for India but for all businesses. Now the design group here in the U.S. is only doing fifteen to twenty percent of the design, and then it goes over to the in-country designers, where they do the other eighty percent. What we've learned is that this gives the in-country design team the opportunity to have input on the design that is going to impact the schedule, cost, and the quality of what we get.

"Our engineers used to complete the design and send it to the in-country design institute for their twenty percent. After that in-country design institute completed their twenty percent, it would be returned to the U.S. design engineers and they would find issues or mistakes. This would then require the U.S. design team to go back to review the changes with the in-country design institute to try to get the design right. The old process took about seventeen weeks. With the new process, our engineers design the twenty percent, and then the design team travels to the in-country design institute to ensure not only that the design intent is clearly understood but for both teams to meet face-to-face to establish a working relationship and open lines of communication. Once these lines of communication are open and the design intent is understood, the foreign design firm has freedom within that framework to design the building. Now the design is completed in about ten weeks instead of seventeen. This means about a forty percent reduction in calendar time, and it's also about a forty-five percent reduction in hours spent doing the design phase.

"Our colleagues in other countries now feel that they have an opportunity to influence and to have an impact. If I had been in their shoes with the previous system, I think I would have been frustrated.

「しかし、インドでの経験は、彼らにとってすばらしい教訓となった。この教訓についていえることは**『何を知らないのかを知らない』**ということだ。異文化間の業務では、何を知らないのかを把握していないことが多い。インドのプロジェクトは、スケジュール通りに適切な品質とコストで完了させるのに多大な困難が伴った。つまり、従来と同じ設計・建設管理プロセスが機能しなかったのだ。同社はこの教訓を活かして、海外のあらゆる事業へのアプローチを劇的に変更した。現在では、本社の設計グループは全設計の15%から20%を担当し、約80%を現地が担う。これによって、プロジェクトについての意見を現地の関係者が述べる機会を与えることができた。

「この新しい体制が確立し設計の意図が理解されると、海外の設計事務所はその枠組み内で自由に設計できるようになる。17週間かかった設計が今では約10週間に完了できる。これは、カレンダー上の時間が約40%短縮され、設計フェーズに費やす時間も約45%短縮されたことになる。しかも、他国のスタッフたちも、自分たちが影響力を発揮する機会があると前向きになる。副社長はいう。

「もし、以前の体制で、自分が彼らの立場であれば、不満だったろう。すでに80%完成した設計図が送られてきたら、影響力を行使したり考え方を変えさせたりする機会がないからだ。彼らが実際に送ってきたメッ

I wouldn't have felt like I had an opportunity to influence and change the thinking, because they had been sent drawings already eighty percent complete. I'm not sure if they were sending us this message but my gut tells me they were—there were times where we would take the drawings and we'd do our eighty percent, which was about six hundred drawings. We'd send it to them, they would work on it for their four weeks, and when we got the packet back there were only thirty drawings. We'd ask them, 'What did you do with all of our drawings and design?' I think their response was basically, 'Well, there's nothing we can do with this so here are your thirty drawings back.' I think they were giving us that message, but we were just not hearing it.

"I find that as soon as you have the concept, that's when you get on the plane and get in front of them at their desk and start talking. This way they have input into the concept and it's not so complete that we have to say, 'Well, we do it this way, and I'm sorry but the train has left the station.' It's taking the concept and going to them to get that mutual understanding and input as early as possible. After we have had the face-to-face meetings, it is then that we can start having the conference calls, which will be much more meaningful and productive. First, take the concept and hold a face-to-face meeting to get a clear understanding. As I've been taking this approach and doing it over and over again, I have learned that it doesn't matter if it's at the plant manager level or at the country president level—I'm just amazed at the acceptance of some of the things we want to do."

Training to Develop Future Leaders

Although the need to develop future global leaders seems obvious, knowing whom to select and how to develop them is less clear. Many companies still depend upon a group of "global leaders" all from the same country or ethnic background, whether they are the head of Asia Pacific, the Americas, or Europe, the Middle East, and Africa (EMEA).

Participants in a global leadership training program can benefit from considering whether the process for selecting future leadership candidates

セージだったかどうか確かではないがこんなことがあった。設計の80%を終えて、約600枚の図面を作成した。私たちはそれを現地に送ったが、現地での4週間の作業期間を経て、返送された図面はたった30枚だった。『こちらで作成した図面とデザインに対して一体何をやったのか？』と尋ねた。『こちらでできることは何もないので、30枚の設計図をお返しします』というのが彼らの答えだった。私たちは彼らの答えの裏にある不満に気づかなかった」

「まず、コンセプトを打ち出し、直接会って話し合い、理解を得ることが大切だ。この方法を何度も繰り返しているうちに、工場長レベルでも現地社長のレベルでも情報が共有される。私たちがやりたいことの一部が受け入れられていることに驚いている」

次世代リーダー育成研修

将来のグローバルリーダーを育成する必要性があるのは明確なようだが、誰を選び、どう育成するかということはそれほど明確ではない。多くの企業では、アジア太平洋、南北アメリカ、ヨーロッパ、中東、アフリカ（EMEA）のトップであるかどうかにかかわらず、いまだに同じ国、または民族的背景を持つ「グローバルリーダー」グループに依存している。

研修プログラムの参加者は、各組織の次世代リーダー候補者の選出プロセ

in their own organization provides a balanced view of each person's leadership potential. Such balance is usually best achieved by incorporating multicultural perspectives in the assessment team.

There are a number of training and development opportunities that should be considered for employees who have been targeted for their future leadership potential. One way to begin planning the development of global leadership capabilities is to weigh the degree of difficulty and the degree of difference presented by any opportunity in connection with the candidate's present state of readiness. The objective over time is to work with each future leader to arrange a series of increasingly challenging experiences. These continue to test the candidate's potential while better enabling him or her to quickly find firm footing and accomplish business objectives even when presented with radically different market circumstances.

The following list identifies some standard practices for cultivating global leadership skills that can stimulate discussion and planning efforts.

- Hiring people with previous successful experience of living and working abroad
- Traveling with short-term immersion in local markets or operations
- Training and development opportunities with global content
- Working on a short-term project assignment abroad

スにおいて、各自のリーダーとしての潜在能力について、バランスよい見解を提供し検討しなければならない。最良の方法は、評価チームに多文化的視点を持つ人を加えることだ。将来のリーダーを目指す従業員向けに、多くの研修や開発の機会を検討すべきである。グローバルリーダーシップ能力開発を始めるにあたって、候補者の現在の心構えに関して、どの程度の困難さと異文化での相違点を認識できるかを比較検討することもひとつの方法だ。

長期的な目標は、各リーダー候補者と協力して、徐々に厳しくなる一連の経験を整理してゆく。この方法によって、候補者の潜在能力を引き続き検証する一方で、全く異なる市場環境においても、より迅速に足場を見つけ、事業目標を達成できるようにする。

計画を促進できるグローバルリーダーシップ・スキルを育成するための標準的な方法の一部を以下に示す。

- 海外生活や海外勤務経験者の採用
- 現地の市場や業務に短期的に深く関わる出張
- グローバルコンテンツを使用した研修と開発の機会
- 海外での短期プロジェクトに派遣

CHAPTER NINE

Coaching the Ten Behaviors

Global leaders work at the crucial point between strategy and implementation. It is here that **executive coaching** becomes a powerful lever to help leaders develop global capabilities. This chapter features examples of the key behaviors in the context of executive coaching.

Executive coaching is a **one-on-one development process** that increases the capability of key talent to achieve business objectives and leadership skills. Coaching is a short- to medium-term, goal-focused form of learning for executives who wish to improve their performance by working through organizational challenges and change initiatives with the help of a skilled partner.

There are many frameworks for coaches to choose from in this work. Most often we find that coaches use a mixture of techniques depending on the client (coachee) and the situation. Frameworks such as **Appreciative Inquiry,**[*1] **Ontological Coaching,**[*2] **GROW (Goals, Reality, Options, Will),**[*3] and **Brain-Based Coaching**[*4] are all useful in working with global executives.

Most of these coaching models involve bringing clients to their own insights through a structured listening process. The coach focuses on the other person, draws out thoughts and feelings related to an issue or opportunity, encourages the coachee to generate options for action, and then seeks a commitment to act on a chosen direction. Coaches may support such structured listening with other techniques, including feedback, suggestions,

＊1 積極的に強みや真価を見つけ、それを最大限に活かすプロセスを用いてコーチする。

＊2 自分自身の在り方や認識を気づかせることで、それを変化させ、クライアント自身が問題を解決できるようにする。

第9章

「10の行動」のコーチング

グローバルリーダーは、戦略を立て、それを実行するために重要な役割を担う。**エグゼクティブ・コーチング**は、そんなリーダーがグローバルな能力を開発するための強力な手段である。

エグゼクティブ・コーチングは、**一対一の能力開発**のためのものである。コーチングは短期から中期の目標に焦点を当てた学習形態で、組織的課題を克服して業績を改善し、有能なパートナーの支援によって業務遂行を目指す管理者のためのものである。

コーチには、様々なフレームワークの選択肢があり、クライアント（コーチング受講者）や状況に応じて様々な手法を組み合わせて学習させる。**アプリシエイティブ・インクワイアリー**、**オントロジカル・コーチング**、**GROW（目標設定、現状把握、行動計画作成、動機付け）**、**ブレイン・ベースド・コーチング**などのフレームワークはどれもグローバル・エグゼクティブのコーチングに役立つものである。

これらのコーチングモデルの多くは、体系化されたリスニングプロセスを通じて、クライアント自身の気づきを引き出すことを目的としている。コーチは相手に焦点を当て、問題や機会に関連する考えや感情を引き出し、行動のための選択肢を生み出すように促し、選択した方向に向かって行動することを約束してもらう。コーチは、このような体系化されたリスニングを、フ

＊3 目標を決め、それに向けた行動をコーチとクライアント（受講者）の双方で作っていく。
＊4 脳科学に基づき、プロセスに焦点を当てた手法で、成果を重視する。

instruction, challenges, advice, and guidance. All of these methods are most effective when the coach is equipped with a solid understanding of the leader's **business objectives, potential obstacles**, and **organizational context**.

Coaching at Citi

To test the efficacy of the key behaviors in relation to coaching, the authors worked with a group of executive coaches at Citi who were interested in learning more about coaching across cultures, the global leader's role, and the use of this new framework in their work with executives. The coaches attended training sessions on coaching across cultures and the **global leadership behaviors**, which they then put into practice with their current coaching clients.

Citi has a huge global operation. The company does business in 160 countries, with a physical presence in over 100, and employs 259,000 people globally. In recent years, Citi has gone through its share of challenges related to the financial crisis, including changes in leadership, strategy and organizational structure. However, Citi has been able to pay back the TARP loan from the U.S. government, redesign its business model with a focus on banking as a **core competency**,[*1] restructure its remaining businesses and functions into a blend of centralized and globally dispersed operations, and return to profitability.

In addition, the leadership team has focused on key competitive differentiators that are difficult to replicate in today's market. Its post-crisis global strategy defined a path forward for the company as well as the specific skills its leaders would need to develop.

This strategy signaled a need to change the **organizational culture** within the company. For the Executive Development group at Citi, the priorities became global mindset, customer-centricity, responsible finance, the development of leaders capable of directing the change, and cultivating other leaders for key next-in-line roles in the organization.

Citi saw an opportunity to accelerate its leaders' global capabilities by training their coaches on key leadership behaviors. "Citi Coach" is the in-house branding for the **Center of Excellence** (COE)[*2] that provides **thought leadership**[*3] and oversight for the seventy executive coaches comprising the internal coaching practice. The Citi Coach group is composed of mostly

ィードバック、提案、指示、異議、助言、ガイダンスなどの手法でサポートする。これらの方法はすべて、コーチがリーダーの**事業目標**、**潜在的な障害**、**組織の状況**をしっかりと理解している場合に、最も効果を発揮する。

シティグループにおけるコーチング

コーチングに関連した重要な行動の有効性を検証するために、著者はシティグループのエグゼクティブコーチ陣の協力を得た。コーチたちは、文化を超えたコーチングや**グローバルリーダーシップ行動**に関する講習会に参加し、コーチングを受けているクライアントにこれを実践した。

シティは、大規模なグローバル企業だ。世界160カ国で事業を展開し、100カ国を超える拠点を持ち、世界で25万9千人の従業員を擁している。当時、シティは、リーダーシップ、戦略、組織体制の変化を含めた金融危機に関連した課題に直面していた。しかし、シティはアメリカ政府からTARP(不良資産救済プログラム)で受けた融資を返済し、銀行業務を**コア・コンピタンス**として中心に据えるビジネスモデルを再構築し、他の事業と機能を再編し、中央集権型の事業と世界中に分散した事業を統合し、収益性を回復させた。

さらに、リーダーシップ・チームは、金融危機後のグローバル戦略の中で、同社の進むべき道とリーダーが習得すべき具体的なスキルを明確にした。

この戦略は、社内の**組織的文化**の変更を推し進めるものだった。シティのエグゼクティブ・ディベロップメント・グループにとっての優先事項は、グローバルなマインドセット、顧客中心主義の徹底、責任ある財務、変革を指揮できるリーダーの育成、組織内で次世代の主要な役割を担うリーダーの育成であった。

シティは、リーダーシップの鍵となる行動についてコーチをトレーニングすることで、リーダーのグローバルな能力を加速する機会を得た。「シティ・コーチ」は、社内のコーチング業務を構成する70人のエグゼクティブ・コーチに**ソート・リーダーシップ**と監督機能を提供する**センター・オブ・エクセ**

＊1「核となる能力」から、その企業が他社を圧倒的に上回る得意分野のこと。
＊2 組織を横断する取り組みを行うための中心となる部署。
＊3 組織内の才能、経験、情熱を活用して特定のトピックに関する疑問に答えること。

Human Resources practitioners who, besides their "day jobs," which include coaching, take on an additional forty to fifty hours of ongoing professional coaching development each year. The coaches are nominated by the regional senior Human Resource officers who preside over HR for a business or region. The coaches work their way up the "coach pipeline" through a combination of training, supervision, and job experience.

Training Event for Coaches

One aspect of the training curriculum for the coaches is the annual Citi Coach Conference, which brings the coaching community together for a development event at the company's training center in Armonk, New York. The main theme of the most recent Coach Conference was enhancing the coaches' understanding of how the company's new global strategy translates to the developmental needs of Citi's leaders.

Two of the central training modules were "**Coaching Across Cultures**" and "Coaching Global Leaders." The Coaching Across Cultures session highlighted the dimensions of culture, cultural self-awareness, and skills for bridging differences among nation states, functions, product lines, and geographies. For this segment, the coaches filled out the GlobeSmart® Assessment Profile, which plotted their work-style preferences on six dimensions of culture. They compared their own profiles to those of other cultures and program participants, and learned techniques for bridging differences between themselves and clients from other parts of the world.

The Coaching Global Leaders session was centered on the **ten key behaviors** described in this book. For this module, the coaches were given the Global Leadership Online survey, which they completed as both a self-assessment and a **360-degree evaluation**, inviting key business partners to rate their global leadership performance. The results of the survey, comparing self-assessment results with feedback from coworkers, were used in the session, which also included case study analysis and role playing. The objectives of the training modules were to build the coaches' understanding of global leadership as well as their skills for increasing the global leadership competencies of their clients.

Three months later, we met with the coaches to ask how they were using the ten key behaviors in their practice, and what, if any, new insights and behavioral changes they were helping clients to attain.

レンス（COE）の社内ブランディングである。「シティ・コーチ」は、主に人事部の職員で、コーチングを含む「本業」の他に、毎年40～50時間の継続的なプロフェッショナル・コーチングの開発を行っている。コーチは、事業や地域の人事を統括する管理者によって指名される。コーチは、研修、監督、職務経験などを組み合わせて、「コーチ・パイプライン」を形成していく。

コーチ向け研修

コーチ向けの研修カリキュラムのひとつは、コーチング・コミュニティが集まって年に一度開催されるシティ・コーチ・カンファレンスだ。直近のメインテーマは、シティの新しいグローバル戦略を同社リーダーの育成ニーズにどのように落とし込むかという課題について理解を深めることだった。

中心となる研修モジュールは、「**文化の違いを超えたコーチング**」と「グローバルリーダーのコーチング」であった。「文化の違いを超えたコーチング」のセッションは、国、機能、製品ライン、地理的位置の違いを乗り越えるための文化、文化的自己認識、スキルに焦点を当てた内容だった。このセッションでは、コーチは自分の働き方を文化的に分析しプロフィールを作成する。次に自分のプロフィールを他の文化やプログラム参加者と比較し、自分自身と世界の他地域から来た参加者との違いを乗り越える手法を学んだ。

コーチング・グローバルリーダーズ・セッションでは、本書で説明されている**10の重要な行動**に焦点が当てられた。このセッションでは、コーチにグローバルリーダーシップ・オンライン調査を行い、自己評価と自らの周囲からの**360度評価**を実施し、自己評価結果と同僚からのフィードバックを比較した調査結果を開示し、事例研究分析やロールプレイなども実施した。

3カ月後、私たちはコーチたちに会い、10の重要な行動を実践の中でどのように使っているか、またもしあれば、クライアントの目的を達成させるために役に立った洞察と行動の変化は何かを尋ねた。

Coaching in a Global Context

The coaches we interviewed found the frameworks from the training—the **dimensions of culture** and the ten key leadership behaviors—useful both for their own professional development and in working with their coaching clients. With respect to their development as coaches, they noted that these frameworks had provided ways of better understanding and applying their prior experience.

COACHES: PERSONAL LEARNING EXPERIENCES

Each of the coaches we spoke with had a long history of working in other countries and with a culturally diverse client base of globally minded executives. These experiences made them open to learning how to be more effective in the global arena. The Global Leadership Online survey provided the opportunity for the coaches to assess their own strengths and skill gaps as global leaders. The coaches spoke at length about the need for a global mindset as a requirement for their success in coaching across cultures. They most commonly cited **cultural self-awareness**, invite the unexpected, and frame-shifting as critical behaviors for their work as coaches.

Cultural Self-Awareness

Larissa Durant has been in Human Resources since 1994, working mostly for U.S. financial institutions in Switzerland, England, Belgium, and Denmark. Today, she is a regional HR business partner for Citi in EMEA. Early in her career, beginning in Geneva, Switzerland, she worked for another large financial institution.

> "Being French and French-speaking, I went to Geneva confident of our commonalties, but had underestimated the differences in mentality, culture, and behavior. I alienated a lot of people in the office by using 'tu' [the familiar form of address], as we had in the French office. I used this for everyone, and the senior bankers were not impressed. I had not earned the right to be familiar with them. No one would tell me. I found out by accident. I was twenty-eight years old and quite young to be heading up the HR practice. It took three months to recover. In the end, my stay there was a success, but it started as a disaster."

グローバル視点からの研修

インタビューしたコーチたちは、研修で得た**文化の次元**と10の主要なリーダーシップ行動というフレームワークが、自分自身の専門的な開発と、コーチングの仕事の両方に役立っていることを実感した。コーチとしての成長に関しては、これらのフレームワークが、これまでの経験をよりよく理解し、適用する方法を提供してくれたと述べている。

コーチの個人的経験

私たちが話を聞いたコーチたちは、他国で働いた経験が十分あり、グローバル志向で多文化的な基盤を持っていた。今回の経験によって、彼らはグローバルな領域でより効果的に業務を遂行する方法を学ぶことを受け入れられるようになった。グローバルリーダーシップ・オンライン調査は、コーチ自身のグローバルリーダーとしての強みとスキルのギャップを評価する機会となった。彼らは、**文化的自己認識**を例に、コーチとしての任務を遂行するための重要な行動として、想定外の事象に対処することと、フレームシフトを挙げた。

自文化への認識力

ラリッサ・デュランは、1994年から人事に携わっており、現在ではEMEAのシティの地域人材開発部門でビジネスパートナーを務めている。

「私は、フランス人で、フランス語を話すため、ジュネーブの人たちとギャップはないと信じてジュネーブに赴任したが、考え方、文化、行動の違いを過小評価していた。私は、フランスにいた時と同じように親しい相手の呼びかけに使う『tu』をジュネーブのオフィスで使って多くの人を遠ざけてしまった。私は誰に対しても『tu』を使ったが、上級銀行員からはよく思われなかった。私は彼らと親しくなる権利を得てなかったのだ。誰も私に教えてくれなかった。それを知ったのは偶然のことだった。私は28歳で、人事業務の責任者としてはかなり若かった。回復するのに3カ月かかった。最終的には、私のジュネーブでの勤務は成功したが、最初はひどいものだった」

When Larissa moved from Geneva to the London office, she observed instances when she and others would attribute too much meaning to cultural differences. Her own self-awareness has continued to evolve, helping her to understand not only which kinds of issues may be cultural in origin, but also which are not.

> "I initially thought that everything was due to cultural differences, and then thought maybe very little, and now I am more balanced in my approach. I realize that global leadership always calls for different approaches. Today, on my own team, I have to be very culturally self-aware. I have to have flexibility, especially when I think about developing my own people. I want to develop HR leaders from places other than the U.K. or the U.S. because our presence in Eastern Europe and Russia is growing. We have to think about the competency model we are using in our organization. Does the framework need to change to address the realities and needs of where our employees will be coming from in the future? Moving from one region to the next means dealing with such ambiguities, finding different solutions, and making sure you understand your colleagues and clients—plus listening and clarifying to a much greater degree."

In any new coaching engagement, forming a relationship takes time, but coaching across cultures requires even more time and careful focus on getting to know the client. Learning about how one's cultural background influences coaching is a lifelong process for coaches.

Invite the Unexpected

Abigail Kwong's early experiences working for a large U.S. multinational in Korea taught her the value of understanding her cultural assumptions as well as inviting the unexpected to be able to better anticipate difficulties. As the country HR leader at that time, originally from Taiwan, she was called upon to work through union issues during an acquisition of the company's Korean business partner. In South Korea, where the union was very strong and an important part of the country's culture, the negotiations were difficult, and she was surprised by what happened next.

> "We ended up with a strike on our hands for sixteen months. This was a very good learning experience for me personally. I realized afterwards there

ジュネーブからロンドンオフィスに異動してきたラリッサは、自分と他の人々の間における文化の違いが非常に多くのことに影響することに気づいた。自己認識を高めたことで、どのような問題が文化的なことに起因するのかを理解できるようになった。

「はじめは、すべてが文化的相違点によるものだと思っていたが、そのうちに必ずしもそうではないと思うようになった。今では、以前よりバランスのいいアプローチができる。人材育成について考える際は、柔軟性を持たなければならない。東欧やロシアでのプレゼンスが高まっているため、イギリスやアメリカ以外で人材開発のリーダーを育成したいと思っている。今後従業員となる人の出身地によって現実とニーズに対応するためにフレームワークを変更する必要があるか？ 他の地域に移ると、あいまいなものに対応し、異なるソリューションを見つけ、同僚と顧客を理解し、彼らの言葉に耳を傾け、多くのことを明確にすることが求められる」

新しいコーチングに取り組む上で、関係構築に時間がかかるが、異文化コーチングでは、クライアントを知ることにさらに時間をかけて注意深く集中する必要がある。自分の文化的背景がコーチングにどのように影響するかを学ぶことは、コーチにとって生涯続くプロセスである。

予期せぬ事態を招き入れる

アビゲイル・クオンは、韓国でアメリカ系の大手多国籍企業に在籍していた初期の経験から、自分の文化的先入観を理解することと、困難を予測するために予想外の事態を想定することの大切さを学んだ。当時、台湾出身だったアビゲイルは、勤務先の韓国のビジネスパートナーを買収する過程で、労組問題に対処するよう求められた。韓国では、組合の力が非常に強く、交渉が難しく、先の読めない事態に驚かされた。

「私たちは自分たちの責任で16カ月間ストライキをすることになった。この経験は個人的にはとてもいい勉強になった。後になって、この交渉を円

were things we could have done to make this deal smoother and to have avoided the strike. I had to learn how to win the hearts and the minds of business leaders."

Frame-Shifting

Citi coach Brian Goodman cites differences in communication style he experienced early in his professional career to illustrate how he learned to play a useful role in facilitating frame-shifting between cultural groups.

> "I was a translator for an oil company. One of the clients was a brokerage planning a joint venture with a company from the U.K. The U.K. company sent a global head of operations. He came into the Mexico office and needed to make things happen in a culture he didn't know well. He decided to keep me on to help support him and I became his chief of staff, acting as a liaison between the North American, Mexican, and U.K. offices. It was a very important learning experience, straddling these cultures. I tried hard to create positive working relationships between New York, London, and Mexico City executives. Each group had its own biases that would become apparent during the negotiations. For instance, the Mexican team would have a very hard time saying 'no' and had a strong desire to please. The U.S. and U.K. teams were very straightforward, making concessions in response to what they thought were concessions from the Mexican team. Then later, when the deal was nearly done, the Mexicans would reopen the negotiations. These became sore points that would flare up in future discussions. I started to recognize that an outside perspective was valuable, and that I could make an important contribution by staying 'outside' and giving my views on the situation."

Larissa Durant links frame-shifting with another global leadership behavior, **core values and flexibility**.

> "'Frame-shifting' is a skill that I like and use. This is also linked with 'core values and flexibility.' I am inclined to build my coaching practice around this: What are the coachee's core values and beliefs and how does this inform their perspective? With this as my frame of reference, I am in a position to help them come to a good decision. I think that, for me, frame-shifting means broadening my horizon in terms of understanding human behavior and human nature."

滑にし、ストライキを回避できる方法があったことに気づいた。ビジネスリーダーたちの心をつかむ方法を学ぶ必要があったのだ」

フレームシフト力

シティのコーチであるブライアン・グッドマンは、働きはじめた頃に経験したコミュニケーションスタイルの違いを例に挙げ、異文化間のフレームシフトを促進する役割をどのようにして身につけたかを語った。

「私は、石油会社の通訳だった。顧客のひとつだったブローカーは、イギリス企業との合弁事業を計画していた。イギリス企業はグローバルな経営責任者を派遣した。メキシコのオフィスを訪れた経営責任者は、慣れない文化の中で業務を遂行する必要があった。私は彼のサポートを続けることになり、北米、メキシコ、イギリスのオフィス間の連絡担当として彼の補佐のトップになった。それは３カ国の文化に触れるとても貴重な経験となった。私は、ニューヨーク、ロンドン、メキシコシティの役員たちの間での良好なビジネス関係を構築しようと努めた。地域独自の偏見が交渉の過程で明らかになった。例えば、メキシコのチームは、「No」と言うことに抵抗があり、他者を喜ばせることを強く望んでいた。アメリカとイギリスのチームは非常に率直で、メキシコチームからの譲歩だと思ったことに応じて、自分たちも譲歩した。その後、取引がほぼ成立しようという時になって、メキシコチームは再交渉をはじめた。この現象は、その後の話し合いの場でも再発し、障壁となった。私は、客観的視点で物事を見ることの重要性に気づき、外部にいながら、状況に対する見解を述べることで大きく貢献できるようになった」

ラリッサ・デュランは、フレームシフトを別のグローバルリーダーシップ行動、**コアバリューと柔軟性**に結びつけている。

「『フレームシフト』は私が好んで使う手法だ。これは『コアバリューと柔軟性』とも関連がある。私はこれを中心にコーチング法を確立したいと思っている。コーチのコアバリューと信念は何か？　彼らの考え方をどのように伝えるものなのか？　これを評価基準として、私は、彼らが適切な決定を下せるよう促す立場にある。私にとって、フレームシフトとは、人間の行動と本質を理解する上で視野を広げることだと思う」

COACHES: SUPPORTING GLOBAL LEADERS

Since the Citi Coach Conference, the coaches have also been using the ten key behaviors as a framework for coaching in their work with business partners. Results through **relationships, adapt and add value, influence across boundaries**, and **third-way solutions** were among the behaviors they cited most often.

Results through Relationships

Pio Arcuni's clients are mostly chief country officers (CCOs) and regional heads who represent the bank in local markets. His CCO clients must be able to work within the constraints of the local market while still meeting the demands of headquarters. They share the common challenges of needing to quickly establish credibility with not only the local offices, but with governmental officials, clients, regulators, and other outside constituencies. Obtaining results through relationships is a **common challenge** for these clients.

Adapt and Add Value

Leaders not only need to get started on the right foot and take the time to build relationships, but also demonstrate the value they bring and ultimately take action. Adapt and add value is a common challenge for these leaders, as Pio continued:

> "They need to understand the environment first. It is risky to make changes without first understanding what is going on and creating common ground from which to implement your changes. The leaders must have an open agenda from the beginning. They must learn to build bridges with the local team, be approachable, think about what scares people and deal with their anxieties from the very beginning, creating a secure environment. You make an impression in the first thirty seconds but it can take a lifetime to undo it if it is not right. I coach my clients that it is important to establish that you know what you are talking about from the very beginning. Yet these initial steps also require a lot of humility in order to understand the environment. The locals are always asking global leaders, 'Why do I need you?' The leader needs to make clear, 'This is the help I can provide to you and the help that I need from you.' They need to enter a contract where there is an exchange."

グローバルリーダーをサポートする

シティ・コーチ・カンファレンス以来、コーチたちは、ビジネスパートナーとの共同のコーチングのフレームワークとして10の重要な行動を使用している。**人間関係**の構築、**適用価値と付加価値**、**国境を越えた影響**、**第三のソリューション**による成果は、最も多く引用された行動であった。

人間関係を通した目標の達成による成果

ピオ・アークニの顧客の大部分は、チーフ・カントリー・オフィサー（CCO）や現地市場で銀行を代表する地域のトップである。CCOの顧客は、本社の要求に応えながら、現地市場の制約内で業務を遂行する必要がある。彼らは、迅速な信頼性確立の必要性を現地オフィスだけではなく、政府関係者、顧客、規制機関、その他の外部機関と共有している。関係構築によって結果を得ることは、これらの顧客にとって**共通の課題**である。

適用と価値を付加する能力

リーダーは、幸先のよいスタートを切り、時間をかけて関係を築くだけでなく、自分が価値をもたらすことを示し、行動を起こす必要がある。適用と付加価値はリーダーにとって共通の課題である。ピオは次のように述べている。

> 「リーダーは自分の置かれた環境を理解しなければならない。何が起こっているかを理解し、共通基盤を構築してからでないと、改革を進めるのは危険だ。リーダーは最初からオープンでなければならない。現地スタッフとの懸け橋を築き、親しみやすく、彼らが何を恐れているか考え、懸念に対して最初から対応し、安全な環境を作り上げる。第一印象は最初の30秒で決まるが、これがうまくいかなければ取り戻すのに一生かかることもある。私はクライアントに、最初から何について話しているのかわかっているかを確認することが重要だと指導している。しかし、このような最初のステップでは、十分な謙虚さも必要だ。現地スタッフは常にグローバルリーダーに『なぜ私たちにはあなたが必要なの？』と問いかけている。リーダーは、『私が支援できるのはこれで、あなたから支援してもらう必要があるのはこれ』と明確にする相互支援協定が必要だ」

Influence across Boundaries

Bandwidth, which in this context means the leader's ability to exert influence across organizational functions and layers, is another common challenge for the global clients of our coaches. Larissa Durant noted that this bandwidth challenge involves both ambiguity and complexity.

> "The global leader has to deal with ambiguity in terms of the problems, which tend to be a lot more complex, spanning countries and business matrices."

Third-Way Solutions

The coaches all said that they were impressed at how their clients dealt with third-way solutions, walking the line between accepting the policies and business drivers of headquarters while being open to new ways of doing business that would benefit the local office.

Pio described the challenge of bridging different priorities and perspectives in an **even-handed way**, which requires leveraging a global network of relationships while working within a particular organizational culture.

> "I was working with a client in Central Europe once who was originally from India. He needed to leverage relationships across product lines and regional centers to get more support for the local office. Sometimes people get bogged down with local requirements and don't prioritize these relationships with the other offices and businesses. I have noticed that people on assignments spend most of their energies locally, but I tell them that they need to work with the matrix and regional centers and have good relationships across boundaries; otherwise, they cannot make things happen. The leader needs to make the regional stakeholders aware and get their support. We all need these relationships to navigate the complexity in organizations today. I coach them to have regular one-on-one calls with these remote managers. The ideal country manager is someone with local and international experience, with good knowledge of the matrix. They must have local relationships but not be driven by the local culture. You don't need to be a dictator to be a leader in Russia, but you need to be aware of the culture."

境界線を越えた影響力の発揮

影響力とは、ここでは、リーダーが組織の機能や階層を超えて影響力を発揮する能力を意味する。ラリッサ・デュランは、この影響力の課題には、「あいまいさ」と「複雑さ」の両方があると指摘する。

「グローバルリーダーは、国やビジネス上のマトリックスを超えて、より複雑になりがちな問題のあいまいさに対応しなければならない」

第三のソリューション

コーチたちは口をそろえて、クライアントが第三のソリューションに取り組んでいることに感銘を受けたと言う。彼らは現地オフィスに利益をもたらす新しいビジネス手法を取り入れながら、本社の方針とビジネス戦略を受け入れるという境界線上でバランスを取って業務を進めている。

ピオは、異なる優先事項と考え方の橋渡しを**公平に行う**ためには、グローバルな人間関係のネットワークを活用しながら、特定の組織文化の中で仕事をする必要があると語った。

「インド出身の顧客と中欧で仕事をしたことがあった。顧客は、各製品ラインや地域センターとの連携を活用して現地オフィスに対する支援を強化する必要があった。地域の要件にとらわれて、他のオフィスや企業との関係を優先しない人もいる。業務に携わっている人がエネルギーの多くを地域にのみ費やしていることに気づいた。そういう人に対し、私はマトリックスや地域センターを活用して、境界を越えて良好な関係を築く必要があると助言した。リーダーは、地域のステークホルダーに気づいてもらい、支援を得る必要がある。このような関係は、今日の組織の複雑さに対応するためには不可欠だ。私は彼らに現地のマネージャーと定期的に一対一で電話会議を行うように指導している。理想的なカントリー・マネージャーは、地域および国際経験の双方があり、マトリックスの知識を豊富に持っている。地域の関係は必要だが、その土地の文化に操られてはならない」

Brian Goodman also spoke about developing integrated solutions, even across silos and functional subcultures.

> "There are cultures within cultures in the bank. My clients are highly evolved leaders, but their success is intertwined with these environments, and these **interdependencies** are so embedded. It comes down to a virtuous cycle or a vicious cycle. In my coaching, I encourage the virtuous cycle: getting the coaches to check all stakeholder needs first before developing solutions."

Brian works with clients to help them to both frame-shift in terms of communication style and signal to others that they are willing to strive for solutions with **collective benefits**.

> "I was coaching a client from South America who was working in the Miami office, with Latin America [LATAM] responsibilities. This person's strengths were her clarity of thinking, incisiveness, and an analytical mind. But many of the cultures had an issue with her delivery, her directness, and they said that she did not appear to respect their competence and expertise. Then link this to being part of a company with its headquarters in New York, and there is a complex interplay of all these cultures that she has to navigate. Sometimes the question of bridging boundaries is a matter of signaling intentions. If she wants to move up, she will have to move beyond herself and the team's interest and think about the larger, collective 'we.'"

COACHING PRACTICES

The Citi coaches portrayed in this chapter indicate a number of ways that they have incorporated the ten key leadership behaviors into their work with clients to better grasp their challenges or to help them achieve their goals. The following more specific examples, based upon previous executive coaching work, were presented to them during their training conference. Analyzing these scenes can help coaches from any organization strengthen their coaching repertoire by diagnosing and addressing the need for particular global leadership behaviors.

ブライアン・グッドマンは、サイロや機能的サブカルチャーを超えた統合ソリューションの開発についても語った。

> 「銀行には文化の中に文化がある。私のクライアントは、優れたリーダーだが、彼らの成功は自身の置かれた環境と密接に関係しており、その**相互依存関係**はしっかり根付いたものである。結局は好循環か悪循環になるが、私のコーチングで好循環を導きたい。コーチにはソリューションを開発する前に、全てのステークホルダーのニーズをまず確認するよう指導している」

ブライアンはクライアントと協力して、コミュニケーションスタイルにおけるフレームシフトと、**包括的利益**を伴うソリューションを目指して取り組む意思を他の人に伝えることの両方を支援している。

> 「南米出身で、マイアミでラテンアメリカ（LATAM）を担当するクライアントがいた。彼女の長所は思考の明晰さ、鋭敏さ、分析力だった。しかし、彼女の話し方と率直さを問題とする文化環境も多く、現地の人の能力と専門知識を尊重していないと言われることもあった。これをニューヨークに本社がある企業の一員であることと関連付けると、こうした文化の複雑な相互作用に対応していかなければならない。境界を越えるという問題は、意思伝達の問題である場合もある。もし彼女が昇進したいのであれば、自分自身やチームの利益を超えてより大きな包括的な「We（私たち）」について考える必要がある」

コーチング手法

本章で紹介したシティのコーチたちは、今までのエグゼクティブ・コーチングをもとに、より具体的な事例を研修会議で発表した。これらの事例を分析することで、どんな組織のコーチも特定のグローバルリーダーシップ行動の必要性を精査し、それに対応することで、コーチングの守備範囲を広げることができる。

EXAMPLE 1: **THE DRIVER**

Client A is a driver. He likes to get things done, and he will run over people, if necessary, to do it. In his mind, the tough management approach he takes reflects the company's corporate culture, and employees either need to learn to deal with it or find a different place to work. He tends to speak directly and forcefully to people, with little variation depending upon with whom he is speaking. Some of his company colleagues and direct reports, particularly those from Asia Pacific, say they prefer to avoid him because they are uncomfortable with his temper. In addition, he frequently misinterprets positive-sounding messages as indicating agreement or commitment, when others are simply trying to please him but do not necessarily agree. Most seriously, he has developed negative relationships with two other functional groups that his own team needs to collaborate with smoothly in order to be effective.

Possible Interpretation and Coaching Strategy: The colleagues and direct reports of this team leader—most notably those from Asia—are likely to have a less direct approach to communication and be put off by his forceful communication style. Their **indirect approach** to communication might also be the key to comprehending the missed deliverables. They could be saying "no" to project deadlines in a way that cannot be heard by the leader, who is taking their silence or positive-sounding messages to signify assent.

This client could benefit from learning all of the ten key leadership behaviors, and he is unlikely to be successful without them. An effective coaching approach would probably combine concrete feedback based upon solid evidence with an invitation to learn more about global leadership in order to advance to the next career step. Cultural self-awareness would be a good place to start. This coachee seems to assume that his personal communication style and values are in line with the company values and therefore are universal. He is coming to premature conclusions about the level of agreement he is getting from team members and the capabilities of other groups. Asking his colleagues in a more open-ended way about the extent

事例１：ドライバー（推進者）

Ａは「ドライバー」である。Ａは物事をやり遂げるのが好きで、必要となれば、他の人を犠牲にすることもいとわない。自分の厳しい管理手法は会社の企業文化を反映しており、従業員はそれに応じる方法を学ぶか、別の職場を見つける必要があるというのがＡの考え方だ。人に対して直接的に説得力を持って話す傾向があり、相手によって話し方を変えることはほとんどない。同僚、直属の部下、特にアジア太平洋地域出身の人の中には、Ａの短気さが気になり避けたがる人もいる。単にＡを喜ばせようとしているだけで、必ずしも賛成していない人たちの肯定的にみえる言動を同意やコミットメントを示すものだと誤解することがよくある。最も深刻なのは、Ａのグループが効果的に業務を進める上で円滑な連携が必要な他の２グループとネガティブな関係を築いてきたことである。

想定される解釈とコーチング戦略：同僚と直属の部下、中でも特にアジアの人たちは、あまり直接的なコミュニケーションスタイルを取らず、Ａの説得力あるコミュニケーションスタイルに嫌悪感を持つ可能性が高い。彼らの**遠回しなアプローチ**が、成果を出せなかった原因となっている可能性もある。彼らはプロジェクトの締め切りに対して「ノー」と言っているのかもしれないが、リーダーは沈黙や肯定的なメッセージを同意を意味すると考えているかもしれない。

Ａの場合、10の重要なリーダーシップ行動すべてを学ぶことなしに成功することは難しい。効果的なコーチング手法は、確かな根拠に基づく具体的なフィードバックと、次のキャリアステップに進むためにグローバルリーダーシップについてもっと学んでみないかという誘いを組み合わせることだろう。まず、文化的自己意識を形成することから始めてはどうか。彼は、自分のコミュニケーションスタイルや価値観が会社の価値観と一致しており、そのためこれらが普遍のものだと考えているようだ。チームメンバーから得られる同意の度合いや他グループの能力について、拙速な結論を出そうとして

to which they have the resources and time to meet commitments would be a good way to discern if "yes" really means "yes" or rather "I hear you." Cultivating frame-shifting and a balance between core values and flexibility might also be among the subsequent steps for this leader; the coaching dialogue with him could include questions about what is most important to him in the workplace and what he is willing to let go.

EXAMPLE 2: **THE SUCCESSFUL EXECUTIVE**

Client B is a relatively high-ranking and successful executive. He set several key objectives for himself six months ago that he has now achieved. As you speak with him today in your coaching session, you notice he seems to be very pleased and satisfied with the progress he has made, and does not express an urgent need to do further work on the areas that you have discussed thus far. His sense of satisfaction makes you wonder whether you have come far enough in this coaching relationship to bring it to a conclusion. However, you also know from speaking to some of this executive's direct reports in Central Europe that they feel he is not sufficiently well-informed about market conditions there—he seems to assume these markets are similar to other markets he has already encountered. Meanwhile, several rapidly growing local competitors have become very nimble and innovative in meeting customer needs. To expand his line of business, a next step could be to develop a more differentiated set of product offerings for this region.

Possible Interpretation and Coaching Strategy: This client may be **overly complacent** in light of the market situation in Central Europe. While congratulating him on his success to date, the coach could also ask whether he is satisfied with the situation in Central Europe, and inquire how he might find out more and take action if necessary. There are many ways for the coachee to determine whether serious concern is justified: spending time

いる。コミットメントを達成するためのリソースと時間がどの程度あるかをよりカジュアルに同僚に尋ねることは、「イエス」が本当に同意を意味するのか、それとも「わかっているよ」を意味するのかを識別するのによい方法である。コアバリューと柔軟性のバランスとフレームシフトスキルを培うことも、このリーダーにとって次のステップのひとつかもしれない。コーチングにおける対話では、職場で一番大切なことは何か、また気にしなくていいことは何かといった質問をするのもいいだろう。

事例2：**成功を収めたエグゼクティブ**

Bは比較的地位が高く、成功したエグゼクティブである。Bは、6カ月前にいくつかの重要な目標を設定しそれを達成してきた。コーチングセッションでBと話すと、Bは自分の成果に非常に満足しているように思われ、これまで議論してきた分野でさらなる取り組みの必要性が緊急にあるようには思われない。彼の満足感は、コーチング関係を終わらせるのに十分ではないかとまで思わせる。しかし、中欧におけるBの直属の部下の一部に話を聞いたところ、彼らは現地の市場状況についてBから十分な情報を得ていないと感じていることがわかった。Bは、中欧市場が、今までに対応してきた他の市場と同じだと思っているようであった。一方で、急速に成長している現地の競合企業の中には、顧客のニーズを満たすために非常に迅速に革新的な戦略を取っているところもある。Bの業務範囲を拡大するためには、次のステップとして、この地域向けにより差別化された製品を開発することが想定される。

想定される解釈とコーチング戦略：中欧の市場環境を考慮すると、Bは**過度に自己満足**している可能性がある。コーチは、Bのこれまでの成功をほめながら、中欧の状況に満足しているかどうかを尋ね、どうすればより多くのことを知り、必要に応じて行動を起こすことができるかを尋ねる。Bが深刻な懸念が正当なものかどうかを判断するには、現地で時間をかけて自分の目と

on-site to see and hear for himself; seeking out fresh sources of competitive data; and/or cultivating deeper relationships with employees, customers, or outside advisors who are willing to speak frankly. The most crucial factor is for him to consider if he should invite the unexpected and then to listen carefully to any data that emerge. If the client decides to take on this challenge, knowing that the situation in this market could be different from what he has been accustomed to, the result might be a **new-found sense of urgency** about competitors and product offerings.

Although in this chapter we have used the terms "coach" and "client" (coachee), the applications are much broader than a formal coaching relationship with an external or internal coach. Nearly every executive who seeks to foster the growth of future global leaders must assume the role of a coach, identifying both the strengths and skill gaps of possible successors along with other high-potential talent, and working together with them to develop new capabilities. The ten key behaviors provide executives, too, with a practical roadmap for evaluating and developing future global leaders that they can use in their day-to-day coaching work. This framework is also applicable in more structured formats such as leader-led action learning.

耳で確かめたり、競合に関する新しい情報源を探したり、率直に話してくれる社員や顧客、外部のアドバイザーとの関係を深めるなど様々な方法がある。何より大切なのは、クライアントが「想定外」を求めるかどうかを考え、出てきた情報に耳を傾けることだ。もし、Bが、現地の市場環境が慣れ親しんできたものと異なる可能性があることに気づき、この課題に取り組むことを決意したならば、競合や製品に対する**新たな危機感**を持つことになるかもしれない。

将来のグローバルリーダーの育成を目指すほとんどのエグゼクティブは、コーチの役割を担う必要がある。後継者候補の強みとスキルのギャップを他の潜在的才能とともに見極め、彼らと連携して新たな能力を開発しなければならない。10の重要な行動は、将来のグローバルリーダーを評価し、育成するための実用的なロードマップとなり、日々のコーチングに活用することができる。このフレームワークは、リーダー主導の行動学習など、より体系化されたフォーマットにも適用できる。

CHAPTER TEN

Teaming the Ten Behaviors

Leveraging the Leadership Behaviors for Shared Vision

For the global leaders involved in our research, the most significant challenge is creating and maintaining a shared focus.

Differences in market environments and commonsense assumptions about how to do business are more pronounced for members of global teams than for teams whose participants work in the same domestic environment. In our work with hundreds of global teams, a lack of **knowledge-sharing systems** has been mentioned as one of the key obstacles to implementing shared goals. Global team members typically lack sufficient insight into their colleagues' skills and **potential contributions**. This fosters isolation and duplicate work, and sets up obstacles to the exchange of best practices, preventing team members from working together toward a common goal.

Global organizations also typically have a matrix structure in which it is quite common for individuals to belong to a number of teams simultaneously. This means that team members are linked with a variety of "**stakeholders**,"* each having competing priorities that reflect the needs of different functions, business units, and regions. For all these reasons it is more difficult for the individual members of a global team to consistently identify how their efforts fit into the "big picture," and a shared vision becomes both more essential and more challenging to create and maintain.

Virtual communication challenges further contribute to the issues global leaders face when trying to create a shared vision and goals for their teams. Our interviewees indicated that a clear sense of direction, even in the midst of **tremendous complexity**, is a crucial factor in the success of **globally dispersed teams**.

第10章

10の行動を組み合わせること

ビジョンを共有するためのリーダーシップ行動

グローバルリーダーにとって最も重要な課題は、共通のビジョンを策定し維持することである。

市場環境の違いやビジネス手法や常識についての相違は、同じ国内環境で働くチームよりもグローバルチームのほうが顕著である。**知識共有システム**の欠如は共通の目標を達成しようとする上で重大な障害のひとつとなる。

グローバルチームのメンバーは、自分以外のメンバーのスキルや**潜在的貢献**について十分な洞察を持っていないことが多い。これが原因で、作業の分離と重複が加速され、ベストプラクティスの交換の障害となり、チームメンバーが共通の目標に向かって協働することができなくなる。

グローバル組織は、個人が同時に複数のチームに所属していることがあり、チームメンバーが様々な**ステークホルダー**と結びついている。それらの一つ一つが異なる機能、事業部門、地域のニーズを反映した競合する優先順位を持つマトリックス構造の中にある。従って、グローバルチームの個々のメンバーにとって自分たちの取り組みが全体像にどのように適合するかを特定することはより困難であり、共通のビジョンを策定し維持することが重要な課題となる。

インタビューでは、**非常に複雑な**状況の中でも、方向性を明確に提示することは、**世界に分散したチーム**を成功させるために大切だとの指摘があった。

＊利害関係者。直接的にはクライアント、社員、消費者などで、間接的には政府、会社・支社のあるコミュニティなど企業活動の影響を受ける相手。

While recognizing the heightened importance of establishing shared direction within a global, virtual team, the more traditional team literature seldom speaks of the distinct skills required to accomplish this in a global environment. The global team leaders in our study stressed the unique nature of their roles and the inadequacy of domestic leadership models to prepare them to be successful in a truly global environment.

Leadership Behaviors for Global Teams

Which leadership behaviors are the most crucial for achieving a common direction within a globally dispersed team? All ten behaviors play an important role in the success of a global team leader, but our research suggests that the most important behaviors to leverage are:

- *Invite the unexpected*
- *Frame-shifting*
- *Influence across boundaries*

While we will look at each of these global leadership behaviors individually as they relate to creating and implementing a shared sense of team direction, they are actually interconnected and mutually dependent.

INVITE THE UNEXPECTED

What does a global team leader need to know to create a vision and goals that will resonate with team members from around the world? Team leaders must of course carefully consider the complex functional, market, and regulatory factors already mentioned, including how these issues will influence the ways team members interpret and implement common goals. Moreover, the leader must take into account other factors, such as what motivates team members as well as the best means to tap into this kind of vital information.

Global Leader: Birgit Masjost, Roche

Dr. Birgit Masjost leads the technical development team at Roche, a major pharmaceutical company, and is based at Roche headquarters in Basel, Switzerland. Her first language is German, and she also speaks French,

インタビューに応じたグローバルチームリーダーたちは、自らの役割の独自性を強調し、本国のそうした役割を支えるための対応が不十分であると指摘した。

グローバルチームに対するリーダーシップ行動

世界に分散したチーム内で共通の方向性を認識するために、最も重要なリーダーシップ行動はどれか？　10の行動は全て大切だが、本調査では、以下の行動が特に重要なものであることが明らかになった。

- 予期せぬ事態への受容性
- フレームシフト力
- 境界を越えた影響力の発揮

これらはチームに共有すべき方向性を策定し、実行するために必要な概念だが、実際には相互に連携し、依存するものである。

予期せぬ事態への受容性

グローバルチームリーダーが、世界中のチームメンバーの共感を得られるビジョンと目標を策定するためになすべきことは何だろうか。チームリーダーは、前述の複雑な機能、市場、規制などの要素を考慮し、チームメンバーが共通の目標を目指す際に、これらの要素がどんな影響を及ぼすかを検討しなければならない。さらに、リーダーはチームメンバーのモチベーションを引き出す方法や、重要な情報を活用するための最良の手法なども考慮する必要がある。

バジット・マスジョストの事例

バジット・マスジョストは、大手製薬会社であるロシュの技術開発チームリーダーであり、スイスのバーゼルの本社に勤務している。彼女の

but she works primarily in English with her team members.

Birgit's technical development team is a subset of Roche's overall development team, and her team members are based across the globe, representing all of Roche's global sites for technical activities. These sites include Germany, Japan, Switzerland, and four sites in the United States. She is also working closely with Chinese team members from the company's new development center in China. Within the Basel, Switzerland, site alone, her team members represent a diverse group, hailing from the United Kingdom, Germany, France, and Italy. As the technical development leader (TDL), Birgit also works broadly across several departments and teams located around the globe.

A primary challenge for Birgit is creating alignment around a shared vision. Most of Birgit's team members, including Birgit herself, speak English as their second or third language, and misunderstandings are common. In addition, team members working at various sites and partner companies often have different organizational systems in place within their respective environments. Birgit's team must create technical procedures that work for all these locations and their different needs. She says, "Some people have different systems in place in their environment, but others don't have the context on that system. Team members should have a chance to explain the context and what they really need."

The circumstances under which Birgit leads her team could easily become fragmented, clouding the team's vision and slowing down the team's progress. Their overall goal is to bring drugs and medical devices through the trial process as quickly as possible while meeting all legal requirements, and thereby gain a competitive advantage in the market. It is crucial for Birgit's team members to each "know what they don't know" so they can have the essential context for understanding their colleagues' different systems and requirements.

Within this global, virtual environment, Birgit has tapped into practices that help her to **invite the unexpected** as a means of gaining alignment. Fundamental to these practices are strong relationships. Birgit insists on a face-to-face meeting to start things off. She wants team members to know one another and to have the chance to bond through team-building exercises. Thanks to such events, subsequent communication with one another improves immensely in their normal virtual, dispersed interactions. Through the **initial face-to-face meetings**, Birgit has also created

母国語はドイツ語で、フランス語も話せるが、チームメンバーとは主に英語で仕事をする。

彼女の技術開発チームのメンバーは、同社のドイツ、日本、スイス、およびアメリカの4拠点をはじめ、世界中の技術開発拠点に点在する。スイスのバーゼルだけでも、チームメンバーにはイギリス、ドイツ、フランス、イタリア出身者がおり、グループの多様性を象徴している。技術開発リーダー（TDL）として、バジットは世界中の様々な部署やチームで幅広い業務に取り組んでいる。

バジットにとっての難題は、共通のビジョンを中心に連携体制を構築することだ。バジット自身を含めチームメンバーのほとんどは英語が母国語ではなく、誤解が生じることも多い。また、各拠点やパートナー企業で業務を行っている多くのチームメンバーは、それぞれの環境内で異なる組織体制を持っている。彼女は、これら全ての場所と多様なニーズに対応できる技術を確立する必要がある。

バジットのチームの環境では、チームを分裂させ、共通のビジョンを曇らせ、業務の進行を遅らせる可能性がある。チーム全体の目標は、法的要件を満たしながら、できる限り迅速に治験プロセスを経て医薬品と医療機器を市場に提供し、それによって市場での競争優位を獲得することだ。バジットのチームメンバーにとっては、各自が「知らないことを知る」ことによって、同僚たちの持つ異なる体制や要件を理解するために必要な要素を把握することが不可欠である。

このグローバルな仮想環境の中で、バジットは**予期せぬ事態を招き入れる手法**を利用して、連携を強化している。これらの手法の基本となるのは、メンバー間の強固な関係である。バジットは、物事を進めるにあたって、直接会うことにこだわっている。チームメンバーがお互いを知り、チームビルディング活動を通じて結束するチャンスを得るためである。これによって、バーチャルで地理的に分散した連携体制においても、その後のメンバー間のコミュニケーションを大きく改善できる。**最初の**

a shared sense of meaning that influences her team's work patterns even when she is not present. As the TDL, Birgit herself gains insights into her team members' different working styles through these face-to-face meetings. For example, when working with her Japanese colleagues with the company Chugai in Japan, Birgit often struggled with how to include them in the team's decision-making process. When she would address an issue during a meeting, her Japanese colleagues would often remain silent. By learning her colleagues' working style, Birgit now knows to wait a couple of days after the official meeting before rolling out a solution in order to receive this feedback.

Birgit also uses several **knowledge-sharing practices** as a means of addressing the "unexpected" aspects of her team members' diverse contexts. When working with the different sites, a TDL often does not know the standard procedures in other countries. However, it is essential to navigate these regulations for a successful project. "As a team leader," she says, "it is essential to understand the background of what my team members are saying and be able to make sound judgments on that basis."

In addition to Birgit's personal efforts, Roche has set up a successful one-year exchange program between Japan and Basel, Switzerland, that has allowed both Japanese and European employees to spend time working in one another's environments. Roche also hires many Chugai employees directly into positions in Basel as a means of instilling their knowledge within company headquarters.

Birgit has also been able to overcome some of the challenges of the "unexpected" by participating in a knowledge-sharing system specifically created for her twenty-two fellow TDLs. The TDL group uses workshops to invite presenters from other parts of the company to share interesting developments and gain a holistic picture of the organization's work.

As a global team leader, Birgit strategically positions herself and the entire team to invite the unexpected, ensuring that her team members have a shared sense of meaning and common goals across their various functional, geographical, and cultural borders.

The pharmaceutical industry provides a good picture of the intricacies involved when working across borders—Birgit experiences a degree of complexity that is a reality for a number of different industries. Team members hail from a wide range of professional and educational backgrounds,

対面ミーティングを通して、バジットがいなくてもチームの業務パターンに影響を与える関係を構築した。TDLとして、バジット自身が対面ミーティングによって、チームメンバーの様々なワークスタイルを知ることができた。例えば、日本の中外製薬のメンバーと仕事をする際、バジットが苦労したのは、日本人のメンバーをチームの意思決定プロセスに関わらせることだった。会議で課題について話し合う際、日本人メンバーはたいてい沈黙したままだった。彼らのワーキングスタイルを知ったバジットは、公式な会議の数日後にソリューションを展開する前に、フィードバックを得られることがわかった。

バジットは、チームメンバーの多様な背景の予期せぬ側面に対応する手段として、いくつかの**知識共有の手法**も活用している。異なる拠点で業務に取り組む際に、TDLが他国の標準的な手続きを知らないこともよくある。しかし、プロジェクトを成功させるためには、その土地の規制に対応することは不可欠だ。「チームリーダーとして、チームメンバーの発言の背景を理解し、それに基づいて正しい判断をすることが不可欠だ」とバジットは言う。

彼女自身の取り組みに加えて、ロシュは日本とスイスのバーゼルで1年間の交流プログラムの立ち上げに成功し、日本とヨーロッパの従業員がお互いの環境で働けるようになった。同社は、中外製薬の多くの社員を直接バーゼルに派遣し、彼らの知識を本社に浸透させている。

バジットはまた、22人のTDL向けに設けられた知識共有制度に参加することによって、想定外の難題の一部を克服することができた。グローバルチームリーダーとして、バジットは自分自身とチーム全体を、予期せぬことに対応するために戦略的に配置し、メンバーが機能、地理、文化などの様々な枠組みを超えて共通の意義と目標を持つようにした。

ロシュの例は、国境を越えて業務を遂行する際に直面する複雑性を的確に表している。バジットの経験は、多くの異なる業界にも共有できる。チームメンバーは、薬理学、化学、生理学、生物学、マーケティングなど様々な職

including pharmacology, chemistry, physiology, biology, and marketing. How can a team leader build a shared picture of the future when heading up a team that holds such enormous diversity of perspectives and will rarely meet in person? The rich array of methods used by Birgit's team for inviting the unexpected are worth keeping in mind, and include the following:

- Face-to-face initial meeting to build personal relationships
- Broad involvement of team members in decision making
- Rotation of team meetings among different market locations to promote broad team member awareness
- Long-term people exchange between key locations

There are additional ways for global team leaders to invite the unexpected by asking the right questions of team members and listening with a new intensity. Like the knowledge-sharing systems created by Birgit's technical development team at Roche, these questions will help to develop a shared sense of meaning and context from which to create a common vision and goals. Our interviewees agree that for global team leaders, the questions they ask of team members are important, particularly in the early stages of team development.

Many of these questions can also be used to structure conversations among team members as they are getting to know one another. It is important for the team to retain and build upon not only the formal exchanges between team members, but also the conversations that happen more naturally.

ORGANIZATIONAL QUESTIONS INCLUDE

- Where do you fit in the organizational matrix?
- Who are your key stakeholders and what do they expect and require of you?
- What would a future picture of this team's success look like for you?
- Do you have objectives related to this team already? How do your objectives fit with the overall organizational vision?

歴と学歴を持っている。非常に多様な視点を持つ実際にはほとんど会うことがないチームメンバーを統率する場合、チームリーダーはどのようにして共有の将来像を描くのか？　バジットのチームが予期せぬ事態に対応するために使用している豊富な手法は覚えておく価値がある。以下はその一部である。

■ 個人的な関係を築くための対面による最初のミーティング
■ 意思決定におけるチームメンバーの広範な関与
■ チームメンバーの意識向上のため、異なる拠点間でのチームミーティングのローテーション
■ 主要拠点間の長期的人材交流

リーダーには、メンバーに適切な質問を投げかけ、情熱を持って耳を傾けることで予期せぬことを受容する方法もある。グローバルチームのリーダーにとって、チームメンバーへの質問は特にチームを育てる初期段階で重要だという点について、インタビューに応じた人たちは同意している。

これらの質問の多くは、お互いを知ろうとする際にチームメンバー間の会話を組み立てる上でも活用できる。チームメンバー間の正式な意見交換だけでなく、自然に発生する会話を維持し積み重ねることがチームにとって重要だ。

組織に関する質問例

- あなたは組織のマトリックス構造のどこに当てはまるか？
- 主なステークホルダーは誰で、彼らはあなたに何を期待し、要求しているか？
- このチームの将来像はどのようなものだと思うか？
- チームに関連する目標をすでに持っているか？　あなたの目標は組織の全体的なビジョンにどう適合しているか？

LOCAL ENVIRONMENT QUESTIONS INCLUDE

- What is your history with the organization? Is there any historical context that might affect your participation and your goals on this team?
- With whom have you worked previously? To whom do you report locally?
- How is our organization structured locally, and how does this impact you?
- Are there local resource, technical, or infrastructure constraints that could affect your ability to meet team goals?

PERSONAL EXPERIENCE QUESTIONS INCLUDE

- What is your understanding so far of this team's vision and goals? Is there anything missing? What would you like to add?
- What particular knowledge or experience do you have to contribute to the team?
- In the best teams you have participated on before, what were the standard team methods for:
  - Getting to know each other
  - Sharing information
  - Holding meetings
  - Making decisions
  - Identifying and resolving conflicts
- Were there any best practices by a previous team leader or the team as a whole that you would like to see used on this team?
- What hours do you normally work? How do you try to balance your work and other parts of your life?

現地の環境に関する質問例

- この組織でどんな経験があるか？　このチームに影響を与えるようなバックグラウンドはあるか？
- 以前は誰と働いていたか？　現地では誰が上司か？
- 現地の組織構成はどのようなもので、それはあなたにどんな影響を与えるか？
- 現地のリソース、技術、インフラストラクチャの制約の中で、チームの目標を達成するためのあなたの能力に影響を及ぼしそうなものはあるか？

個人的な経験に関する質問例

- チームのビジョンと目標を現時点でどのように理解しているか？　何か足りないもの、追加したいものはあるか？
- チームに貢献できる具体的な知識や経験を持っているか？
- これまでに参加した中でベストなチームは、どのようなものだったのか？
  - 互いのことをよく知る
  - 情報の共有
  - 会議の開催
  - 意思決定
  - 不一致の特定と解決
- 以前のチームリーダーやチーム全体のベストプラクティスで、このチームで採用したいものはあるか？
- あなたの普段の勤務時間は？　仕事と仕事以外の生活のバランスを取るにはどうしたらよいか？

FRAME-SHIFTING

The global leaders interviewed in our research each encountered the unexpected in a variety of ways. As the organizational, local, and interpersonal circumstances of team members became more evident to them, these leaders were able to **put themselves into others' shoes** more readily and to shift their approach. Frame-shifting can occur on several levels: communication style, leadership style, and strategy.

Birgit Masjost altered her communication habits to better incorporate the input of Japanese team members into decisions. She learned to wait for their post-meeting contributions, allowing this to occur in a more private exchange rather than in the general team meeting. In addition, she invested time in building closer relationships to foster more direct communication at an earlier stage.

In terms of leadership style, Birgit positions herself as a learner. She seeks to establish a team culture wherein each team member is trained to ask about and incorporate local constraints and processes before creating project plans.

The overall goal of her team is clear: to bring new drugs to the market quickly while ensuring product safety and compliance with local laws. Her technical development team needs to establish work flows, policies, and procedures that support this goal, and she actively solicits team members' ideas on how the team can best meet its targets.

Birgit's consensus-building leadership style appears to work well for the types of teams she heads up. However, if a team leader with similar assumptions were to take on a different type of team and embark upon a more formal vision-building effort, asking team members to help create a "**shared picture of the future,**" he or she could meet with a surprising response. For example, members of other global teams have expressed the following views.

Team Member Perspective #1: The team leader is from headquarters and knows the company well, and those of us on the team are younger and have less experience. Why is she asking us for our opinion? It would be better for her to just tell us what to do and teach us the skills we still need to learn.

フレームシフト力

インタビューに応じたグローバルリーダーたちは、各自が様々な形で予期せぬ事態に遭遇していた。チームメンバーの組織的、地域的、対人的な状況が明らかになるにつれ、リーダーたちは**他者の立場に立って**アプローチを変えることができるようになった。フレームシフトは、コミュニケーションやリーダーシップのスタイル、戦略など、いくつかのレベルで実施できる。

バジット・マスジョストは、日本のチームメンバーの意見を意思決定にうまく取り入れるために自分のコミュニケーションスタイルを変えた。バジットは、会議後の発言を待つことを学び、通常のチーム会議ではなく、より個人的な交流の中でインプットを得られるようにした。また、より早い段階で直接的なコミュニケーションを促進するために時間をかけて緊密な関係を築いた。

バジットは自分自身を常に学習者と位置づけている。各チームメンバーが訓練を受け、プロジェクト計画を策定する前に、現地の制約や手続きなどについて質問し、それを組み込むことができるチーム文化の確立を目指している。

彼女のチームの全体的な目標は、製品の安全性と現地の法律の遵守を確保しながら、新薬を迅速に市場に投入することである。技術開発チームは、ワークフロー、ポリシー、手順を確立する必要があり、バジットは目標を達成するための最善の方法についてチームメンバーのアイデアを積極的に求めている。

このようなコンセンサス形成型のリーダーシップ・スタイルは、バジットが率いるチームのタイプにはうまく機能するようだ。しかし、同じような仮説を持つチームリーダーが、別のタイプのチームを担当することになり、より正式なビジョン構築の取り組みに着手した場合、チームメンバーに「**共有の将来像**」を描くのを手伝うように頼むと、驚くべき反応が返ってくることがある。例えば、他のグローバルチームのメンバーは次のような見解を示している。

チームメンバーの見解1：本社から来たチームリーダーは会社のことを熟知しているが、私たちのチームメンバーは、リーダーより若く経験が少ない。なぜ私たちの意見を求めるのか？　何をすべきかと、学ぶべき知識や技術を教えてくれるだけでいいのに。

Team Member Perspective #2: When the team leader asks for our input, it is always the same few people who speak up and dominate the conversation, even though they don't know this market well. This process is a waste of time.

Team Member Perspective #3: We have a perfectly good set of goals for our country operation already that our country director has provided and that the previous team leader used. We do not need a new direction for the team—this is too confusing.

Team Member Perspective #4: Our team leader wants us to have a shared vision, but the whole idea of vision is a fashion introduced by smarty-pants consultants who don't know what it's like to work in a real company. We don't need a fancy vision; we just need to make a good plan and implement it.

Faced with these kinds of views, a consensus-building team leader must choose between attempting to persist with a style that team members are not yet accustomed to, or at least temporarily turning to a different style that might be more directive, tactical, or technically oriented. Other forms of frame-shifting might include teaching versus learning, or being an agent of stability versus an agent of change.

As for strategy, frame-shifting typically means modifying products, services, processes, supplier relations, and so on to fit the needs of different markets.

In our work with clients from a variety of industries, we have had success with a very simple strategy-building tool which lends more structure to the kind of process that Birgit has experienced. The frame-shifting approach involves (1) identifying differences in the local market that may impact the implementation of the team vision, (2) analyzing the business impact those differences may have, and (3) strategizing about how the team may need to frame-shift and modify its implementation plan in response to the identified differences.

INFLUENCE ACROSS BOUNDARIES

Both invite the unexpected and frame-shifting support a third behavior that

チームメンバーの見解2：チームリーダーが私たちの意見を求めると、いつも少数の同じメンバーが、市場のことをよく知っているわけでもないのに発言し会話を独占する。こんなのは時間の無駄だ。

チームメンバーの見解3：この国のビジネスに対する完璧な事業目標はすでに存在している。それはカントリー・ディレクターが設定し、以前のチームリーダーが使ってきたものだ。チームに新しい方向性なんて必要ない。ややこしすぎる。

チームメンバーの見解4：チームリーダーは共通のビジョンを持たせたいと思っているが、そんなアイデアは、現実の会社で働くことがどんなものか理解していない知ったかぶりのコンサルタントによって導入されたものだ。私たちには立派なビジョンなんて必要ない。必要なのは実現可能な計画を立て、それを実現することだ。

このような見解に直面した場合、コンセンサス形成型のチームリーダーは、チームメンバーが慣れていない手法に固執するか、少なくとも一時的により指示的、戦術的、技術的な別の手法に切り替えるかを選択しなければならない。その他のフレームシフトとして、教育/学習、維持/変革などの形態が挙げられる。

戦略に関する限り、フレームシフトとは通常、異なる市場のニーズに応じて、製品、サービス、プロセス、サプライヤーとの関係などを変えることを意味する。

フレームシフトのアプローチとは、チームのビジョン実現に影響を与える可能性のある現地市場の相違点を特定し、それらの相違点が事業にもたらす影響を分析し、特定された相違点に応じてチームがどのようにフレームシフトし、実施計画を修正する必要があるかについて戦略を立てることである。

境界を越えた影響力の発揮

予期せぬ事態を招き入れることと、フレームシフトとは、3番目の行動、

is important for global team leaders: influence across boundaries. Leading in complex global organizations calls for skillful influence and collaboration across the various "boundaries" within the organization and the team. These boundaries may be national, cultural, linguistic, functional, or organizational.

Our interviewees stressed the need for global team leaders to "keep their finger on the pulse of changes" and the ways those changes might affect their teams. When working across boundaries with an unfamiliar set of environmental cues, it is important to be able to read situations accurately and to predict future scenarios. Two areas have proven to be especially worthy of attention: engaging key stakeholders and facilitating the flow of knowledge and information across boundaries.

Engaging Key Stakeholders

Most team members are simultaneously involved in a number of different teams at any given time. It is important that the team leader knows both what other teams his or her team members are a part of and how those teams fit into the overall organizational context. Without this **holistic picture**, team leaders will not know whom to influence or why. They will not be able to grasp the origins of competing priorities pulling at their team members and affecting the team's success. Global team leaders have to work much harder in this environment to create and maintain alignment. At the same time, the imperative that they do so is far greater. As a corporate executive cited in one study commented:

> "When I'm working with a matrixed team, I always start by emphasizing that they have to be clear and aligned on the strategy, goals, structure, and rewards; and most importantly link their goals to [those] of their key stakeholders. They have to understand how what they want to do affects others."

Team leaders should work with participants to analyze:

- Who are the people outside the team that each team member feels responsible to satisfy?
- What are each stakeholder's requirements or priorities in terms of team outcomes?

境界を越えた影響力の行使を支えてゆく。複雑なグローバル組織をリードするには、組織内と、チーム内の境界線を越える優れた影響力との連携が必要である。国籍、文化、言語、機能、組織の境界線である。

インタビューでは、グローバルチームリーダーが「変化の脈動を指で押さえ続ける」必要性と、その変化がチームに与える影響が強調された。未知の環境信号によって境界を越えて業務を遂行する際には、状況を正確に読み取り、将来のシナリオを予測することが重要である。主要なステークホルダーを関与させること、境界を越えた知識と情報の流れを促進するという2つの手法に注目したい。

主要ステークホルダーとの関係

ほとんどのチームメンバーは、常に複数の異なるチームの業務を同時に遂行している。チームリーダーは、自分のチームメンバーが他にどのチームに所属しているか、またそのチームの組織の中でどのような位置づけにあるかの両方を把握することが重要である。この**全体像**を認識していなければ、チームリーダーは、誰になぜ影響を与えるべきなのかを理解できないだろう。その緊急性は非常に高い。以下は、ある調査を実施した際に企業幹部から寄せられたコメントだ。

> 「マトリックス化されたチームと働く際はいつもまず、メンバーが戦略、目標、構造、報酬について明確に理解し、これに沿って取り組むべきだということを強調する。一番重要なのはチームの目標を主要なステークホルダーの目標に結びつけることだ。自分のやろうとしていることが他人にどう影響するか理解しなければならない」

チームリーダーは、メンバーと協力して以下の点を精査しなければならない。

- 各メンバーが、満足させる責任があると感じるチーム外の人は誰か？
- チームの成果において各ステークホルダーの要件と優先事項は何か？

- How do stakeholders' priorities, including those unrelated to the team, support or conflict with team goals?
- Does the team need to reprioritize or modify its own goals to better serve stakeholder requirements?

For teams that are in the **formative stages**, it is even better to anticipate the needs of at least some key stakeholders and to reach out to them before the team's labors begin. The preferred approach for gaining alignment is usually to reach "up and across." An executive at a higher level in the team leader's organization who is sponsoring the team's activities may be best positioned to contact an executive counterpart, gain mutual alignment about team objectives, and make the proper introductions. Sometimes there are several levels of hierarchy and rank that must be considered.

Facilitating Knowledge Sharing across Boundaries

The **knowledge exchange** supported by Birgit Masjost of Roche also helps her team to exert influence. It is important to stress that such exchanges need to take place across boundaries of all kinds. Global team leaders often need to act as a "bridge" between their team members and other parts of the organization, enabling the knowledge they share among themselves to be disseminated across the company. This helps to set realistic expectations both inside and outside the team, and provides information crucial to the success of a global enterprise.

Successful team leaders work to create an expanding "memory" within and beyond the team, including a mental map of who knows what in order to augment team resources and remove barriers. In the case of Birgit's technical development team, team members had the opportunity to learn their colleagues' unique culture and work environment, and brought their own expertise and best practices into this new collaboration as well.

- チームに関係のないものを含めたステークホルダーの優先事項は、チームの目標をどのように支えたり離反したりするか？
- ステークホルダーの要件によりよく対応するために、チーム目標の優先順位を再設定または変更する必要があるか？

形成段階のチームの場合、チームの活動を開始する前に、少なくとも一部の主要なステークホルダーのニーズを予測し、コミュニケーションを取る方がいい。チームの活動を主導するチームリーダーの組織でより高い職位のエグゼクティブは、カウンターパートと連絡を取り、チームの目標について相互の連携を図り、適切な紹介を行うのに最適な立場にあるかもしれない。場合によっては、考慮しなければならない階層やランクのレベルがいくつかある。

境界を越えた知識共有の促進

ロシュのバジット・マスジョストが提唱する**知識の交換**は、チームの成長に欠かせない。重要なのは、あらゆる種類の境界を越えた知識交換の必要性を強調することだ。グローバルチームリーダーは、チームメンバーと組織のその他の部分との間で「橋」としての役割を担う必要がある場合が多く、メンバー間で共有する知識を会社全体に広めることができる。これは、チーム内外の現実的な期待値を設定することに役立ち、グローバル企業の成功に不可欠な情報を提供する。

成功を収めたチームリーダーは、チームのリソースを増やし、障壁を取り除くために、誰が何を知っているかのメンタルマップを含めて、チーム内外で拡大する「メモリ」の作成に取り組んでいる。バジットの技術開発チームの場合、チームメンバーは、同僚の独自の文化と職場環境を学ぶ機会を得て、この新しい協働体制に自身の専門知識とベストプラクティスをもたらした。

CHAPTER ELEVEN

The Future of Global Leadership

Global leaders today face more imposing tasks than ever as they work across multiple geographies, functions, product lines, and national cultures. Many leadership development programs in corporate universities and business schools have not yet integrated the **focus**, **content**, or **methodology** for developing global capabilities. In this final chapter, we will examine some of the potential obstacles and solutions to the challenge of global leadership development.

How Global Leaders Learn: What's Different?

Global leaders must be able to scan the environment for meaningful information, events, or commercial possibilities that allow them to formulate effective strategies and plot new courses of action. These may stem from unexpected sources in another part of the company or the world, from cultural influences that shape differences in local business practices, or from combining products and services in a new way for an emerging market. Leaders, therefore, need to be able to "see" and process information in new ways, making connections between phenomena that have never been linked before in their minds.

INDIVIDUAL TRANSFORMATION

Helping global leaders to make sense of their work experiences means that leadership development efforts should focus leaders on "thinking about their thinking." Thinking about thinking calls for a holistic view of the leader, leadership competencies, and the models, frameworks, and methods for development. Global leadership is a **transformational learning experience.**[*1] As Jack Mezirow[*2] explains, "Transformational learning refers to the

第11章

将来のグローバルリーダーシップ

今日のグローバルリーダーは、複数の地域、職務、製品ライン、国の文化にまたがって業務にあたっている。企業内大学やビジネススクールにおけるリーダーシップ開発プログラムの多くは、グローバルな能力を開発するための**対象**、**内容**、**手法**をまだ統合できていない。

グローバルリーダーはいかにして学ぶか

グローバルリーダーは、そうした複雑な状況の中で、効果的な戦略と新たな行動方針を策定しなければならない。異文化環境での予期せぬ相違、地域の事業慣行の違い、新興市場での新しい方式の製品とサービスの組み合わせなど、リーダーは今までに心の中で関連付けたことのない現象を結びつけ、新しい方法で情報を読み取り、処理できなければならない。

個人的な変革

グローバルリーダーが自分の職務経験を理解できるよう支援するということは、リーダーシップ開発の取り組みにおいて、リーダーに「考え方について考える」ことに集中させなければならないことを意味する。考え方につい

＊1 積み重ねてきた知識を活かしつつ、自身や世界の見方をシフトさせる学習。

＊2 大人の変容的学習の理論で有名。

process by which we transform our taken-for-granted frames of reference (meaning perspectives, habits of mind, mind-sets) to make them more inclusive, discriminating, open, emotionally capable of change, and reflective so they may generate beliefs and opinions that will prove more true or justified to guide action."

Transformational learning can have uncertain outcomes. Some organizations have learned firsthand that regionally disparate working groups not trained to understand regional, cultural, or functional differences can become polarized in their values, beliefs, and assumptions about how to get work done. This can widen differences rather than help participants learn to work together effectively. As one Human Resources practitioner stated, "Because we don't teach leaders how to understand and leverage diversity in the workplace, there's the potential for a lot of damage to be done."

ORGANIZATIONAL TRANSFORMATION

At the organizational level, global leadership development faces many **challenges and obstacles**. The fact that global leaders learn most of what they need to know on the job means that the organization's culture has a direct influence on learning. Much has been written on "**the learning organization**," which refers to firms that are quick to integrate the lessons of leaders. Such activity leads to new ways of organizational problem solving and, ultimately, to a new corporate culture. The learning that global leaders must do is, in fact, an organizational development initiative through which the culture of the organization not only affects the ways in which leaders learn but is also affected by that learning.

Defining Global Competency

To better understand the organizational complexities for developing global leaders in multinational companies, one of the authors conducted a separate set of in-depth interviews and focus groups over a two-year period with senior leaders in Human Resources, Learning and Development, Organizational Development, and Diversity from Fortune 100 companies, as well as with cutting-edge leadership academics and consultants. The study asked these practitioners and academics to (1) define global leadership competency, (2) identify global competency gaps in organizations, and (3) identify the obstacles to closing these gaps.

て考えるためには、リーダー、リーダーシップ能力、開発のためのモデル、フレームワーク、手法の全体像が必要となる。グローバルリーダーシップは、**変容的学習の経験**である。ジャック・メジローは、「変容的学習は、一般的に認められている評価基準（視点、思考習慣、マインドセット）を、より包括的、識別的、解放的、感情的な側面から見直し、変容し、新たな行動を導くためによりしっかりとした真実性や正当性を証明する信念と意見を生み出すプロセスである」と述べている。

しかし、変容的学習の成果は不確実なこともある。ある人事担当者も指摘していたが、職場の多様性を理解し活用する方法をリーダーに教えていない場合、変容的学習は多くの弊害を引き起こす可能性がある。

組織改革

グローバルリーダーシップを開発するためには、組織レベルでの多くの**課題と障壁**を乗り越えなければならない。グローバルリーダーの経験は、ほとんど実務を通じて習得されているという事実からみればそれは明らかだ。リーダーの学習をいち早く取り入れことができるよう、『**学習する組織**』について考えなければならない。このような活動を通して、組織の問題を解決し、進化させ、新しい企業文化を育てることができる。グローバルリーダーが学ぶべきことは、実は組織文化がリーダーの学習方法に影響を与えるだけでなく、そうしたグローバルな影響を受容できる組織開発を行うことにも繋がっている。

グローバル・コンピテンシーの定義

多国籍企業でグローバルリーダーを育成するための組織的な複雑性をより深く理解するために、本書の著者の一人は、フォーチュン100企業の中で人事、人材開発、組織開発、ダイバーシティ担当の上級リーダーや、最先端のリーダーシップ研究者やコンサルタントを対象に、2年間詳細な調査を実施した。その中で

（1）グローバルリーダーシップ・コンピテンシーの定義
（2）組織におけるグローバル・コンピテンシー・ギャップの特定
（3）ギャップを埋める障害となるものの特定

The data from these interviews were remarkably consistent. Participants unanimously noted that:

- Their firms did not have adequate global competencies.
- These organizations lacked knowledge about culture in the workplace (which was especially apparent at the executive levels).
- Siloed thinking among support functions and academic disciplines had a negative effect on their ability to design and support training interventions.

Though the multinationals that participated in the research did have a defined set of leadership competencies, most did not specifically address global leadership, the competencies were often vague, and they were not vetted for applicability in the national cultures in which they did business. Competencies such as "**values diversity**" or "**leverages diversity on teams**" illustrate the very general level at which many organizations qualified global leadership behavior. Similarly worded phrases such as "**bold, game-changing strategy**" and "**increased velocity of execution**" are not only vague but do not translate, as demonstrated by the response of one company's Japanese office:

Bold game-changing strategy: "Bold is not necessarily good in Japan. It reminds us of an impudent approach, and Japanese dislike that."

Increased velocity of execution: "Velocity is not a common English word we learn in Japan, and so it does not land well. Rushed work is not considered good. Sometimes we need to take time to make sure that we achieve high quality."

To develop global leaders more effectively, practitioners need to define and assess more precisely key success factors for global leaders. As suggested in the preceding chapters, there is a set of leadership behaviors that is easy to recognize; these behaviors are also linked with underlying traits, attitudes, beliefs, and cognitive abilities that are more difficult to pinpoint or to socialize. Practitioners should be able to understand and appreciate all of these competencies—both dynamic and stable—in order to design appropriate interventions and sustainable support systems.

の3つのテーマでインタビューを行い、以下のようなコメントが集まった。

- 自分たちの会社は、十分なグローバル・コンピテンシーを持っていなかった。
- 組織は、職場の文化に関する知識に欠けていた（これは特にエグゼクティブレベルで顕著だった）。
- 支援機能と学問領域の間の連携の伴わない考え方は、研修の設計や支援にマイナスの影響を与えた。

この調査に参加した多国籍企業は、一連のリーダーシップ能力の開発は行っていたが、ほとんどの企業はグローバルリーダーシップ開発には具体的に取り組んでおらず、概念についても曖昧なことが多く、事業を展開している国の文化への適応性を精査していなかった。「**多様性の尊重**」、「**チームの多様性の活用**」といった概念は、多くの組織で理解されるものの、「**大胆な革新的戦略**」や「**実行速度の向上**」といった言い回しは曖昧であるだけでなく、理解されていないことが、ある企業の日本支社の回答でも明らかになった。

大胆な革新的戦略：「日本では大胆が必ずしもよいとは限らない。日本人が嫌いな生意気なアプローチを思い起こさせる」

実行速度の向上：「ベロシティ（方向性を持って速度を上げてゆくこと）は日本では一般的な用語でないため、定着しにくい。やっつけ仕事はよくないと考えられている。質の高い成果を達成するために時間をかけることが必要な場合もある」

グローバルリーダーをより効果的に育成するためには、育成担当者はグローバルリーダーの成功要因をより正確に定義し評価する必要がある。

前述したとおり、リーダーシップ行動には認識しやすいものもある一方で、これらの行動は、特定したり業務に活かしたりすることが難しい特徴、態度、信念、認知能力とも結びついている。育成担当者は、適切な介入と持続可能な支援体制を構築するための動的、安定的な戦略が必要だ。

The key global leadership behaviors described in this book provide a road map for understanding the **conflicting data**, demands, and perspectives that the global leader must continually balance, including:

- Reducing uncertainty and managing ambiguity
- Decisiveness versus humble inquiry
- Centralized decision making and shared leadership
- Experienced senior leadership and group intelligence

The Organizational Global Mindset

Leaders in every company noted a significant gap between the demand for globally competent leaders and the number of individuals who were ready, willing, and able to perform in a global capacity. The gap was attributed to the absence of a "global mindset" in individuals and the **ethnocentrism of headquarters**.

One HR practitioner summed up the views of many when she said, "We're not U.S.-centric; we're New York-centric!" The business leaders on assignments whom we interviewed abroad were aware of **corporate culture** and are engaged in constant negotiations between the local culture and that of headquarters, but this concept is far more difficult to grasp for the leader who is running a global operation from his or her home country.

Leaders often do not have a framework or language to make sense of or to talk about cultural differences across corporate, functional, product line, regional, or national cultures. The HR practitioners and academics interviewed were unanimous in their views about the problems this caused and the importance of cultural training in helping to close the gap. They also cited the challenge of having very senior executives who, because of their **own ignorance of culture**, were perpetuating the lack of an "**organizational global mindset**" at the most strategic and systemic levels of the corporation. Training alone, however, is not the answer. The authors have on many occasions completed training programs for leaders in organizations with outsourced operations in India, only to be stopped afterward by executives who say, "This is all well and good, but can you go there and train them to work

本書で詳述したグローバルリーダーシップの行動は、グローバルリーダーが継続的にバランスを取るべき**相反した情報**、要求、見解を理解するためのロードマップを提供している。以下にその例を挙げる。

- 不確実性の低減および曖昧性への対応
- 決断力に対する曖昧性の問い
- 一元化された意思決定と共有されたリーダーシップ
- 経験豊富な上級リーダーシップとグループ・インテリジェンス

組織的なグローバル・マインドセット

どの企業も、グローバルレベルで有能なリーダーへの需要と、それに対応できる人材の数との間に大きな差があることを指摘した。この差は、個人の「グローバルマインド」の欠如と**本社の自民族中心主義**に起因している。

海外赴任中の現役のビジネスリーダーは、**企業文化**を意識し、現地と本社の文化の間で常に交渉を行っている。しかし、母国でグローバルな業務に携わっているリーダーにはこの概念はなかなか理解されない。彼らが企業、職務、製品ライン、地域、国の文化の違いを理解したりそれを伝えたりするためのフレームワークや言語を持ち合わせていないことが多いのだ。

また、上級経営幹部が、**自身の文化に無知なために**、会社の最も戦略的で組織的レベルでの「**組織のグローバル・マインドセット**」が欠如したままであるという問題も指摘された。仮に、こうしたテーマでの研修があったとしても、「すばらしいプログラムだが、現地に行ってもらって私たちと同じように仕事ができるように訓練できないか？」と言われて打ち切られることもある。

more like us?" Ongoing organizational support to help leaders make sense of the cultural lessons they experience on the job is what makes training a sustainable and worthwhile investment.

OBSTACLES: SILOED THINKING OF LEADERS

Global leaders must be able to think and collaborate across products, regions, markets, and cultures in order to be effective. The structure of the typical organization, however, is one of separate business units that were built around accumulated technical expertise.

Many senior executives learned their leadership skills during a different business cycle, when reaching across these "silos" was not vital. They now have mental maps that were charted for another era. This is why leaders today tell us they need to think hard about the way they think—testing assumptions, striving to make new connections, reflecting, and being open to new ideas.

Thinking about thinking is especially important at higher levels in the organization for a number of reasons. For one, senior executives have made it to the top based on a mix of skills to which they now owe their success. Being open to new ways of thinking, however, allows senior executives to acquire new skills for a new era. This is crucial because the sphere of influence one has within the company is much greater at the higher levels, extending far beyond **formal job responsibilities**.

OBSTACLES: SILOED APPROACHES TO LEADERSHIP DEVELOPMENT

The Human Resources leaders we interviewed consistently said that the lack of a cohesive strategy among the **Performance Management**, **Talent**, **Organizational Development**, **Learning and Development**, **Diversity**, **Expatriate Administration**, and **Compensation** groups was a serious obstacle to the development of global leaders. Though there was great thought leadership in one or two of these functions in some companies, their progress was limited due to a lack of support from other groups.

The HR leaders indicated that, even with targeted talent initiatives for executive development, there was little connection between assessment, selection, succession planning, development, and reward systems. In most instances, functional support groups (such as Learning and Development, Expatriate Administration, and Compensation) did not even know one

障壁：自己中心的な考え方

ここで、経営幹部の課題も指摘したい。

グローバルリーダーは、製品、地域、市場、文化を横断して物事を考え、関係者と連携しなければならない。しかし、多くの経営幹部は、自らの個々の「サイロ」を超えることが重要ではなかった時代に、現在とは異なる景気循環の中でリーダーシップ・スキルを学び、策定されたメンタルマップを持っている。

「**考え方について考える**」ことは、組織の上層部にとって様々な理由で特に重要だ。なぜなら、上級経営幹部は成功の要因となったスキルの組み合わせによって、その地位に上り詰めた。新しい考え方を受け入れることで、経営幹部は新たな時代に向けてさらに新しいスキルを習得することができる。企業内での影響力の範囲は、上層部であるほど大きく、**本来の職務責任**をはるかに超えて広がっているため、これは非常に重要なことである。

障壁：グローバルリーダー育成

また、インタビューに応じた人事部門のリーダーたちは、**業績管理**、**人材**、**組織開発**、**学習と開発**、**ダイバーシティ**、**海外駐在者管理**、**報酬**を担当するグループ間に一貫した戦略がないことが、グローバルリーダーの育成の重大な障壁になっていると述べている。一部の企業では、これらのグループのひとつかふたつに優れた考え方のリーダーシップがあったが、他のグループからの支援が不足していたため、完全には機能できなかった。

人事部門のリーダーたちは、幹部育成のため人材育成の取り組みにおいても、同様の連携がないことを指摘した。多くの場合、学習と開発、海外勤務者管理、報酬などの各職務サポートグループは、連携どころかお互いを知ることさえない。グローバルな職場の複雑性に対応するには、リーダーと育成

another, let alone collaborate. The complexity of the global workplace calls for leaders and practitioners alike to draw together an equally complex mixture of solutions from multiple sources.

Developing Global Leaders: Implications

We now know the key behaviors of successful global leaders, what is different about developing them, and where individuals and organizations encounter the greatest obstacles in cultivating global capabilities. What other practical steps can be taken to foster the development of outstanding global leaders? The future of global leadership is likely to involve a closer look at how global leadership development can be integrated with everyday job roles.

ON-THE-JOB LEARNING OPPORTUNITIES

Given the nature of the work that leaders perform in the global theater, it is difficult to imagine that a fixed classroom curriculum alone could provide enough relevant content to meet their learning needs. There are many **on-the-job learning** opportunities that, if identified and supported, can provide a rich forum for developing the key behaviors described in this book while simultaneously complementing properly designed training. When properly supported through the mechanisms of nomination, assessment, selection, performance management, compensation, succession planning, classroom training, and coaching, on-the-job learning opportunities offer powerful and effective ways to develop the individual's and the organization's global mindsets.

WHAT INDIVIDUAL LEADERS CAN DO

Leadership development has often been likened to the **work of the alchemist** who makes gold out of common materials. The leader, however, needs to be able to see the opportunities for making gold in the moment—out of the ordinary things that happen on the job. This is not always easy in a work world that moves at a fast pace and where leaders are constantly under pressure to move on to the next task or crisis. However, since one of the most frequently cited personality traits of accomplished leaders is lifelong learning, we know that reflection is an important ingredient.

担当者は、複数のソースから複雑なソリューションを組み合わせることが求められている。

将来に向けたグローバルリーダーの育成

傑出したグローバルリーダーを育成するために、他にはどのような方法があるのだろうか。グローバルリーダーシップの将来のためには、その開発を日常業務にどのように組み込めるかを精査する必要があるだろう。

実地学習の機会

リーダーがグローバルな環境で遂行する業務の性質を考えると、授業形式の固定されたカリキュラムだけで、彼らの学習ニーズを満たすのに十分な内容を提供できるとは考えにくい。OJL（**実務を通じた学習**）の機会は多いが、それを特定して個々に具体的に支援する必要がある。任命、評価、選定、業績管理、報酬、後継者育成計画、授業形式の研修、コーチングなどの手法を通じて適切に支援できれば、OJLの機会によって個人と組織のグローバル・マインドセットを育成する強力で効果的な方法を提供できる。

リーダーができることは何か

リーダーシップ開発は、一般的素材からゴールドを作り出す**錬金術師の仕事**にたとえられる。しかし、リーダーは仕事上で起こる通常のことから、その瞬間にゴールドを作るチャンスを見抜けなければならない。これは、速いペースで次の任務や危機に対応するようプレッシャーを受けている現場では必ずしも容易ではない。この能力は経験とそれを整理する学習の繰り返しで育成される。

WHAT ORGANIZATIONS CAN DO

In order for organizations to leverage on-the-job learning, a shift in perspective needs to occur to best support the development of future leaders. A fixed curriculum has natural limitations. This curriculum may or may not have direct relevance to participants' jobs, current capabilities, or learning objectives. One of the main reasons learning budgets are subject to cuts is that the business leaders making spending decisions do not see how learning is aligned with implementation of their near-term business objectives. **Learning cycles** and **budget cycles** are not coordinated, which makes learning "nice to have" but not essential in the eyes of at least some decision makers. Whereas **classroom learning** includes frameworks with which participants can make sense of past and current experiences, it is seldom effective in providing tools for future learning and for changing one's approach to daily business decisions.

Alignment with the individual learner's needs is also important to consider because research on generations in the workplace and in emerging markets tells us that customized, ongoing learning is a crucial factor in recruiting and retaining key talent. **Career development**, in many parts of the world today, is viewed as another perquisite along the same lines as **job title and level**, **compensation**, or **vacation** time. In fact, the reputation of a company as a "learning organization," as having a "leadership performance culture," or as employing leaders with high levels of expertise and a willingness to train their direct reports are among the top features that attract recruits. The capability of a corporation to design **learner-centered training** is increasingly becoming a point of competitive differentiation in global markets.

Leader-Led Action Learning

We propose a model for implementing the global leadership behaviors that can put both the learner's development and the organization's global business objectives in the center of the frame. We use the term "leader-led action learning" and believe that, for target groups of mission-critical, high-potential talent, it may provide a meaningful path forward.

Leader-led action learning has the potential to transform corporate learning in a way that goes far beyond its standard applications, but this requires a shift in mindset and skills on the part of those who are driving

組織ができることは何か

一方、組織がOJLを活用するためには、考え方をシフトする必要がある。固定されたカリキュラムには当然限界があり、受講者の職務、現在の能力、学習目標に直接関連する場合とそうでない場合がある。学習予算が削減の対象となる主な理由のひとつは、事業目標の達成に関する**学習サイクル**と**予算サイクル**に整合性がないことにある。また、**授業形式の学習**には、参加者が過去と現在の経験を理解するためのフレームワークが含まれているが、将来の学習のためのツールや、日々のビジネス上の意思決定へのアプローチを変えるためのツールの提供との連携を考えなければならない。

個々の学習者のニーズとの整合性を考慮することも大切である。今日、**キャリア開発**は、**役職やレベル**、**報酬**、**休暇**などと同じようにひとつの特典なのだ。実際、「学習する組織」であるという評判や、高レベルの専門性と部下育成の意欲を持つリーダーを雇用したりているという評判は、就職希望者を引きつける大きな要素である。**学習者中心のトレーニング**を計画する企業の能力は、グローバル市場での差別化のポイントとなりつつある。

リーダー主導の行動学習

私たちは「**リーダー主導の行動学習**」という概念で、業務上必須で潜在能力の高い人材のターゲットグループに対して有意義な道筋を提供できると考えている。これを実現するためには、推進する側の意識変革が要求される。

it. Traditional action learning typically occurs in the context of a leadership "program" that lasts for six months or a year, structured around two or three face-to-face gatherings of current or future leaders at headquarters or in a key emerging market location. During the course of the program, corporate executives are called upon to share information about the business and its future direction, tell their personal stories, and talk with participants. In addition, such executives are often asked to propose and sponsor action-learning projects that are carried out by small teams of participants during the interim period between face-to-face meetings; later, these executives may listen and respond to presentations by project teams of their results.

However, the very structure of this kind of leadership development program places limitations on the potential of leader-led action learning. Although these constraints are natural enough in the context of a leadership development program, what if they were removed? More specifically, consider the impact if leader-led action learning were to include:

- **Objectives:** Vital strategic projects with **high levels of visibility** and support; focus on key corporate objectives for business growth and performance, with complete integration of business and leadership development objectives
- **Duration:** As much time and resources as needed to accomplish the task
- **Executive sponsors:** Full executive sponsorship and accountability for results
- **Scope:** Teams are able to design the scope according to what is necessary to ensure full implementation and lasting results

On-the-job action learning can of course occur without any formal structure, but learning can also be accelerated and enhanced through a structured approach that creates a project "crucible" for optimum results. The project's business objectives are more likely to be achieved because the leader and participants receive special visibility, guidance, coaching, and support. Leadership development is intensified because the team is working on a strategically vital project, and the team leader is doing, learning, and developing other project members at the same time.

Leader-led action learning employs a **just-in-time approach** to

従来の行動学習は、本社や主要な新興市場の拠点で、現在あるいは将来のリーダーが2、3回会合を持つように構成された半年から1年のリーダーシップ「プログラム」として実施される。

しかし、この種のリーダーシップ開発プログラムの構造そのものが、リーダー主導の行動学習の可能性を制限している。もしその制限を取りのぞいたらどうなるのか。リーダー主導の行動学習の内容について具体的に検討してみよう。

- **目標: 高レベルの可視性**とサポート体制を備えた重要な戦略プロジェクト。事業目標にリーダーシップ開発目標を完全に組み込み、事業の成長と業績に関する企業目標に焦点を合わせる
- **期間とリソース:** タスクを完了するのに必要な十分な時間とリソース
- **経営幹部の支援:** 経営陣の全面的なサポートと結果に対する説明責任
- **適用範囲:** チームは完全実施と永続的成果を実現するための要件を考慮して適用範囲を設定できる

実務を通じた行動学習は、形式的な構造がなくても可能だが、最大限の成果を得るために「厳しい試練」を伴うプロジェクトを立ち上げ、構造化された手法によって学習をスピードアップし、強化することもできる。リーダーと参加者に焦点をあてて、指導、コーチング、支援を継続できれば、プロジェクトの事業目標自体が達成できる。チームが戦略的に重要なプロジェクトに取り組み、チームリーダーも業務を遂行し、学び、同時に他のプロジェクトメンバーを育成するため、リーダーシップ開発を強化できるのである。

リーダー主導の行動学習では、**ジャスト・イン・タイムの手法**を活用する。

curriculum development. It is based on linking organizational strategy to specific business unit goals and then to the people skills required to execute these objectives. This form of learning puts the business, the business leaders, and their teams in the center of the learning and development frame. It also coordinates efforts among the business leaders, global talent leads, and practitioners from Training and Development, Human Resources, and Organizational Development (OD), whose jobs are to identify the top business needs, the specific skills required to achieve them, and to design learning interventions.

To ensure the relevance and impact of the learning project, it must be aligned to very specific and discrete business objectives that can be measured. The learning objectives are inseparable from the objectives of the business. The learning points describe the way in which the leaders need to behave to successfully meet the targeted business objectives. The learning leader is a manager in the business unit who has demonstrated an aptitude for the identified competencies, has further room to grow, and is willing to focus on developing these skills in selected team members. The functional support groups working in a concerted and integrated team design the learning infrastructure.

Leader-led action learning provides significant advantages, especially during tough economic times, by bringing the right people and the required level of resources together to advance global strategic objectives. By integrating high-profile projects with on-the-job learning opportunities, action-learning projects provide an intensive developmental experience for team leaders and participants with minimal added expense, and they are readily scalable across the organization to achieve major goals.

RETHINKING INTERNATIONAL ASSIGNMENTS

The leader-led action-learning framework offers a fresh way of viewing at least some international assignments, underlining the substantial investment they entail as well as their critical value for both accomplishing global business objectives and developing global leaders. Expatriates in executive roles, like the people we interviewed, have enormous leadership responsibilities that include developing future leaders across a country or region. Although some companies have sought to reduce costs by decreasing the number of expatriates around the world and outsourcing many services for

これは、組織の戦略を事業単位の具体的な目標と、その目標達成に必要な人的スキルを結びつけるカリキュラムだ。この形式の学習では、ビジネス、ビジネスリーダー、そのリーダーのチームが学習と開発のフレームの中心となる。また、ビジネスリーダー、グローバル能力開発リーダー、および研修、開発、人事、組織開発（OD）の担当者の間で取り組みを調整して、上位のビジネスニーズ、そしてニーズを満たすために必要な具体的なスキルを特定し、学習の介入を検討する。

学習プロジェクトの妥当性と効果を実現するには、測定可能で非常に具体的な個別の事業目標と整合させる必要がある。学習目標は、事業目標と切り離すことはできない。学習ポイントは、対象となる事業目標を達成するためにリーダーがどのように行動すべきかを示すものである。専門的な知識と適性を持ち、さらに成長の余地があり、選ばれたチームメンバーのスキル開発に注力する意欲を持つ事業部門のマネージャーが学習リーダーとなる。機能サポートグループは、協力し一体となってチームで学習基盤を構築する。

リーダー主導の行動学習は、特に厳しい経済状況下では、適切な人材と必要なレベルのリソースを結集して、グローバルな戦略目標を推進することが大きな利点に繋がる。行動学習プロジェクトは、注目度の高いプロジェクトとOJLの機会を組み合わせることによって、チームリーダーや参加者に最小限の追加費用で集中的な開発経験を提供し、主要な目標を達成するために組織全体で容易に拡大縮小できる。

海外勤務についての再考

リーダー主導の行動学習のフレームワークは、少なくとも一部の海外勤務を新たな視点でとらえる方法を提供する。それは、グローバルな事業目標を達成し、グローバルリーダーを育成するためには、どのように投資をし、重要な価値とはなにかを明確にするものである。経営幹部の役割を担う海外駐在員は、国や地域を越えて将来のリーダーを育成することを含めた、多大な責任を負っている。一部の企業は、世界中の駐在員の数を減らし、駐在員とその家族向けの多くのサービスをリロケーション・サービスプロバイダーに

assignees and their families to relocation service providers, there is a countertrend that views international assignments, either short-term or long-term (often defined as at least two or three years), in a more strategic light. Due to the transformational nature of the culture shock experience and the resourcefulness required from the global leader at work outside his or her home country, expatriate assignments are increasingly being reevaluated as a prime development opportunity. In some of the world's most advanced global enterprises, a work assignment in another region has long been considered to be a fast-track opportunity for leadership development and a necessity for attaining executive status—the trend in many other organizations as well is now to invest in ensuring the rapid learning, adjustment, and success of key assignees. These assignees in turn are often charged with retaining and accelerating the cultivation of emerging market leadership talent, and play a crucial role in this high-stakes endeavor.

When properly supported and coached, expatriates can develop intercultural insight, systems thinking, skill and comfort in working across functions, and a sound understanding of the firm's operational capabilities and opportunities on a worldwide basis. This experience results in a mindset of cross-border collaboration and coordinated activity that is often linked with organic growth and innovation. Expatriate assignments are indeed costly; however, the cost of the missed opportunity to leverage these work assignments as vehicles for global leadership development is even greater.

The project team for a leader-led international assignment project should be composed of representatives from all the groups connected with such assignments, and they must work together in a deliberate and strategic way like with other forms of leader-led learning. The planning team members would work in alignment to address the business objectives and targeted performance goals for the assignment; in the selection, development, and compensation of the expatriate; and to achieve the organizational goals related to knowledge transfer and innovation.

Aligning the different functions that support expatriate assignments is just as essential as for other forms of action learning. Unfortunately, "ownership" of expatriate talent is like a **hot potato** in many firms: the tracking of career goals, accomplishments, next-in-line job opportunities, and succession plans are tossed between home and host locations, usually being dropped altogether at some point along the way. Handling at least the

委託することによってコスト削減を図ろうとしている。しかし、この傾向とは逆に、より戦略的観点から、短期または長期（少なくとも2、3年と定義されることが多い）の海外勤務をとらえている企業もある。カルチャーショック体験の変革的性質や、母国以外で業務を遂行するグローバルリーダーが必要とする臨機応変さによって、海外勤務は人材開発の貴重な機会として再評価されつつある。世界で最も先進的なグローバル企業の一部では、母国以外での勤務はリーダーシップ育成の出世コースに乗る機会であり、経営幹部の地位を得るために必須であると長い間考えられてきた。それ以外の多くの組織でも、現在では、主要な任務を与えられた人材が迅速に学習し、適応し、成功してゆくための投資に積極的である傾向がある。このような任務を与えられた人は、新興市場のリーダーにふさわしい人材を発掘し、その人材を確保し、育成する役割を担うことに重要な役割を果たす。それはリスクを伴う貴重なミッションだ。

適切な支援と指導を受けた海外駐在員は、異文化間の洞察力、他文化でのシステムへの思考力、機能横断的業務におけるスキルを安定的に行使する能力、そして世界規模での企業の経営能力とチャンスにチャレンジするための適切な知識を身に付けることができる。この経験によって、国境を越えた協働と協調的な活動というマインドセットが生まれ、それが有機的な成長と改革に結びつく。

従業員を海外赴任させることは、確かにコストがかかる。しかし、これをグローバルリーダーシップ開発の手段として活用する機会を逃した場合、コストはさらに大きくなる。

リーダー主導の海外勤務プロジェクトチームは、そのような業務に関係するすべてのグループ代表者で構成されるべきであり、他の形態の学習と同様に、計画的で戦略的な方法で協働しなければならない。プランニングチームのメンバーは連携して、任務に対する事業目標と業績目標に対応し、駐在員の選抜、育成、補償において、知識の移転と改革に結びつく組織的目標を達成するべきだ。

残念ながら、駐在員に「オーナーシップ」を付与育成することは、多くの企業で**やっかいな課題**のようだ。キャリア目標、業績、次の仕事の機会、後継者育成計画の追跡が自国と赴任地の間で行われるが、途中で全面的に放棄さ

most crucial international assignments in a form similar to leader-led action-learning projects would help to bring structure and accountability to this vital form of talent development.

The global leaders we interviewed gave numerous examples of how their organizations could better utilize expatriate assignments as developmental initiatives. There is a sharp contrast between companies that have learned to leverage international assignments strategically and those that have not.

Assignee comments about nonstrategic approaches include:

- "[People at headquarters] are bored if you say too much about your experience."
- "[During an expatriate assignment,] you weren't there; you were on vacation as far as people at headquarters were concerned."
- "No one cares about where you've been."
- "There is no career planning for expatriates."

Assignee recommendations for more strategic approaches include:

- Share success stories. Talk about what happened and why it is beneficial.
- Send high-potential employees on international assignments early in their careers so they can start right away; recruit for this kind of experience.
- Do not send someone abroad who displays a lack of curiosity or interest.
- Appoint former assignees to top executive posts.

Leadership in a complex and connected world can only be developed with the mindful participation of all stakeholders. There are many ironies in global leadership development, and many fallacies that companies must outgrow in order to become truly global in their thinking. Nonstrategic

れてしまうことが多い。リーダー主導の行動学習プロジェクトと同様の形態で、少なくとも、最も重要な海外業務に対応することは、人材育成の重要な形態に対する枠組みと説明責任を伴うからだ。

インタビューに応じたグローバルリーダーたちは、自分たちの組織がどのように海外駐在員の業務を人材開発への取り組みとして有効に活用しているか多くの事例を挙げた。海外業務を戦略的に活用することを学んだ企業とそうでない企業とでは明確な差がある。

海外業務を戦略的に活用していない企業に対する駐在員のコメントの一部を以下に紹介する。

- 「駐在員の体験談に本社の人たちはうんざりしている」
- 「海外勤務中は、本社にいなかったわけで、本社の人から見ると休暇中だったのと同じことだ」
- 「他人がどこにいたかなんて気にする人はいない」
- 「海外駐在員向けのキャリアプランニングが確立されていない」

駐在員が推奨する戦略的活用方法は以下のとおりである。

- サクセスストーリーを共有し、何が起こったか、なぜそれが有益かを伝える。
- 有望な従業員をキャリアの早い段階で海外に派遣し、すぐに活かせるようにする。また、このような経験を持つ人を採用する。
- 好奇心や興味を示さない人材を海外に派遣してはならない。
- 海外勤務経験者を経営幹部に任命する。

複雑につながり合う世界でリーダーシップを育成するには、ステークホルダー全員の意識的参加が不可欠である。

皮肉にもグローバルリーダーシップ開発には多くの過ちが伴う。企業が真のグローバルな思考を持つためには、多くの誤った考え方から抜け出す必要

approaches to expatriate assignments, for example, only serve to insulate an organization and its leadership from the experiences of the people who have firsthand knowledge of vital growth markets.

The assumption that international assignments are a separate administrative realm that is not at the heart of global leadership development is absurd, and the idea must be reversed: How can the hard lessons and the everyday experiences of global assignees be transmitted most efficiently and effectively to everyone in the organization who touches global business or even domestic diversity in any form?

The advantage of leader-led action learning is that it not only helps to hasten the implementation of business strategies, but also begins to alter the culture of an organization through careful collaboration and transmission of new knowledge. The iconic companies of the future will achieve business results and build a true global leadership performance culture through the focused development of employees across boundaries of every kind.

がある。例えば、海外駐在員に対する非戦略的アプローチは、重要な成長市場について直接の知識を持つ人々の経験を組織とリーダーシップから遠ざけるだけである。

国際業務がグローバルリーダーシップ開発の中心から外れた管理領域だという仮説はばかげており、その考えを変えなければならない。どうすれば、海外駐在員の厳しい教訓や日々の経験を、グローバルな事業や国内の多様性に関わっているすべての人に効率的かつ効果的に伝えることができるのか？

リーダー主導の行動学習は、事業戦略の実施を早めることができるだけでなく、徹底した協力体制と新しい知識の移転によって組織文化を変革するためのものだ。今後の模範となる企業は、あらゆる種類の境界を越えて従業員の育成に注力し、そのことで業績を上げ、真のグローバルリーダーシップを発揮できる文化を構築できる企業であろう。

About the Authors

Ernest Gundling, Ph.D.,
Founder & Managing Partner,
Aperian Global

Dr. Gundling has been involved with the organization Aperian Global since its inception in 1990. He is a Senior Asia Specialist and consults with clients on strategic approaches to global leadership development and relationships with key international business partners. He coaches executives with global responsibilities and works with multicultural management teams to help them formulate business plans based upon strong mutual understanding and a joint commitment to execution.

Dr. Gundling holds a Ph.D. and a Master of Arts degree from the University of Chicago, and a Bachelor of Arts from Stanford University. He is also a Lecturer at the Haas School of Business at the University of California, Berkeley, where he teaches a course called Global Management Skills. He is the author of numerous publications, including several books: The 3M Way to Innovation: Balancing People and Profits, Working GlobeSmart: 12 People Skills for Doing Business Across Borders, and Global Diversity: Winning Customers and Engaging Employees within World Markets.

Terry Hogan.
Director, Citi Executive Development

Terry Hogan is Director of Executive Development at Citi where she is responsible for the design and delivery of global executive development, team training, and other organizational support interventions. In addition to her responsibilities for the company's Business Leadership Program, Chief Executive's Forum, and the Global Executive Leader Program, Ms. Hogan heads up the

著者について

アーネスト・ガンドリング

Aperian Global社　創立者兼マネージングパートナー
1990年の創立以来、Aperian Global社を率いてきた

シニア・アジア・スペシャリストとして、グローバルリーダーシップ開発に対する戦略的アプローチや主要な国際ビジネスパートナーとの関係構築についてのコンサルティングを行っている。グローバルな責任を持つ経営者を指導し、多文化経営チームと協力して、強固な相互理解とその実践への共同コミットメントに基づいた事業計画の策定を支援している。

シカゴ大学で博士号と文学修士号、スタンフォード大学で文学士号を取得。カリフォルニア大学バークレー校ハース・スクール・オブ・ビジネスの講師として、グローバル・マネジメント・スキルと呼ばれるコースで教鞭を取っている。以下を始めとする多数の著書がある。“The 3M Way to Innovation”（邦題『3M：超発想法』）“Balancing People and Profits, Working GlobeSmart”（「人々と利益とのバランス、GlobeSmartの機能」）“12 People Skills for Doing Business Across Borders, and Global Diversity”（「国境を越えてビジネスを行うための12人のスキルとグローバルな多様性」）“Winning Customers and Engaging Employees within World Markets”（世界市場で顧客を獲得し、従業員を引きつける方法）

テリー・ホーガン

ディレクター、シティ・エグゼクティブ・ディベロップメント

テリー・ホーガンは、シティグループのエグゼクティブ・ディベロップメントのディレクターとして、グローバルな経営者の育成、チーム研修、その他の組織的支援インターベンションの設計と実施に携わっている。同社のビジネス・リーダーシップ・プログラム、最高経営責任者フォーラム、グローバル・エグゼクティブ・リーダーズ。プログラムを担当している。また、シティ・コーチ・センター・オブ・エクセレンスの責任者でもある。

Citi Coach Center of Excellence. She joined Citi in 2009 from Aperian Global, where she managed the firm's Global Leadership Development Practice.

Previously, Ms. Hogan was a global General Manager for Cendant Corporation, where she led the development of new markets and products globally. Ms. Hogan has a Bachelor of Science degree from Oregon State University and holds a Master's degree in Intercultural Relations and Global Leadership from the University of the Pacific and the Intercultural Communication Institute.

Karen Cvitkovich,
Senior Consultant, Aperian Global

Karen Cvitkovich has worked in intercultural consulting, coaching and multinational team-building for more than fifteen years. She has designed and facilitated seminars for intact teams, team leaders and individual contributors on subjects including globalization, multinational teambuilding, global leadership and virtual communications.

Ms. Cvitkovich has a Bachelor's degree in Business and Human Resources from the University of Massachusetts Amherst and a Master's of Science in Training and Organizational Development from Lesley University. She is a frequent speaker at global conferences including SHRM, ASTD, and the Summer Institute for Intercultural Communication.

2009年にAperian GlobalからCitiに移り、同社のグローバルリーダーシップ・ディベロップメント・プラクティスを管理した。

以前は、Cendant Corporationのグローバル・ジェネラル・マネージャーとして新しい市場と製品の開発をグローバルに指揮していた。オレゴン州立大学で理学士号を取得し、パシフィック大学および異文化コミュニケーション研究所で異文化関係とグローバルリーダーシップの修士号を取得している

カレン・チヴィトコヴィッチ
Aperian Global シニアコンサルタント

カレン・チヴィトコヴィッチは、異文化間のコンサルティング、コーチング、多国籍チーム育成に15年以上取り組んできた。グローバル化、多国籍チーム育成、グローバルリーダーシップ、バーチャルコミュニケーションといったテーマについて、チーム全体、チームリーダー、一般社員向けのセミナーを企画し支援してきた。

マサチューセッツ大学アマースト校でビジネスと人事の学士号を、レスリー大学でトレーニングと組織開発の修士号を取得している。SHRM（米国人材マネジメント協会）、ASTD（米国人材開発機」）、Summer Institute for Intercultural Communication（暫定訳：異文化コミュニケーションのための夏期プログラム）を始めとする多くの国際会議で講演を行っている。

日本語ナビで読む洋書
What is Global Leadership?

2021年 7 月 4 日　第 1 刷発行

ナビゲーター　山久瀬洋二

原 著 者　Ernest Gundling, Terry Hogan, Karen Cvitkovich

発 行 者　浦　晋亮

発 行 所　IBCパブリッシング株式会社
〒162-0804 東京都新宿区中里町29番3号 菱秀神楽坂ビル9F
Tel. 03-3513-4511 Fax. 03-3513-4512
www.ibcpub.co.jp

印 刷 所　株式会社シナノパブリッシングプレス

Printed in Japan

ISBN978-4-7946-0665-5